STUDIES IN LITERARY MODES

BY

ARTHUR MELVILLE CLARK

M.A., D.PHIL.

Lecturer in English in the University of Edinburgh

OLIVER AND BOYD

EDINBURGH: TWEEDDALE COURT

LONDON: 98 GREAT RUSSELL STREET, W.C.

1946

PRINTED AND PUBLISHED IN GREAT BRITAIN BY
OLIVER AND BOYD LTD., EDINBURGH

TO
MY MOTHER

PREFACE

THE eight essays in this book are all discussions either of literary kinds or of literary mechanisms. Of the first three essays I need say only that they are each self-contained and independent. The other five, though each is likewise complete in itself, together form a group. They are among the products of a study of the origin, justification, and use of rhyme, its varieties, its cognates (assonance, alliteration, parallelism, the refrain, and the like), the part played by these various devices on the formal side of poetry, their bearing on poetic diction and style, and their relation to the ultimate nature of poetry and its kinds and to the artistic impulse generally.

In the fifth, the sixth, and to some extent the eighth of the essays published here the pursuit of the ramifying subject of rhyme has carried me out of English which is my province into the literature of other languages in which I make no pretence to move with the same freedom. Accordingly I offer my opinions on these languages and literatures with hesitation and all the diffidence becoming to a student of English who has gone where his research has led him, no doubt far afield but perhaps not too far astray.

With great pleasure I acknowledge my debt to my friend and colleague, Mr John Purves, M.A., Reader in Italian in the University of Edinburgh. Not only did he read the first proofs of this book with vigilant attention, but, as is his generous wont, he gave me freely of his ripe scholarship and rich suggestion.

A. M. C.

EDINBURGH, *July* 1945

v

CONTENTS

THE HISTORICAL NOVEL

> Goe, and catche a falling starre,
>   Get with child a mandrake roote,
> Tell me, where all past yeares are,
>   Or who cleft the Divels foot.
>
> John Donne, *Song*, 1-4.

I

AMONG the favourite clichés of to-day are " the pages of history "
and " the book of the past." The historian is popularly supposed
only to read this book. But in fact it is largely his composition.
The further back he goes in the book of the past, the more tattered
does he find the pages of history, the more interlineation and
conjectural addition he has to make, and the more mounting
he must supply to hold the authentic relics in place. Sometimes
he may even be suspected of following the lead of the German
professor who reconstructed a whole tragedy of Euripides from
a few fragments found on potsherds and then came to like his
own reinforcements so much that he threw away the originals.

The actual past and the written history of the past are two
different things. Even if, as I must admit, historical fiction is a
tertium quid, the historian is just as much an imaginative
reconstructor as is the novelist ; and there never was a novelist
to pervert history till there had first been a historian to (shall we
say ?) invent it, or a wrong picture of the past in fiction without
a wrong view of it in preceding history.

One of Signor Croce's dicta is that the criticism of poetry
is always the criticism of previous criticism.[1] He holds that every
age has a peculiar relationship to every existing work, that each
new age sees *La Divina Commedia*, for example, or *Hamlet* from
a new angle and in a new perspective, and that a work of criticism
is fully valid only for the age which produces it. Thus the
critics bandy an author about in a dialectical process in which
they expose the outmoded notions of their predecessors.

---

[1] *Conversazione Critiche*, 1932.

I submit, then, that the writing of history is likewise a criticism of the mistakes, omissions, wrong emphases, and disproportions of previous history. I am so little of a sceptic that I can well believe our historians, like our literary critics, thus grow better and better every day and in every way. But I am also so much of a sceptic that I must expect B's explosion of A to be followed by C's explosion of B. The historian is " the priest who slew the slayer And shall himself be slain." [1] And if " Man never is, but always to be blest," [2] the historian never is, but is only becoming, true.

His aim at any given time is the closest approximation to the truth possible for him and his generation. That, however, is seldom or never the historical novelist's aim in the first place or indeed in any place before the nth. A fiction is a fiction and has, notionally at any rate, all the rights and privileges of a creative kind. It is a variety of poesy. But, as Aristotle says, " the poet's function is to describe, not the thing that has happened, but a kind of thing that might happen, *i.e.* what is possible as being probable or necessary. The distinction between historian and poet is not in the one writing prose and the other verse—you might put the work of Herodotus into verse, and it would still be a species of history ; it consists really in this, that the one describes the thing that has been, and the other a kind of thing that might be. Hence poetry is something more philosophic and of graver import than history, since its statements are of the nature rather of universals, whereas those of history are singulars." [3]

The same thing with a Renaissance difference that will, I hope, excuse another long quotation is said by Bacon :—" Poesy is . . . in measure of words for the most part restrained, but in all other points extremely licensed, and doth truly refer to the Imagination ; which, being not tied to the laws of matter, may at pleasure join that which nature hath severed, and sever that which nature hath joined, and so make unlawful matches and divorces of things. . . . It is taken in two senses, in respect of words or matter. In the first sense it is but a character of style. . . . In the later it is . . . nothing else but Feigned History, which may be styled as well in prose as in verse. The

---

[1] Macaulay, *The Battle of Lake Regillus*, 175-6.

[2] Pope, *An Essay on Man*, i, 96.

[3] *Aristotle. On the Art of Poetry*, ed. Ingram Bywater, 1909, p. 27.

use of this Feigned History hath been to give some shadow of satisfaction to the mind of man in those points wherein the nature of things doth deny it, the world being in proportion inferior to the soul ; by reason whereof there is, agreeable to the spirit of man, a more ample greatness, a more exact good-ness, and a more absolute variety, than can be found in the nature of things. Therefore, because the facts or events of true history have not that magnitude which satisfieth the mind of man, poesy feigneth acts and events greater and more heroical. Because true history propoundeth the successes and issues of actions not so agreeable to the merits of virtue and vice, therefore poesy feigns them more just in retribution, and more according to revealed providence. Because true history representeth actions and events more ordinary and less interchanged, therefore poesy endueth them with more rareness, and more unexpected and alternative variations. So as it appeareth that poesy serveth and conferreth to magnanimity, morality, and to delectation. And therefore it was ever thought to have some participation of divineness, because it doth raise and erect the mind, by sub-mitting the shows of things to the desires of the mind ; whereas reason doth buckle and bow the mind unto the nature of things." [1]

It is, I admit, only a pure fiction that can have all the creative liberty which Aristotle and Bacon allow it. A fiction which compromises its integrity by an intrigue with history can claim only a modified freedom. Nevertheless even of the historical novel the essence remains fictitious and it is only the accidents that are historical. The historical novel professes to tell a story of a past age and in so doing to give some sort of savour of that age to those who want a particular bouquet in their fiction— not to historians in their professional capacity, but to anybody with an imagination capable of a historical sympathy. It exists to give what Aristotle would have called " its own proper pleasure." [2] That is all it should be asked to do, not to teach history ; and in the process of adjusting and reconciling the components it must be the history that yields to the fiction, not the fiction to the history.

The " wise ones, the grave and the precise ones " [3] of historical

---

[1] *The Advancement of Learning* in *The Works of Francis Bacon*, ed. James Spedding, R. L. Ellis, and D. D. Heath, 1870-2, iii, pp. 343-4.

[2] *Aristotle. On the Art of Poetry*, ed. cit., p. 39.

[3] Sir John Denham, *Martial. Epigram*, 4-5.

scholarship may dislike any playing fast and loose with facts. Well, if facts they are that may be overset by the next issue of *The English Historical Review* just as much as by an ignorant novelist, the grave historians have the remedy in their own hands : they are not forced to read historical novels. As to the general public many of them have been broken in to history proper by historical fiction, and for every potential historian seduced from fact by fiction a score have come through fiction to fact. Nor should it be forgotten that one historical novelist at least, Sir Walter Scott, by peopling the past with real human beings and insisting on the past as something more than *memorabilia* influenced for good all subsequent historians.

II

In a sense all fiction is historical fiction, unless like Hudson's *Crystal Age* (1887) and Wells's *War of the Worlds* (1898) it is prophetic. For it is bound to be set in some period of past time. I say " past time " advisedly, since even a novel that is about to-day when written will be about yesterday when read.

It is true that in most novels written more or less contemporaneously with the supposed period of the action the characters live and act apart from any obtrusive historical circumstances. But in the course of time such novels acquire the status of a historical document. We can see now, for instance, how the lives of even the detached Jane Austen's heroes and heroines were modified to a degree of which she was unaware by the social, economic, and political facts of Georgian England, though those same facts are seldom more than implicit in the novels.

Many novelists, mostly but not only in the twentieth century, have by design so treated the life of their own period as to produce fiction that was historical from the outset. Disraeli in such novels as *Coningsby : Or The New Generation* (1844) and *Sybil : Or The Two Nations* (1845), Mrs Gaskell in *Mary Barton, a Tale of Manchester Life* (1848) and *North and South* (1855), and Trollope especially in his political novels from *Phineas Finn* (1869) to *The Duke's Children* (1880) found their themes in a narrative presentation and interpretation of Victorian England which is more in the nature of social history than are the novels of any of their contemporaries, even Dickens and

Thackeray. In the twentieth century the social revolutions and the political and international upheavals have provided novelists with a very rich field for fiction dominated by the actual affairs and circumstances of the time. Such are Galsworthy's *Forsyte Saga* (1906-21) with its sequel, *A Modern Comedy* (1924-28), and Bennett's *Clayhanger* chronicle (1910-16).

Perhaps the last war which brought to millions tragic, comic, or romantic experiences such as the imaginations of all previous story-tellers had never dreamed of, the uneasy interbellic peace with its alarms and sensations which left no nerve unstrung, and its shattering economic changes which made the most indifferent aware of his share in the national destiny, and then the new war which insists with a still grimmer insistence on our absorption— perhaps these catastrophic events have, for the time being at least, made it almost impossible for fiction above the level of " holiday reading " to be anything but historical. " The time-enclosures exist. A novel may end in July 1914, or in August 1939, and contain no reference to war, but even such stories are inevitably part of war's prelude or aftermath ; narrative, as it runs, is always in danger of bumping its head against one time-barrier or another ; and the interaction of personal destinies, which formerly was regarded as being either self-contained or subject to the influence of a continuing Fate, has for many years been dominated by catastrophe, discontinuous but repetitive." [1]

Whatever may be the relation of novels in the future to the actual context of the future, the existing fiction in which the action and characters are involved in a historical time-scheme and period environment are on the whole exceptional. It is, however, this very involution which makes a historical novel in the usual meaning of the phrase and constitutes its *raison d'être*. It is not enough to introduce historical events and persons to date the story, and to describe historical accessories and manners. The characters, the action, the dialogue, and the sentiments must be in such an intimate relation to a particular time-factor and all which derives from it and manifests it as to be modified or even determined by it. I think it can be said of most historical novels, including those discussed in the previous paragraph, that the characters are less free agents in the conduct of their lives than are the characters in most non-historical novels. The

[1] *Menander's Mirror. A Problem of Story-Telling* in *The Times Literary Supplement*, 7th August 1943, 375.

often-noted passivity of Scott's heroes whose fortunes are made for them more than by them is only an extreme illustration of what is a feature of historical novels generally, however artistically it may be disguised. So far from its necessarily detracting from the interest, it may make the interest a dual one—the conflict of character with character, and the conflict of character with the historical circumstances.

III

It is quite possible to have a historical novel without any definite historical event or even the echo of one and without a single person known to history. Thus in Scott's *Guy Mannering* (1815) only the general social conditions of a fairly well-defined time, not particular events and persons, are historical. The prose romances of William Morris do not even define the time beyond making it of the dark or the middle ages in *The Roots of the Mountains* (1890) or in *The Well at the World's End* (1896) respectively.

But as a rule historical events and historical persons, either or both, provide some or much of the substance and motivation. However the historical and the fictitious may be associated, the importance of either is sometimes a little ambiguous. For historical events on the one hand, or historical persons on the other, or both together may be central ; or subordinate but still important ; or merely peripheral ; with the fictitious events and the fictitious characters or both peripheral, or subordinate, or central contrariwise—to say nothing of other more complex combinations ; but even when the historical is ostensibly of less importance for the plot it may be actually of more general interest, as in Scott's *Abbot* (1820). The historical may be so blended with the fictitious that history provides some of the events but few or no persons, as in Thackeray's *Vanity Fair* (1847-48) and Dickens's *Tale of Two Cities* (1859). Conversely historical persons may appear in what are purely or largely fictitious events, as in Scott's *Fortunes of Nigel* (1822) and Pater's *Gaston de Latour* (1896). Or historical persons may be called in to transact historical events, as in Lytton's *Rienzi* (1835), *The Last of the Barons* (1843), and *Harold* (1848).

Lytton, indeed, was the inventor of this type in which instead of " lending to ideal personages, and to an imaginary fable, the additional interest to be derived from the historical groupings," the author extracts " the main interest of romantic narrative from History itself," [1] and gives to history " that warmer interest which fiction bestows, by tracing the causes of the facts in the characters and emotions of the personages of the time . . . what remains for him, is the inner, not outer, history of man—the chronicle of the human heart ; and it is by this that he introduces a new harmony between character and event, and adds the complete solution of what is actual and true, by those speculations of what is natural and probable, which are out of the province of history, but belong especially to the province of romance." [2] Lytton may have taken a hint from Defoe's *Journal of the Plague Year* (1722) and *Memoirs of a Cavalier* (1724) in which history provides practically everything but the uninteresting narrator who has no inner life to speak of and whose outer life is merely to participate inconsiderably in the action and to record minutely the historical events and conditions. But both works are descriptive rather than narrative and such narrative as there is is entirely without plot. In Lytton's three novels in which he practised his new method, and in such later examples of it as Kingsley's *Hypatia* (1853) and *Hereward the Wake* (1866) and Mr Robert Graves's novels of imperial Rome, the lacing of invention with the history is enough to keep them in the province of fiction, though Mr Graves would object to incorporation in the province of romance.

On the other hand, out of this type has developed the anomalous *vie romancée* in which the boundaries of fact and fiction are deliberately blurred and for which the literary classifications of history or biography and novel are alike inappropriate.

A more legitimate effect has sometimes been secured by novelising fact by means of transposing it from one age and setting to another and by altering names and details—not just as novelists in general work over their own or other people's experience, but after the manner of historical novelists in particular. Scott frequently derived material from family history and private life, as he admits in his introductions.[3] But he always " studied to generalize the portraits, so that they should

---

[1] *Harold*, preface to the third edition, Knebworth Edition, n.d., p. xi.

[2] *Rienzi*, 1848 preface, Knebworth Edition, 1848, p. xi.

[3] *Cf.* e.g. *Chronicles of the Canongate*, introduction in *Waverley Novels*, ed. 1829-33, xli, pp. xii-xxiv.

still seem, on the whole, the productions of fancy," [1] even if the disguise was sometimes penetrated, as in the case of Monkbarns in *The Antiquary* (1816); and he always altered the facts freely and deliberately in order no doubt both to heighten the effects and to afford a still better disguise, if circumstances made that desirable. Stevenson in *Weir of Hermiston* (1896), on the other hand, did not attempt to mystify his public about the original of his hanging judge, dead *sine prole* for nearly a hundred years. But Robert MacQueen, Lord Braxfield, was a relatively unknown person. Not so Byron and Shelley whose stories, elaborately contraposed and shifted to the seventeen-seventies and eighties, were retold by Disraeli in *Venetia* (1837), in order to interpret them sympathetically and to stimulate the public's interest by setting it an easy problem of identification. Instead of antedating real persons Dickens resurrected Lord Chesterfield to play the sinister part of Sir John Chester in *Barnaby Rudge* (1841), and Thackeray threw the contemporary Marquis of Hertford back into history as his Marquis of Steyne in *Vanity Fair* (1847-48). Disraeli's Marquis of Coningsby, another and even more brilliant portrait of Lord Hertford, is to be regarded as contemporaneous with the novel in which he appears (1844). He is typical of the many studies from living notabilities in *Coningsby* itself and Disraeli's other *romans à clef*, which with other similar novels scarcely come into the scope of my survey.

IV

It is a kind of paradox that, in whatever proportions and by whatever means the historical and the fictitious are mixed, that which makes a novel a convincing picture of the past is less the use made of real persons and events than the creation of a historically plausible environment by means of details of setting and accessories on the one hand and of speech and sentiment on the other. In these features fact and fiction should be fused : they should be on the one hand historically appropriate and on the other fictitiously applied.

Let me consider in the first place, then, the language put into the mouths of the characters.

---

[1] *Chronicles of the Canongate*, introduction, xli, *ed. cit.*, p. xvii.

No doubt novels have been written with next to no dialogue at all. Smollett's *Peregrine Pickle* (1751), for instance, gives most of the speeches in *oratio obliqua* ; and the psychological novelists from Meredith and Henry James downwards have been partial to characters who say little but think a lot, like the Irishman's parrot. Perhaps the historical novelist, too, could rub along with indirect speech (which does not purport to give the *ipsissima verba*) or internal discourse (which can be entirely in the author's own terms). But there are many people who feel that a novel of any kind without dialogue is worse than an egg without salt—indeed is scarcely a novel at all ; and certainly a historical novelist deprives himself of one of the subtlest means for creating a historical atmosphere and illusion if he evades the choice of an appropriate dialogue and gives nothing but indirect speech for conversation or internal discourse for soliloquy.

The different kinds of dialogue which have in fact been adopted by historical novelists may, I think, be reduced to three or four :—(1) the speech of the day in which the story is set ; (2) the speech of an unspecified yesterday, not always easily distinguishable from (3) the speech of no day at all ; and, lastly, (4) the speech of to-day.

Naturally the ideal dialogue for the historical novel is the speech of the period chosen for the plot. The accepted masterpiece of this method is Thackeray's *Henry Esmond* (1853) which is said not to use one word that might not have been used at the court of Queen Anne. I am not quite sure if, while all the separate words are period-pieces, all the phraseology is likewise antique. For a phrase made up of Augustan words may never have been so arranged under Queen Anne and may convey a thought never entertained till the days of Queen Victoria. Be that as it may, *Henry Esmond* is certainly a *tour de force*, all the more remarkable because description and narration as well as dialogue are kept within the Augustan orbit. Thackeray was just as scrupulous in his *Barry Lyndon* (1844) and his unfinished *Denis Duval* (1864). But these fictitious autobiographies and *The Virginians* (1857-59) deal with events no more remote than the eighteenth century ; and Thackeray had an abundance of the right kind of literature to soak himself in.

Obviously the novelist can use the speech of the day only for fairly recent historical periods and for stories set in the country to which the language in use belongs. For most historical

periods and for all stories set in foreign countries another kind
of dialogue has to be employed.

Scott realised this when he considered the reasons for the
failure of one of his predecessors in historical fiction, the antiquary
Joseph Strutt whose *Queenhoo Hall*, a romance of the fifteenth
century, Scott himself finished and published (1808). " Every
work," he says, " designed for mere amusement must be expressed
in language easily comprehended ; and when . . . the author
addresses himself exclusively to the Antiquary, he must be
content to be dismissed by the general reader with the criticism
of Mungo, in the Padlock [1] . . . ' What signifies me hear, if
me no understand ? ' " [2] What indeed ? A question to be asked.

Scott himself was faced with the problem of dialogue in no
very acute form till he wrote *Ivanhoe* (1819). None of his earlier
novels from *Waverley* (1814) to *The Legend of Montrose* (1819)
went any farther back than the middle of the seventeenth century
and no farther afield than his native Scotland or, for one or two
scenes, the contemporaneous England. In these earlier novels
such characters as do not speak the Doric use a bookish language
of a slightly formal and old-fashioned cast. Such variations as
he makes in it are to suit the individual characters rather than
to indicate the different epochs to which they belong. But in
Ivanhoe and in later novels handling the sixteenth or earlier
centuries, either at home or abroad, he had to find a better means
of suggesting archaic speech, whether Scots, English, Anglo-
Norman, Provençal, or what not.

His view was that " He who would imitate an ancient language
with success, must attend rather to its grammatical character,
turn of expression, and mode of arrangement, than labour to
collect extraordinary and antiquated terms, which . . . do not
in ancient authors approach the number of words still in use,
though perhaps somewhat altered in sense and spelling, in the
proportion of one to ten." [3] It will be noticed that Scott is
thinking in that passage only of the imitation at a later stage
of an earlier stage of the same language : he does not say what
sort of English is to be the equivalent of Louis XI's French or
King René's Provençal. His actual practice in suggesting all
kinds of bygone speech was to give to the dialogue " a little of

---

[1] A comic opera by Isaac Bickerstaffe, 1768.
[2] *Waverley Novels*, general preface, *ed. cit.*, i, pp. xvi-xvii.
[3] *Ivanhoe*, dedicatory epistle, *ed. cit.*, xvi, p. xxxvi.

the colour of that of our grandparents, a slightly archaic tint." [1]

I have to admit that Scott was not very successful in this. The fact is that he was not a master of dialogue in general at all. His forte in dialogue was restricted to those who, be they princes like James I and VI or peasants like Cuddie Headrig, spoke the Scots lowland dialect which not only was racy and vigorous but could be used for some of the characters in any Scottish novel from the sixteenth to the eighteenth century.

Scott's own derivation of his non-dialectal dialogue from the speech of his grandparents is a little open to question. Listen to this from *Ivanhoe* :—

> " ' By Saint Thomas of Kent,' said [the Friar], ' an I buckle to my gear, I will teach thee, sir lazy lover, to mell with thine own matters, maugre thine iron case there ! '
>
> " ' Nay, be not wroth with me,' said the Knight ; ' thou knowest I am thy sworn friend and comrade.'
>
> " ' I know no such thing,' answered the Friar, ' and defy thee for a meddling coxcomb ! '
>
> " ' Nay, but,' said the Knight, ' . . . hast thou forgotten how, that for my sake (for I say nothing of the temptation of the flagon and the pasty) thou didst break thy vow of fast and vigil ? '
>
> " ' Truly, friend,' said the Friar, clenching his huge fist, ' I will bestow a buffet on thee.' " [2]

I am afraid that I cannot believe Robert Scott of Sandy-knowe or Professor John Rutherford of Edinburgh University spoke in these-like accents. What Scott called the speech of his grandparents was really a sort of Wardour-Street modification of the speech that his grandparents might have spoken if they had been English born and bred and, if, like their grandson, they had been mighty readers of romances and Elizabethan plays.

In short it came near to being, if indeed it did not actually sometimes become, the speech of no day at all. By that phrase I do not mean merely what Stevenson called " tushery," the flat-footed repetition of a few obsolete expletives and tags, but

---

[1] Sir H. J. C. Grierson, *Sir Walter Scott : II, History and the Novel* in *University of Edinburgh Journal*, November 1941, p. 86.

[2] *Ivanhoe*, ed. cit., xvii, pp. 166-7.

the kind of pseudo-poetic, metaphorical roundaboutness which proceeds on the principle that our ancestors never called a spade a spade and that the more allusive, whimsical, quipping, skipping, ranting, and mouthing the dialogue is the more likely it is to bridge " the dark backward and abysm of time." [1]   But nothing will convince me that this passage from Maurice Hewlett's *Richard Yea-and-Nay* (1900) represents the way in which Richard Cœur-de-Lion's mind worked or his lips spoke :—

> " [H]e is old, and passionate, and indifferent wicked. . . . Look, my girl, there were four of us : Henry, and me, and Geoffrey and John, whom he sought to drive in team by a sop to-day and a stick to-morrow. A good way, done by a judging hand. What then ? I will tell you how the team served the teamster. Henry gave sop for sop, and it was found well. Might he not give stick for stick ? He thought so. God rest him, he is dead of that. There was much simplicity in Henry. I got no sop at all. Why should I have stick then ? I saw no reason ; but I took what came. If I cried out, it is a more harmless vent than many. Let me alone. Geoffrey, I think, was a villain. God help him if He can : he is dead too. He took sop and gave stick : ungentle in Geoffrey, but he paid for it. He was a cross-bred dog with much of the devil in him ; he bit himself and died barking. Last, there is John. I desire to speak reasonably of John ; but he is too smug, he gets all sop. This is not fair. He should have some stick, that we may judge what mettle he has. There, my Jehane, you have the four of us, a fretful team ; whereof one has rushed his hills and broken his heart ; and one, kicking his yoke-fellows, squealing, playing the jade, has broken his back ; and one, poor Richard, does collar-work and gets whip ; and one, young Master John, eases his neck and is cajoled with ' So then, so then, boy ! ' " [2]

As Ben Jonson said of Spenser's diction,[3] this of Hewlett's is no language at all. It is not English, and it is not a translation from Anglo-Norman because it is not even human.

---

[1] Shakespeare, *The Tempest*, I, ii, 50.

[2] N.d., p. 21.

[3] *Timber, or Discoveries* in *Critical Essays of the Seventeenth Century*, ed. J. E. Spingarn, 1908, i, p. 34.

To come now to the use of the speech of to-day for every period and every setting at home or abroad. This is a cutting of the Gordian Knot. It is the bold method adopted by Mr Robert Graves, Mr Masefield, and Mrs Naomi Mitchison, and may have been learned by them from Mr Shaw's employment of it in his historical dramas. There is much to be said for it. It has vivacity. It makes us realise that people in the past were human beings. It gives, as compared with the effect of any other kind of dialogue, the same sort of reality which a photograph gives as compared with a woodcut or a steel-engraving. And it is perhaps the simplest way of providing a manner of speech for historical novels set abroad or for foreigners.

But, then, the risk in using the language of to-day is of introducing at the same time the feelings of to-day. In fact it is almost impossible to avoid this. And something far more ruinous to the historical illusion may come through a word or phrase from the modern idiom, which, just because it is from that idiom, calls up instantly the modern feeling, than from the (more or less supposed) speech of yesterday or even from the speech of no day at all which, if they do not call up the past very successfully, at least do not release the present on us.

This passage from Mr Shaw's *St Joan* (1923) will illustrate the incongruity :—

> " Bishop Cauchon. . . . I see now that what is in your mind is not that this girl has never once mentioned The Church, and thinks only of God and herself, but has never once mentioned the peerage, and thinks only of the king and herself.
>
> " Earl of Warwick. Quite so. These two ideas of hers are the same idea at bottom. It goes deep, my lord. It is the protest of the individual soul against the interference of priest or peer between the private man and his God. I should call it Protestantism if I had to find a name for it. . . . I think you are not entirely void of sympathy with The Maid's secular heresy, my lord. I leave you to find a name for it.
>
> " Bishop Cauchon. . . . I have no sympathy with her political presumptions. But as a priest I have gained a knowledge of the minds of the common people ; and there you will find yet another most dangerous idea. I can express

it only by such phrases as France for the French, England for the English. . . . It is sometimes so narrow and bitter in country folk that it surprises me that this country girl can rise above the idea of her village for its villagers. But she can. . . . Call this side of her heresy Nationalism if you will : I can find you no better name for it." [1]

Mr Shaw's own sufficient defence would probably be along the following lines :—That he was not trying, either in *St Joan* or in any of his non-contemporary plays, to recreate the past for its own sake ; that for him the past was of service merely as a parable for the present and a warning for the future ; that he was quite ready to do the past a metaphorical " injury " which it could not feel ; that he would not " debar himself from the attainment of beauties within his view, by a needless fear of breaking rules which no literary dictator had authority to enact " ; [2] and that he deliberately adopted a style in dialogue that was appropriate to his dialectic and that, by its very incongruity to the speakers and their epoch, yielded a certain witty surprise and comic charm.

This line of argument, however, is not open to historical novelists unless they are writing undisguised tracts for the times like Mr Shaw himself or such *facetiæ* as Thackeray's *Rebecca and Rowena* (1850) and Mark Twain's *Connecticut Yankee at King Arthur's Court* (1889). So long as they intend to present the past for its own sake or mainly for its own sake, they can justify their use of the speech of to-day only on the ground of its contributing to the effectiveness of their historical novels as such, either by its vivacity and truth to nature at one period at least if not at the period depicted, or by its serviceableness as a neutral medium into which any language at any period can be plausibly translated.

V

To come now to the setting and accessories of the historical novel, not the timeless background and details of nature but the changing physical environment of human life and the equally changing spiritual and intellectual atmosphere. Events and

---

[1] 1924, pp. 52-3.
[2] Johnson, *The Rambler*, No. 156, in *The Works of Samuel Johnson*, 1792, vi, p. 100.

characters must be embedded in that environment and enveloped in that atmosphere, and out of the dual matrix the characters must speak if the novel is to call up a convincing picture of the past.

It was with respect to the multifarious milieus, physical and spiritual, of their narratives that all the predecessors of Scott but one failed most signally. The respect for the particulars of the past which even Horace Walpole, the most knowledgeable of them all, had was that of a collector of curios. He thought of the tangible relics of the past—the intangibles he and his school practically ignored—as contributing by their oddity to the amusement of his present, but scarcely as having any rights, as it were, the right to be assigned to their proper century and the right to be regarded as significant without the smug condescension of a later age. Clara Reeve and " Monk " Lewis were even less aware of any scholarly duty to the physical actualities of the past. With a complete irresponsibility they confused the products of the different centuries and went to their very unhistorical imaginations for their accessories as much as for their plots. Mrs Radcliffe, it is true, elaborated her scenic background far beyond any earlier novelist and almost indeed set the example to Scott and through him to all his successors of creating an elaborate natural setting more or less appropriate to the events of the plot. But the scenic is not the historic, and Mrs Radcliffe is as wild in her historic background as any of her contemporaries.

In revulsion from such unhistorical inaccuracy in details Joseph Strutt went to the opposite extreme. He was a didactic antiquary, much more than a novelist, and he drenched his by no means exciting tale with a wealth of verified antiquarian lore that he had gathered for his *Royal and Ecclesiastical Antiquities* (1773), his *Manners, Customs, Arms, Habits, etc., of the Inhabitants of England* (1775-6) and his *Sports and Pastimes* (1801).

Scott had to strike a balance between the too-much and the too-little, to remember that his reader must be made aware of the epoch by suggestion and description, and at the same time to refrain from boring him with antiquarian pedantry. He had to avoid, as he put it, " the repulsive dryness of mere antiquity " without exceeding " the fair licence due to the author of a fictitious composition." [1] He succeeded remarkably well, though those who read him for only one of his components sometimes resent the time he spends on his setting. Moreover, he realised,

[1] *Ivanhoe*, ed. cit., xvi, p. xxxiv.

as his predecessors scarcely did, that what I have called the spiritual atmosphere of his characters and events—the ideas, beliefs, conventions, superstitions, and sentiments—and the manifestation of these in manners and customs were likewise factors in the milieu. Though he may not always have understood the true quality of some of those factors, especially those related to medieval Catholicism, he is generally both clear and interesting ; and he rarely fails in the adequacy with which he illustrates them in manners and practice.

The effectiveness of the historical novelist's physical and spiritual background must result from his gift of selection. While there must be some knowledge due to some research, the illusion of a past age is not necessarily created by the abundance or the accuracy of the historical detail displayed. " [S]uccess," Mr Belloc says, " . . . does not seem to depend upon any great mass of reading. The artist obtains his success in this, as in so many other fields, by some strange process of intuition, integrating, from not many isolated points of knowledge, a whole combined scheme which is true and real. . . . He who would attempt historical fiction must, of course, read something of the period upon which he would touch, but it is astonishing how little is sufficient for the man who has the right kind of genius, and how much remains quite insufficient for the man who has it not." [1] I should not go as far as Mr Belloc in discounting research. It is not a question of research or no research, but of managing the products of research.

Out of the fullness of his knowledge and memory Scott spoke of the physical and spiritual accessories of history. Research, if you can call it such, was his delight. He had, he said, one advantage over all his imitators. " They may do their fooling with better grace ; but I, like Sir Andrew Aguecheek, do it more natural. They have to read old books and consult antiquarian collections to get their information ; I write because I have long since read such works, and possess, thanks to a strong memory, the information which they have to seek for. This leads to a dragging-in historical details by head and shoulders, so that the interest of the main piece is lost in minute descriptions of events which do not affect its progress. Perhaps I have sind in this way myself—indeed, I am but too conscious

[1] *On the Character of an Historical Novel* in *The London Mercury*, November 1923, p. 41.

of having considered the plot only as what Bayes calls the means of bringing in fine things ; so that in respect of the descriptions, it resembled the string of the showman's box, which he pulls to show in succession Kings, Queens, the Battle of Waterloo, Bonaparte at Saint Helena, Newmarket Races, and White-headed Bob floored by Jemmy from town. All this I may have done, but I have repented of it ; and in my better efforts, while I conducted my story through the agency of historical personages and by connecting it with historical incidents, I have endeavoured to weave them pretty closely together, and in future I will study this more. Must not let the background eclipse the principal figures—the frame overpower the picture." [1]

On the other hand, Lytton filled notebooks laboriously with matter that he thought might be useful and to which he was often bound by a mistaken loyalty to his own diligence ; and George Eliot expended so much labour on *Romola* (1862-3), as it discloses only too completely, that she confessed to having " begun it a young woman and ended it an old one." [2]

Such overloading of the background, as in Flaubert's *Salammbô* (1862) and Charles Reade's *Cloister and the Hearth* (1861), not only impairs the interest : it also falsifies the picture and misdirects the eye. After all, in our ordinary experience we are normally aware of the things about us and the ideas at the back of our minds only in a secondary degree. We are more interested in the people in a room than in its furniture, in them as persons than in their clothes, and in their deliberate decisions and actions than in their more or less unconscious responses to the spirit of the age. It is true that in the historical novel the very unfamiliarity of the background of body and mind claims more of our attention. But the best way for the novelist to satisfy our curiosity is like the best kind of annotation—to give the maximum of relevant information with the minimum of distraction. As Dr Johnson says of textual notes, " The mind is refrigerated by interruption." [3] The historical novelist fails who has too obviously a design on us of making sure that we will depart better informed though we came only to be amused and of proving his erudition at the cost of his invention and our patience. He must select not accumulate, hint rather than

---

[1] *The Journal of Sir Walter Scott*, 1825-6, ed. J. G. Tait, 1939, pp. 248-9.
[2] *Cf.* Blanche C. Williams, *George Eliot. A Biography*, 1936, p. 199.
[3] *Preface to Shakespeare* in *The Works of Samuel Johnson*, 1792, ii, p. 138.

B

state, suggest rather than labour. He must have tact and discrimination. By what Mr Belloc calls an " eye-opener " [1] he can reveal a whole world. Out of the great mass of things in the past different from those of to-day, he ought to be able to choose a single detail which may be trivial enough in itself yet which will be the one thing needful, the magic formula of evocation.

Perhaps, says Mr C. S. Lewis, " there is no writer who admits us so intimately into the heart of [his] age as Augustine. Sometimes he does so by accident, as when he comments on the fact—to him, apparently, remarkable—that Ambrose, when reading to himself, read silently. You could see his eyes moving, but you could hear nothing.[2] In such a passage one has the solemn privilege of being present at the birth of a new world. Behind us is that almost unimaginable period, so relentlessly objective that in it even ' reading ' (in our sense) did not yet exist. The book was still a λόγος, a speech ; thinking was still διαλέγεσθαι, talking. Before us is our own world, the world of the printed or written page, and of the solitary reader who is accustomed to pass hours in the silent society of mental images evoked by written characters. This is a new light. . . . It is the very moment of a transition more important . . . than any that is commonly recorded in our works of ' history.' " [3]

Such a detail, then, chosen from a historical source or, by a flash of genius, appropriately invented, is the kind of revelation which the historical novelist needs. It is brief, concrete, unexpected, memorable, and significant. That a novel should contain very many such eye-openers is not to be expected. But even a few will convince the reader as nothing else will. That a novel should contain very many is indeed perhaps not even desirable. A picture can have too many high lights. A style can be too witty. And a historical novel like any other work of art may defeat its own higher purpose of securing the reader's own contribution by leaving him nothing to add.

I was recently asked a question of some interest, namely, Why are historical dramas usually or always less successful than historical novels in calling up the past ? I have to admit the inferiority in this respect of the drama to the novel, but it is not easy to find a simple explanation.

[1] *Op. cit.*, p. 41.
[2] Cf. *Confessions*, VI, iii.
[3] *The Allegory of Love*, 1936, pp. 64-5.

Our most famous historical dramatist kept to periods about which his audience in that age of strong nationalism and interest in the English past possessed the necessary modicum of knowledge. He could rely on their supplementing his history from their own share of tradition, balladry, floating opinion, and prejudice. But Shakespeare wrote when there was no historical perspective for him or for his audience, no reference books in public libraries, no plates and museums illustrating costumes, furniture, and other equipment. He was, therefore, as free to set his historical personages in an Elizabethan world and to dress them in Elizabethan clothes as were the great painters of the Italian Renaissance to pose their Biblical and classical figures in the dress of sixteenth-century Italy and in Florentine or Venetian palaces. His audience felt no incongruity and were, like himself, interested in the past for quite other reasons than the antiquarian.

Ben Jonson was exceptional in his own age for giving chapter-and-verse guarantees of his accuracy, and for long his practice remained unique. In the nineteenth century, however, historical dramatists like Tennyson and Browning did try to be faithful to the details of the past, and as the century advanced stage-managers and producers of the type of Sir Henry Irving and Wilson Barrett lavished money and scholarship, more especially money, on attempts to build up impeccably medieval or antique *mises-en-scène*. The cinema has not only far surpassed the theatre in its elaboration in its own proper sphere, but has also made the theatre try to outdo its nineteenth-century realism on some occasions at least, though the general tendency of modern theatrical producers is towards simplicity and convention.

But whatever dramatists or producers may do, the drama will always remain at a disadvantage in this matter of historical detail by its very nature. The novel can be of any length. Apart from such closet-dramas as Swinburne's *Bothwell* (1874) or Hardy's *Dynasts* (1903-8), the drama cannot be indefinitely long. The novel can devote as much of its space as it requires to describing setting and to suggesting atmosphere. It is true that Sir James Barrie, Mr Shaw, and many other modern dramatists have developed their stage directions to a remarkable degree. But the result is more to satisfy themselves and possible readers of their plays than to convince spectators of them. It is a stealing of the methods of the novel, which, when one comes to think of it, is largely in the nature of " stage-directions," both

in the historical and in the non-historical varieties. But even
if a dramatist had unlimited money for staging and costumes
and were as thorough about details as the man who blacked
himself all over to play Othello, all that the audience *hears* is
the words of the dialogue and all that they *see* is what is before
them. The dramatist must trust the former to their perhaps
intermittent attention, the latter to their perhaps perfunctory
observation, and both to their perhaps lethargic intelligence.
The audience cannot turn back the page for verification. The
dramatist can scarcely emphasise details in the setting at all :
he must leave them to take their chance. He cannot emphasise
details in the dialogue beyond a certain point : he can seldom
or never speak *about* anything in a commenting way because
he can speak only through his characters and they naturally
speak *in and out of* a particular milieu rather than about it. The
matrix of the past which can be provided in a historical drama
is, therefore, too sketchy to create the illusion of the past.

That illusion is weaker in the historical drama for another
subtler reason. Perhaps the most fundamental of all our aware-
nesses are our sense of place and our sense of time. When we
recover from a faint, the two questions we generally ask are,
Where am I ? and How long have I been unconscious ? as if
our primary psychological needs were to reorientate ourselves
in place and time. Now when we are seated in the theatre we
are far too fully aware of the twentieth century to feel with any
profound degree of temporary and voluntary conviction that
the events taking place across the footlights belong to the
thirteenth or fourteenth. We see and hear the thirteenth or
fourteenth century, but it is impossible to think ourselves in it.
As Dr Johnson judiciously says of theatrical illusion in general,
" The truth is, that the spectators are always in their senses,
and know, from the first act to the last, that the stage is only a
stage, and that the players are only players." [1]   " It will be
asked," he goes on, " how the drama moves, if it is not credited.
It is credited with all the credit due to a drama. It is credited,
whenever it moves, as a just picture of a real original ; as
representing to the auditor what he would himself feel, if he were
to do or suffer what is there feigned to be suffered or to be done." [2]
With that proviso it may be admitted that the better the acting,

[1] *Prefaces to Shakespeare* in *The Works of Samuel Johnson*, 1792, ii, p. 97.
[2] *Ibid.*, pp. 98-9.

the more moving will be the representation. But here is the paradox : the more deeply one is stirred emotionally, the more one is aware of being alive there and then in a twentieth-century theatre. One can enter into a thirteenth- or fourteenth-century emotion, but not into its period. Sight and hearing are very practical senses. What the eye sees and the ear hears is happening for them *now*. By 99/100 of our working lives they are habituated to dating anything they see or hear as contemporary. We may be transported imaginatively, but the transport is emotional, not temporal or spatial. On the other hand, when the reader is reading a novel, he knows that what he is reading is historic. He is not asked to believe that it is happening while he reads. The matter-of-fact senses of sight and hearing are in abeyance, except for the purely mechanical use of the eye in reading. It is the mind's eye and ear which are appealed to on a level beyond space and time. That is to say, it is the imagination alone which operates. In a sense it is easier for the imagination to work when the practical senses are lulled as in reading. At least if the emotional transport is less than at a play, the imagination is not asked to function in opposition to the eye and the ear.

VI

Presumably all historical novelists have shared a common interest in the past. But there have been other, perhaps more compelling, reasons for their choosing it as a basis for fiction. Whatever these reasons may have been, and however interesting, much more so are the different ways in which the novelists regard and depict the past. They have been many, but I think that they can all be subsumed under three several methods :—(1) the portrayal of the past as different from the present; (2) the portrayal of it for its own sake; and (3) the portrayal of it as like the present.

It might perhaps be added that so long as novelists see the past as different from the present they almost necessarily reveal it under the glancing lights of romance. In the hands of those who depict the past for its own sake realism and objectivity tend, at least to a certain degree, to dull the romantic colouring. And in the novelists who treat the past as essentially more like the present than different romance is replaced by the light of common day.

Naturally, perhaps, it was the difference of the past from the present that first attracted historical novelists. These late eighteenth-century romantics from Horace Walpole onwards wanted to escape from the sedate rationalism and sober security of their day into a past which might induce a willing suspension of disbelief for otherwise unconvincing narratives by providing a more plausible climate for marvels, thrills, and surprises, physical, psychological, and metaphysical—in short, a world in which anything could be made to happen by the laws of romance. But a novelist whose main desire is escape from the supposed boredom of the life of his day is not likely to deal faithfully with the life of the past when he gets there, especially if like the eighteenth-century escapists he has next to no knowledge and no historical sense. It was certainly an age in which great historians had, practically for the first time in Britain, acquired an effective sense of the past and had made history a recognised department of English literature. Without their work and the taste for history which it created, the eighteenth-century novel might have remained for a long time contemporaneous and realistic. Hume, Gibbon, and Robertson, to name only three practitioners of the historian's art out of many, were undoubtedly contributors to the various literary and other forces which produced the Romantic Revival. But there is a difference between a taste for history and a knowledge of it. Even dilettante historians like Horace Walpole and William Beckford thought of the middle ages in terms of dubious bric-à-brac and sham Gothic. It is little wonder, therefore, that the less knowledgeable Chatterton and Macpherson produced such forgeries as would scarcely take in a modern schoolboy, or that they did take in most of the critics and all the unpretending readers of the day. The eighteenth-century novel-reader knew as much about life in sixteenth-century Italy as the twentieth-century cinema-patrons of life in Brazil or Bali or Baluchistan, however enthralled they may be by the films supposed to reveal them. That is to say, he had all the historical knowledge that his novelists required and nearly as much as they themselves possessed. It was enough that he should want to read about the past and to assume unthinkingly and easily that *The Castle of Otranto* (1764), *The Old English Baron* (1777), and *The Mysteries of Udolpho* (1794) supplied it. Not only did the novelists practically avoid all historical persons and events, but they were wildly anachronistic in all their settings and details. They were really rather hysterical, than historical, novelists, wild romantics and melodramatists, crude sensationalists and sentimentalists. Their predecessors, like Richardson and Fielding, had, in Dr Johnson's phrase, brought " about natural events by easy means, and [kept] up curiosity without the help of wonder." [1] They themselves, on the other hand, stage-managed unnatural and supernatural events by extraordinary means and kept curiosity at a stretch by wonder on wonder. But the majority of readers, then as now, are poor judges of what is *la vérité vraie* either in psychology or in history, and still poorer judges of what may be called historical psychology. What the eighteenth-century reader of historical thrillers wanted was what his fellow-enthusiast to-day wants, a book of sensations rather than thoughts, a tale with simpler and keener passions, brighter colours and costumes, intenser characters, more exciting actions, and loftier dialogue than the drab routine of every day. " Are we never to shed blood ? " asked Stevenson. The answer is " Yes, and get all manner of novelties and risks by identifying oneself with a proxy hero in a historical novel." For the past will always provide the crude novelist and superficial dramatist with disguises for unreal events and false psychology.

In Scott romance and realism were ambivalent and each qualified the other. For all his romantic love of things as they are not, he had his feet planted with unusual solidity and firmness on the ground. The romance of the past, therefore, which was most to his taste was of a less highly coloured and more probable kind than that of the sensationalists. It was related to reality not merely by the introduction of historical events and characters which his predecessors for the most part avoided, but also by a great variety of persons who were fictitious but whose humours and humanity were entirely convincing. And it was given additional confirmation by its setting in actual localities and buildings, most of which Scott had visited and which, whether he had visited them or had only read about them in books, had a reality that Udolpho and Otranto could not afford.

" The romantic feeling," he says, " which I have described as predominating in my mind, naturally rested upon and associated themselves with these grand features of the landscape around me ; and the historical incidents, or traditional legends connected with many of them, gave to my admiration a sort of intense impression of reverence, which at times made my heart

[1] *The Rambler*, No. 4, in *The Works of Samuel Johnson*, 1792, iv, p. 20.

feel too big for its bosom. From this time the love of natural beauty, more especially when combined with ancient ruins, or remains of our fathers' piety or splendour, became with me an insatiable passion, which if circumstances had permitted, I would gladly have gratified by travelling over half the globe." [1] " My principal object in these excursions " of his youth, he continues, " was the pleasure of seeing romantic scenery, or what afforded me at least equal pleasure, the places which had been distinguished by remarkable historical events. The delight with which I regarded the former, of course had general approbation, but I often found it difficult to procure sympathy with the interest I felt in the latter. Yet to me, the wandering over the field of Bannockburn was the source of more exquisite pleasure than gazing upon the celebrated landscape from the battlements of Stirling Castle . . . show me an old castle or a field of battle, and I was at home at once, filled it with its combatants in their proper costume, and overwhelmed my hearers by the enthusiasm of my description." [2]

In the poetic romance perhaps the unlocalised setting of *The Ancient Mariner* or *La Belle Dame sans Merci* may release the imagination better than do the local habitations and names of *Marmion*. But in the prose historical romance a different degree or kind of credibility must be maintained by reference to actuality of persons, places, and things.

After all, however sympathetic Scott was with the romantic tendency of his generation, he was on the other side of his nature a man of the eighteenth century. He knew the novelists of common and contemporary life from Richardson and Fielding to Maria Edgeworth and Jane Austen as well as the true romances of the middle ages and the pseudo-romances of his own day. The fiction into which Scott wove historical material and the romance of the past was closer in many ways to the novels of the realists than to those of the pseudo-romantics.

In the main, therefore, and in his most characteristic work he sought the past, not in a flight from reality at all but for its interesting and piquant differences from his present, differences set off by likenesses. There are many passages in which he draws such contrasts explicitly, quite apart from the implicit contrasts

[1] *Memoir of the Early Life of Sir Walter Scott written by himself* in J. G. Lockhart, *Memoirs of the Life of Sir Walter Scott, Bart.*, 1878, i, p. 12.
[2] *Ibid.*, p. 15.

which he supplies all the time and means us to see.[1] He was singularly well placed, locally and temporally, in a country far from homogeneous in its customs and manners, in which the ways of the more primitive, as they had but recently been, were of absorbing interest to the more sophisticated, and in an age which followed hard on the heels of striking events and was separated from them by general and profound changes. " It naturally occurred to me," he said of *Waverley* (1814), the very subtitle of which *'Tis Sixty Years Since* points the contrast between a past and a present, " that the ancient traditions and high spirit of a people, who, living in a civilized age and country, retained so strong a tincture of manners belonging to an early period of society, must afford a subject favourable to romance." [2] Scott's instinctive wisdom made him choose for his first essays in historical fiction periods of Scottish history remote enough to afford striking differences and yet near enough to be within the memories of persons whom he had known and questioned, like Alexander Stewart of Invernahyle and Mrs Murray Keith.[3] But when in *Ivanhoe* and later novels set in ages long since gone he went farther back in time, he still sought the romance of difference in fundamental likeness. " The passions," he remarks, " . . . are generally the same in all ranks and conditions, all countries and ages ; and it follows, as a matter of course, that the opinions, habits of thinking, and actions, however influenced by the peculiar state of society, must still, upon the whole, bear a strong resemblance to each other." [4]

One result of his pervasive desire to contrast the past with the present is that he always remains outside of the past himself. He sees it across the gulf of years. He calls it up like Prospero—

> Spirits, which by mine art
> I have from their confines call'd to enact
> My present fancies [5]—

to amuse by its differences the more civilised age to which he, somewhat regretfully, and his readers belong. " My own opinions," he makes his double, Chrystal Croftangry, say, " are in favour of our own times in many respects, but not in so far

---

[1] *Cf.* e.g. *Rob Roy*, ed. cit., vii, p. viii, and *Ivanhoe*, ed. cit., xvi, pp. xxv-xxvi.
[2] *Waverley Novels*, general preface, *ed. cit.*, i, p. x.
[3] Cf. *Chronicles of the Canongate*, ed. cit., xli, pp. xviii-xxii.
[4] *Ivanhoe*, ed. cit., xvi, pp. xxxvi-xxxvii.
[5] Shakespeare, *The Tempest*, IX, i, 120-2.

as affords means for exercising the imagination, or exciting the interest which attaches to other times. I am glad to be a writer or a reader in 1826, but I would be most interested in reading or relating what happened from half a century to a century before. We have the best of it. Scenes in which our ancestors thought deeply, acted fiercely, and died desperately, are to us tales to divert the tedium of a winter's evening, when we are engaged to no party, or beguile a summer's morning, when it is too scorching to ride or walk." [1]

I used the phrase " to amuse " advisedly. Not that Scott was indifferent to the moral effects of novel-writing and novel-reading. For example, he has an eloquent repudiation, in his large and generous way, of the falsification of life by the so-called poetic justice which would have had him reward the suffering and meritorious Rebecca.[2] But he was almost as little of the conventional moralist as his great master Shakespeare, and he did not seek to make the mere amusement of historical fiction serve didactic ends.

But this didactic use of the past in fiction soon followed. It was no more than adumbrated in Bulwer Lytton's *Eugene Aram* (1832), *The Last Days of Pompeii* (1834), and *Rienzi* (1835), and in Disraeli's *Wondrous Tale of Alroy* and *The Rise of Iskander* (1833). It was rather the *histoire moralisée* of Carlyle in *The French Revolution* (1837) and *Past and Present* (1843) which turned the Victorians to historical fiction for edification, instruction, social criticism, partisanship, and propaganda. Though Carlyle had rejected the literal inspiration of the Bible and the Presbyterian or, indeed any, version of Christianity, he did not abandon the Presbyterian devotion to preachment, and he took his texts from the " book of the past," which Gospel according to Thomas seemed to him as inspired as any Bible. In fact his books are to a large extent the secular sermons of a " stickit minister." The effect of his example can be seen on such typical novels of the period as Charles Kingsley's anti-papal *Hypatia* (1853) with its provocative subtitle *New Foes with an Old Face*, and Newman's Roman Catholic counterblast *Callista ; A Sketch of the Third Century* (1856). But these are only two double-purpose novels out of the many. Indeed it is scarcely an exaggeration to say that practically all the major novelists of

[1] *Chronicles of the Canongate*, ed. cit., xli, pp. 86-7.
[2] *Ivanhoe*, ed. cit., xvi, pp. xx-xxii.

the Victorian heyday, Dickens, Thackeray, Charles Reade, George Eliot, Mrs Gaskell, as well as Charles Kingsley and Newman and a host of minors, depicted the past with more or less of an intention to make it minister something more than thrills and amusement to the present. The Victorians were nothing if not serious-minded ; and their novelists by choosing a past to restate the present in other and simpler terms achieved something like the effect of a parable or allegory. But for that very reason and for others they, like Scott, maintained the distance and difference of the past.

So, too, do those novelists, mostly of recent date and but ephemeral fame, who form what I might call the historical nostalgics.

As the nineteenth century waned, so did the taste for the double-purpose historical novel. As if in direct revulsion from it came the historical novel which concentrated on the interest of the past for its own sake without stressing the thrills and romance, the contrasts to the present, or the significance for it. It is the aim of this kind, not to show us the past at a romantic distance, but to carry us bodily back into it and make us live there for the time being. There is a sense in which Thackeray, especially but not only in *Henry Esmond* (1852), achieved this. But he was, even in *Henry Esmond*, too much of a Victorian moralist and social critic to present the past with complete objectivity ; and I prefer to regard the objective Flaubert as its originator in *Salammbô* (1862) and *The Temptation of St Anthony* (1874). We may take as English examples Shorthouse's *John Inglesant* (1880), Pater's *Marius the Epicurean* (1885) and *Gaston de Latour* (1896), Morris's prose romances or some of them, and George Moore's *The Brook Kerith* (1916) and *Héloise and Abelard* (1921). The method of all of these tried to be more psychologically sensitive than earlier historical novels had cared to be, to give in fact to historical fiction some of the psychological realism which novels of contemporary life had already developed. They tried to admit us into a bygone age through the internal lives of the characters rather than their external lives, however bustling, and to make us understand the furniture of their minds rather than the furniture of their houses and appreciate the beliefs and feelings which coloured and determined their actions. I do not say that many of the novelists of this class have quite achieved their aim.

Perhaps Flaubert in his *Temptation of St Anthony* rather than in *Salammbô*, Tolstoy in *War and Peace* (1868), and Larreta's *Glory of Don Ramiro* (1920) have been most successful in giving life as men and women had lived it in their dead generations, fairly, objectively, and without extenuation, not with any design on the reader or any attempt to mould his judgment, and with the prejudices, superstitions, idealisms, and convictions of the past unqualified and unmodernised. It is probably in the very best specimens of this class that historical fiction would pass most frequently Mr Hilaire Belloc's high test by showing the " power [to solve] the problem of *incomprehensibles* . . . the making understandable these things which had hitherto bewildered " [1] us in history, pious barbarities, furious enthusiasms, repellent conventions, and the like.

Still another way of handling the past in fiction began within the last thirty years or so. It is, like the method I have just been discussing, more psychological than that of Kingsley or Scott. But the psychological quality as such is not its differentia. Instead of seeing the past as different from the present or as possessing an intrinsic interest which requires no support from either likeness to or difference from the present, this most recent school sees the past as more like the present than different from it. Indeed by smoothing down the differences it sees the past ambiguously in terms of the present and deliberately confused with it. Good examples up to a point, but only up to a point, of this reading the present into the past are Mr Robert Graves's *I, Claudius* (1934), *Claudius the God* (1934), and *Count Belisarius* (1938) ; and bad examples are Mr Masefield's *Basilissa* (1940) and *Conquer* (1941).

But even the best example that the method would permit could not be a good historical novel ; and the better it was of its kind the worse it would be as a historical novel, because it would be attempting an impossibility. It needs but little experience of family life and little observation of the two consecutive generations to know that either misunderstands what the other understands, believes what the other rejects, and so on. How much more divided are generations two or three hundred years apart ! The novelists of the new school cannot, of course, press their method to its logical conclusion. They must have labels, as it were, to tell you where and when, since in spite of themselves they

[1] *Op. cit.*, p. 38.

still want to be historical; and a great deal of the past simply will not allow of translation into the present. It is in the psychology of their characters that these novelists take their greatest liberties. For they infuse into these characters modern complexities, indirections, compunctions, and sentimentalities until they feel, think, speak, act, and react in the sophisticated modes of to-day. It is an *ersatz* past which their creators really present. The interest of their stories may be very considerable, but it is not the special kind of interest which the historical novel is calculated to give.

I suppose that the practitioners of this particular type of fiction would justify themselves by saying that since men and women are always the same there is no point in making much difference in their way of life. My own view is that their novels are manifestations of the debunking spirit which has devoted most of its activity to belittling historical individuals but which can turn, as in the novels in question, to removing the glamour of the past by deleting its differences. In any case it is not true that men and women are always the same, except on the ground-floor to which Shylock referred when he asked : " Hath not a Jew eyes ? hath not a Jew hands, organs, dimensions, senses, affections, passions ? fed with the same food, hurt with the same weapons, subject to the same diseases, healed by the same means, warmed and cooled by the same winter and summer as a Christian is ? If you prick us, do we not bleed ? if you tickle us, do we not laugh ? if you poison us, do we not die ? and if you wrong us, shall we not revenge ? " [1] Men's reflex actions, sense organs, appetites, and passions may be the same, fundamentally at least, at all times and in all places. *Quod semper, quod ubique, quod ab omnibus.* But the outward manifestation and accompaniments of all of them can be very different. Take sneezing, for example. Sometimes men have sneezed only involuntarily, and sometimes also voluntarily with the help of snuff. Nowadays a sneeze for most people is a sneeze and, like the primrose, " nothing more," except a warning of a coming cold. But not so long ago a sneeze was supposed to be fraught with a mysterious danger which kind friends averted by a " God bless you ! " As to our sense organs, we need only to look at portraits and landscapes by Van Eyck, Rubens, Whistler, and Derain to realise that, apart from individual differences, no

[1] Shakespeare, *The Merchant of Venice*, III, i, 61-9.

two ages see alike or want to look at the same things. In the matter of the appetites, life may be made up at all times of eating and drinking, as Sir Andrew Aguecheek believed. But how different are the things men eat and drink, the amounts, the preparing and serving, and the significance of it all at different times. Even the passions have their fashions. The way of a man with a maid or of a maid with a man is as different in different ages as one can see from Ovid's *De Arte Amandi*, Mr C. S. Lewis's *Allegory of Love*, and Mr Bernard Shaw's *Man and Superman*. We are born into a world, not of uniformity and sameness, but of infinite differences and perpetual changes. Even birth into it and death out of it differ from year to year in significance and context, and no two lives between these termini are the same. It is in the recording of human differences that the interest of the novel resides ; for manners are its chief ingredient and they are always changing and those other things which may be alike very deep down are of value and interest to the novelist only as they differ on their surfaces from man to man and from age to age.

THE ART OF SATIRE AND THE SATIRIC SPECTRUM

As no thought can be justly said to be fine, unless it be true, I have all along had a great regard for Truth ; except only in passages that are purely satirical, where some allowance must be given : For Satire may be fine and true Satire, tho' it be not directly and according to the Letter, true : 'Tis enough that it carry with it a Probability or Semblance of Truth.

Edward Bysshe, *The Art of English Poetry*, 1718, i, sig. *A4.

We talked of Pope. JOHNSON. " He wrote his ' Dunciad ' for fame. That was his primary motive. Had it not been for that, the dunces might have railed against him till they were weary, without his troubling himself about them. He delighted to vex them, no doubt ; but he had more delight in seeing how well he could vex them."

Boswell's Life of Johnson. Edited by George Birkbeck Hill. Revised and Enlarged Edition by L. F. Powell, 1934–, ii, 334.

I

" HOLDE Satyra, Tochter der gerechten Themis und des bocks-füssigen Pan," as Heine apostrophised it,[1] is a literary anomaly. Though it gathers itself up so compactly in certain works as to have obtained the status of a literary kind, it might be regarded as being not so much a kind as a flavouring or quality like humour, a flavouring which may taste any of the formal kinds whether in prose or in verse.

The satiric quality may be essential to the kind, as in parody, in burlesque, and in regular verse satire. In other species it may be entirely absent ; or it may crop out sporadically ; or it may be of frequent or even constant occurrence. Thus in the essays of Bacon and of Temple it is all-but-negligible, but in the essays of Addison and of Sir Max Beerbohm it is all-but-omni-present. It can add animation to oratory in Burke, piquancy to history in Gibbon, and venom to criticism in Housman. It has had, especially in the seventeenth century, rather than has now, a place in the sermon ; and like an out-thrust of rock in a meadow, it can sometimes appear without incongruity in poetry of a predominantly non-satiric character, as it does in *Lycidas*.

[1] *Reisebilder iv, Italien iii* in *Samtliche Werke*, 1914, v, p. 72.

The novel and the drama can make a freer use of incidental satire than can any other kind except that chartered libertine of letters, the essay. One might perhaps distinguish three classes of fiction and drama according to the degree of satire present. In the first or purely objective class, satire, which in the ultimate analysis is subjective, is completely excluded, at least from every part but the dialogue, or the unspoken thoughts of the characters, being admitted even there only to serve an intrinsic organic requirement; and unpleasant or silly characters, who would otherwise be fair game for satire, are created like any other character as agents in an action which is self-contained and self-sufficient. In the second class the novelist or the dramatist, without disturbing the general effect, permits himself occasional departures of longer or shorter duration from his predominantly objective treatment of the theme and of the characters to the satiric, principally by way of comment and description. In the third class the action and the characterisation have a primarily satiric intention of varying degrees of pungency, and the narrative or the dramatic interest is a means to the end. It is to the second or the third classes that most fiction and drama now belong; and it is in the novel and the play that the modern satiric spirit is most frequently manifested, having become milder as it has become more pervasive.

Whether the satiric quality appears fitfully in, or becomes the *raison d'être* of, a poem or essay, play, narrative, or speech, it is a most volatile and unstable essence, *varium et mutabile semper satura*. For even regular verse satire of the classical variety of Horace and Pope, with which I am chiefly concerned, swings backwards and forwards, on an ellipse about the two foci of the satiric universe, the exposure of folly and the castigation of vice; it fluctuates between the flippant and the earnest, the completely trivial and the heavily didactic; it ranges from the extremes of crudity and brutality to the utmost refinement and elegance; it employs singly or in conjunction monologue, dialogue, epistle, oration, narrative, manners-painting, character-drawing, allegory, fantasy, travesty, burlesque, parody, and any other vehicle it chooses; and it presents a chameleon-like surface by using all the tones of the satiric spectrum, wit, ridicule, irony, sarcasm, cynicism, the sardonic, and invective. Such is the heterogeneity of so-called " regular " verse satire as a species. As for the individual satirist's work, it varies, in the first place,

according to the gravity of his matter; in the second place,
according to the rôle he plays, preacher, friend, eulogist, literary
critic, gossip, politician, patriot, *censor morum*, or *arbiter
elegantiarum*, and the reality or the pretence of feeling or
detachment with which he fills the rôle; in the third place,
according to the civility of the age and the audience for which
he writes; and lastly, according to his mastery of the satiric
design he has chosen and of the satiric tones in which he paints.
It is obvious that the number is very large of the possible per-
mutations and combinations, of the possible functions of so many
variables. Satire, to take a metaphor from music, is not a
simple melody on the G string, but a symphony in discord.

II

Ever since Socrates in *The Republic* came to the reluctant
conclusion that until poetry can be proved to be profitable as
well as pleasurable it ought to be excluded from a well-constituted
state,[1] lovers of poetry have tried to make the Muses out to be
honest women and literature respectable. The Horatian " Omne
tulit punctum qui miscuit utile dulci " [2] may be taken as summing
up the most popular argument in the ancient justification of
literature. The Renaissance seized on the tag and made it one
of the central articles of its literary creed. Nor has it altogether
ceased to operate even to-day. Thus it has passed from Sidney
to Dr Johnson and from Dr Johnson to Mr Middleton Murry.
" Poesy," said the first, " is an art of imitation . . . with this
end, to teach and delight." [3] " Poetry," said the second, " is
the art of uniting pleasure with truth, by calling imagination to
the help of reason." [4] " [T]he simplest fragment of pure poetry,"
says the third, " has its own metaphysical and moral finality " [5];
and " criticism . . . should openly accept the fact that its
deepest judgements are moral." [6]

Since men-of-letters, like other men, are beings whose minds

---

[1] *The Dialogues of Plato*, ed. Benjamin Jowett, 1875, iii, p. 504.

[2] *De Arte Poetica*, 343.

[3] *An Apology for Poetry* in *Elizabethan Critical Essays*, ed. G. Gregory
Smith, 1904, i, p. 158.

[4] *Lives of the Poets : Milton* in *The Works of Samuel Johnson*, 1792, ix,
p. 160.

[5] *Pure Poetry* in *Countries of the Mind*, Second Series, 1931, p. 28.

[6] *A Critical Credo* in *Countries of the Mind*, First Series, 1931, p. 189.

are naturally polarised by good and evil—and since from what one man has thought another may derive, if not a positive, at least a negative accommodation to moral concepts on the liberal principle that to the human being nothing human is alien—it is generally easy to discover in nearly any work some sort of edification *ex postfacto*. But did the men of letters always, or even often, put it there ? There is a difference between what the poet said and what he meant ; between what he said and what the critics think he said ; between what he meant and what they think he meant ; between what he said and the effect it has on different readers at different times. It is quite true that poets have sometimes written with a didactic intention. But more often they have sought no end beyond the work itself and no justification beyond the art and delight thereof. Or, if they did indeed have a didactic intention at the outset, that intention was quickly relegated to the background when once they had actually begun ; it had served their turn and it might come forward again when the work was completed.[1] But in the process of creation a purely artistic intention supervened and displaced the didactic, for the creative process generates an artistic potential far more powerful than any which is not artistic. Poetry is first of all an art and therefore ideally an end in itself, never a means to an end, though, by reason of language which is its medium and which inevitably associates it intimately with the purposive life of man, it may appear to subserve—and in moments, when, however, it ceases to be itself, it does subserve—many purposes not its own.

"What *is* didactic poetry ? " asks De Quincey. " What does ' didactic ' mean when applied as a distinguishing epithet to such an idea as a poem ? The predicate destroys the subject ; it is a case of what logicians call *contradictio in adjecto*—the unsaying by means of an attribute the very thing which is the subject of that attribute you have just affirmed. No poetry can have the function of teaching. It is impossible that a variety or species should contradict the very purpose which contradistinguishes its *genus*. The several species differ partially but not by the whole idea which differentiates their class. Poetry, or any one of the fine arts (all of which speak through the genial nature of man and his excited sensibilities), can teach only as

[1] Cf. *Satire* in *The Times Literary Supplement*, 23rd June 1927, to which article I am indebted for several suggestions.

nature teaches, as forests teach, as the sea teaches, as infancy teaches, viz. by deep impulse, by hieroglyphic suggestion." [1]

III

From the supposed moral function of poetry in general, let us pass to the equally supposititious moral function of satire in particular. It has been oftener and more emphatically justified as a moralising and normative agent than has any of the other literary modes, perhaps because satirists have always been conscious of having somewhat ambiguous motives.

The elusive nature of satire has called forth a great deal of criticism rather rhapsodical than rational, rather oracular than empirical. Its apologists have tended to accept some of the conventions by which it proceeds as literal facts without which it cannot exist or at least have any value. They would make satire out to be a virtual exception to all the other literary kinds, in that they point out as its antecedent *sine qua non* a genuine emotional urge of contempt for, or indignation at, an actual fact or person, the contempt or indignation being not only sincerely felt but justified by the facts of the case. They would naively define satire as the sincere expression, in a style peculiarly fitted to provoke salutary laughter, either of a genuine moralist whose regard for the decencies of public or private life has been outraged, or of an intelligent and cultured man whose fine sense of fitness and propriety induces him to protest chaffingly or forcibly against aberrations from the best standards of good manners, good sense, good feeling, and good taste.

Thus, near the beginning of satire's history, Juvenal declared his own works to be the explosions of a righteous and irresistible indignation which of itself beat out verses :—

Difficile est, saturam non scribere.[2]

The typically moralistic Sidney, distinguishing between the abusive and the bantering methods, held that " the bitter but wholsome Iambick . . . rubs the galled minde, in making shame the trumpet of villanie with bolde and open crying out against naughtines . . . the Satirick . . . sportingly neuer

---

[1] *The Poetry of Pope* in *The Collected Writings of Thomas De Quincey*, ed. David Masson, 1890, xi, p. 88.

[2] i, 30.

leaueth vntil hee make a man laugh at folly, and, at length ashamed, to laugh at himselfe ; which he cannot auoyd, without auoyding the follie." [1] In our own day Mr Gilbert Cannan assigns to the " true satirist . . . no obligation to society but that of showing its individual and collective villainy, cowardice and hypocrisy. To fulfil that obligation," Mr Cannan continues, " he needs to be one man picked out of ten thousand, an honest man." [2] In the same strain of didactic criticism Mr A. G. Barnes insists that " the satirist's greatest difficulty [is] to convince the world that he is sincere. For sincerity is truly the essence of all good satire. Affected indignation is too soon detected for the poet to be able easily to succeed where he does not feel what he writes." [3]

But do the knave and the fool really read satire like guilty creatures sitting at a play and resolving to confess and make amends, to purge and live cleanly and to grow wise ? Does the satirist really chasten whom he loveth, and expect to effect a cure ? Is he disappointed when he does not, and has he any right to look for any other result from so unpersuasive a remedy ? Or is a satire a failure if the world rolls on its wicked or its silly way with not so much as the deviation of a hair ? Has any satirist ever abandoned his art in despair by reason of the non-success he has met in his evangelism of abuse and scorn ? Must the satirist have a passion for the truth ? Does he never knowingly exceed it ? Did all those whom satirists have gibbeted as knaves or tormented as fools actually deserve their punishment ? Have satirists, the Popes, the Churchills, and the Byrons, been men of such unblemished characters that no beam obstructed their vision of the motes in the eyes of others. Or, lastly, must a satire which has all the inventive, literary, and stylistic virtues proper to the kind be pronounced worthless because the author was insincere, his intentions were unprincipled, and his charges were false ?

The answer to all these and many similar questions is Certainly not. At the utmost " Satire is," as Swift said, " a sort of glass wherein beholders do generally discover every body's face but their own ; which is the chief reason for that kind reception it meets with in the world, and that so very few are offended with

---

[1] *Op. cit.*, i, p. 176.
[2] *Satire*, n.d., p. 15.
[3] *A Book of English Verse Satire*, 1926, p. ix.

it." [1]   But the goodness or badness, and the genuineness or falsity
of a satire are qualities which have no direct relation to the
goodness or badness and the genuineness or falsity of the author, his
purpose, and his charges.

IV

Satire, like all the other literary kinds, rests on conventions,
premisses tacitly agreed on by the author and his public, which
are the means of producing the οἰκεία ἡδονή of the kind, and
which may or may not coincide with the external facts. Thus,
just as it is by convention that the love-lyrist treats of love, the
elegist of grief, and the tragic dramatists of the most serious
issues of life, so it is by an exactly co-ordinate convention that the
satirist concerns himself with vice and folly.

It is, too, by convention that the satirist, in relation to his
twofold subject, poses as either the moralist or the social arbiter.
It is not necessary—indeed it is generally inadvisable—to adopt
too lofty a tone on the moral side or one too decided on the
social. When the satire deals mainly with the more serious
offences, the most generally effective pose is that of the honest
man who is forced to break silence and claims no more virtue
than the decent average of his fellow-citizens. Such is the usual
attitude of Juvenal and of Dryden. When the satire is concerned
more with manners than with morals, the more apparently
moderate the author is the better. Like Addison he will hint a
fault and hesitate dislike, or like Horace he will merely remark
on this or that as if they only needed to be called to notice to be
laughingly acknowledged and put right.

By a third convention the satirist is something of an orator
in his more rhetorical, and something of a talker in his more
familiar, moods, always conscious of an audience with which
he has to establish relations and employing a variety of stylistic
devices which originated in speech and still retain much of their
public or oral character. On the other hand most other poetic
kinds are by a different convention supposed not to be heard
but to be overheard, the voices of lonely singers with a

> delight in singing, though none hear
Beside the singer.[2]

---

[1] *The Battle of the Books* in *The Works of Jonathan Swift*, ed. Walter Scott,
1814, xi, p. 220.
[2] Walter Savage Landor, *Robert Browning*, 1-2.

Like the orator and the talker, the satirist has to conciliate his audience and he does so by nearly always accepting their standards. He must have an opposition, his victims ; but he himself pretends to express the opinions of a majority, at least of all those who matter and who would preserve what time has proved and reason has established. He is, therefore, generally a moral and social conservative because the majority in a community will always be ready to suspect changes in morals as wicked and changes in manners as bad form. Occasionally, however, for one reason or another, a satirist realises that he is in a minority. Even so, he may still be a conservative *laudator temporis acti* and appeal to such lovers of the old order as survive. But more probably he will offer himself, like Byron in *Don Juan*, as a left-wing critic of cant and humbug in an outmoded system. In this way he presents a minority view, but he assumes that his audience, fit and few, is with him and that he and they share the same enlightenment.

These three conventions together necessarily involve a fourth. For given the satiric matter of vice and folly, the satirist's *ex officio* manner of indignation and contempt, and the accommodation of the style and the implications to an audience, it follows that satire will be nearly always occasional, particular not general, local not universal. It will take the contemporary world as its frame of reference, the abuses and the absurdities of the age as its topics, and living persons with or without disguise or else types of the period as its victims. The peculiar kinds of interest and of laughter which it seeks to arouse can be provoked, at least in the audience for which it is primarily calculated, only by what I might call the satiric distortion of an existing state of affairs ; and the equally peculiar kinds of indignation and of contempt which the satirist actually or imaginatively feels can be convincing only with respect to his own day and generation, not to historical vice and antiquated folly. The occasional character of satire, its topicality, and its appeal to a contemporary audience, which never consists of Tom, Dick and Harry, result in its need of annotation for certain native readers even in its own day, for every foreign reader from the first, and for every reader whatsoever after a lapse of time. But if it was originally vital enough, it will escape from the limitations of the ephemeral and the local, and will acquire an interest on the second plane for all competent readers anywhere and at any time.

V

If the real purpose of a literary genus can be deduced rather from its actual effect then from what purports to be its aim, then the general purpose of satire is not to cure anything or reform anybody, but to give to the reader a kind of astringent pleasure like an acid drop or a dash of bitters.

The fact is that we all have a vein of malice in us, a capacity for hate with some resemblance to our capacities for love or pity or fear. It may be the negative charge, as it were, in the will to live, or, in other words, a biological necessity to give the organism sufficient self-assertiveness and resistance. We certainly draw on this malicious reservoir, turning the tap on for a few drops or half-cock or full-pelt according as we are merely vigorous or somewhat aggressive or thoroughly angry.

But the three forces of civilisation, morality, and religion have had to curb our malicious egoism and to pronounce it according to their modes as barbaric, anti-social, and sinful. It can be indulged openly only on what the community regards as legitimate occasions ; and except for these rare liberties it must fust in us unused and bottled up.

But in satire, as in the graphical parallel of caricature, a tolerated *modus irascendi, odiendi, invidendi* [1] has been invented. It provides for the satirist himself and for us his readers a licensed cathartic of envy, hatred, and malice, and all uncharitableness. His satisfaction is more or less immediate and particular, ours more or less vicarious and general.

It is possible, too, that satire serves another but corollary function. For some of our evil humours are partly due to a vague awareness of defects and excesses in ourselves which satire enables us to externalise and condemn.

VI

" Aristotle divides all Poetry," says Dryden, " in relation to the progress of it, into nature without art, art begun, and art completed." [2] Such has certainly been the progress of satire. Dryden was under no delusion as to its beginnings, for he discovered them in the mutual hate of Adam and Eve after the

---

[1] *Cf.* Apuleius, *De Dogmate Platonis*, iii, 631.

[2] *A Discourse concerning the Original and Progress of Satire* in *Essays of John Dryden*, ed. W. P. Ker, 1900, ii, p. 45.

Fall. " This original, I confess, is not much to the honour of satire ; but here it was nature, and that depraved : when it became an art, it bore better fruit." [1]

Though hatred of a person, and nothing more respectable, is the urge behind the earliest satire, hatred like all the intenser emotions is naturally nearly inarticulate and must express itself rather physically than verbally. From such an anarchical passion nothing so effective as even the most primitive satire could have originated, until the hater realised how inadequate for the satisfactory expression of his rage was the vocabulary of Yah and Boo. He had to discover the art of articulate hate which could vary and sustain the invective.

It was mainly by assuming a moral superiority to his adversaries and by giving to his hatred the sanctions of morality that the incipient satirist found how rich his stock of abuse could become, how inexhaustible his supply of opprobrium. He learned how to seem to hate only because his enemies had brought down on themselves the merited obloquy of every good man, including himself, by a violation of principles cherished by the whole community ; and how to substitute for the less reputable motives of private enmity the more respectable reasons of a moral code. The satirist thus not only made an art out of his malice, the art of abuse, but also a virtue out of his hate which threw a righteous robe over the ambiguous motives of his art.

As soon as satire became an art, an artistic motive for writing it could at any time supervene, co-operating with, modifying, or even altogether displacing, any others. But some satirists may by actual circumstances be what the conventional pose would indicate, as love-lyrists may indeed love or elegists truly mourn ; there will always be good haters who like Byron abandon their minds to wrath, sincere moralists who like Jonah believe they do well to be angry at the way of the world, or true social reformers who like the Mikado engage in a

> very humane endeavour
> To make, to some extent,
> Each evil liver
> A running river
> Of harmless merriment.[2]

---

[1] *A Discourse concerning the Original and Progress of Satire* in *Essays of John Dryden*, ed. W. P. Ker, 1900, ii, p. 44.

[2] Sir W. S. Gilbert, *The Mikado ; or, The Town of Titipu* in *Original Plays*, third series, 1924, p. 204.

Since the art of satire exists, there is every reason why they should remember its existence and canalise their anger or contempt along the lines which it prescribes. But, be the motives of such satirists as authentic as you please, the dignity of moralist or social arbiter is reflected back on every satirist whatsoever by the mere act of writing satirically on vice and folly ; and satire still remains an art ready for any other practitioner to turn to in the spirit of the self-contained, self-actuated, and self-controlled artist who is drawn to it as a literary exercise, as a suitable means of self-expression, as a concession to the taste of the day, as a way of making money or of winning fame. Whatever other motives may contribute, they belong to the individual satirist, not to the nature of satire, as the moralising apologists hold, except by convention. The artistic motive, however, must be present, and the more it prevails the better the satire will be.

VII

If we were to insist on the sincerity of the satirist, we should in effect separate the kind from the category of the arts, as I have already said, because we should be judging it by moral, not æsthetic, criteria. It is quite true that excellence in any department of literature or any other art is dependent on a certain kind of sincerity, which has nothing to do with the artist's character or his non-artistic motives. I mean that the artist must have artistic integrity, which might be described as a fidelity to the medium in which he works, an acceptance of its conditions, and a genuine attempt to extract from its exigencies the maximum effect. " Art finds her own perfection within, and not outside of, herself," said Oscar Wilde,[1] who, if not a very sincere person in the moral sense, knew well enough what artistic integrity was. The poet in general must feel *what he writes* : he need not *feel what he writes about* ; and the satirist in particular is under no obligation to his subject except to render it with the fullest art at his command, and satire can be as free from a real indignation or contempt as any other kind of poetry can be free from any precipitating cause but the author's imagination and a desire to exercise it and his art. When poets, including satirists, put themselves in more or less imaginary situations, as by the law of wit and the liberty they are perfectly entitled to do, they

[1] *The Decay of Lying* in *Intentions*, 1909, p. 29.

produce work in the same vein as Browning's, "dramatic in principle, and so many utterances of so many imaginary persons," [1] perhaps sometimes approximating to their own, but at other times utterly different. But anyone may write what is conventionally appropriate to a kind, as for example indignation and contempt to satire, without feeling it except imaginatively and without imperilling his artistic integrity. Why should it be imposible to palm off simulated indignation or contempt alone of all the passions of the mimetic poet ? Like an advocate or an actor, the satirist can simulate them to the life, if for some reason it is worth his while, and can couple them with an assumption of righteousness as convincing as it is factitious, or with a purely theoretical sense of propriety belonging to his literary intelligence rather than to his real character.

There is another side to this question of sincerity. A satirist's indignation or his contempt may be sincere in the sense of being genuine. But it may have little or no justification : it may be out of all proportion to the cause.

> Non amo te, Sabidi, nec possum dicere quare :
> Hoc tantum possum dicere, non amo te,

says Martial [2] with what he professes to be a genuine, but apparently causeless, dislike. It was a dislike, however, which, to judge from a later epigram *In Sabidium*,[3] was allowed to invent or to excogitate reasons for its existence. Nor has it ever mattered to the satirist to what lies he stooped so long as he moralised his song. But was he in this false to the spirit of poetry ? " No, truly ; for the truest poetry is the most feigning ; and lovers [and haters] are given to poetry, and what they do swear in poetry may be said as lovers [and haters] they do feign." [4] All poets say more than they would be prepared to avouch in a cool hour ; as Wordsworth says, " The appropriate business of poetry . . . her privilege and her *duty*, is to treat things not as they *are*, but as they *appear* ; not as they exist in themselves, but as they *seem* to exist to the *senses*, and to the *passions*." [5] It might indeed be reasonably argued that this transfiguration

---

[1] Author's Preface in *The Poetical Works of Robert Browning*, 1868.

[2] i, 32.

[3] iii, 17.

[4] Shakespeare, *As You Like It*, III, iii, 19-22.

[5] *Essay, Supplementary to the Preface* (of 1815) in *The Poetical Works of William Wordsworth*, ed. E. de Selincourt, 1944, ii, p. 410.

of things by the passions and the senses will be at least as obvious
in the literature of hatred and contempt as for example in the
hyperbolical literature of love, because hatred and contempt by
their very nature distort, and because satire indulges without
scruple in the most unfair devices from the technique of rhetoric.

From the first extant satirists downwards, whatever moral
professions they have made and whatever lofty aims they have
advertised, there have been few—and these not the most admired
—who have not exaggerated their cases, distorted the facts, and
blackened their victim's characters.   I do not mean simply that
they have been carried away by social zeal, like certain clergy who

> hae been kend,
> In haly rapture,
> A rousing whid at times to vend,
> And nail 't wi' Scripture ; [1]

but that deliberately and with malice prepense they have mis-
represented men and things ; and they may have seemed to be
blind with rage when in fact they were using with consummate
and clear-headed skill all the restraints of artifice and selective
cunning.   Such satire was, is, and ever will be.   If it is suffered
at all in the state, it must be on the understanding that a man is
no more on oath in satires than in lapidary inscriptions.   Artistry
in malice demands it, though few satirists have been candid
enough to admit this.

The Earl of Rochester was one of the few.   Gilbert Burnet
was prepared to concede to him " that a grave way of *Satyr*
was sometimes no unprofitable way of Reproof.   Yet they who
used it only out of spite, and mixed Lyes with Truth, sparing
nothing that might adorn their Poems, or gratifie their Revenge,
could not excuse that way of Reproach, by which the Innocent
often suffer." [2]   To this animadversion Rochester answered, " A
man could not write with life, unless he were heated by Revenge :
For to make a *Satyr* without Resentments, upon the cold Notions
of *Philosophy*, was as if a man would, in cold blood, cut men's
throats, who had never offended him : And he said, The Lyes
in these Libels came often in as Ornaments that could not be
spared without spoiling the beauty of the Poem." [3]   A modern

[1] Burns, *Death and Dr Hornbook*, 3-6.
[2] Gilbert Burnet, *Some Passages of the Life and Death of the Right
Honourable John, Earl of Rochester*, 1692, pp. 25-26.
[3] *Ibid.*, p. 26.

satirist, Lord Alfred Douglas, has been equally candid in his remark that satire " cannot be polite or pleasant writing. If satire is to exist at all, it must be savage, fierce, bitter and perhaps also even occasionally unfair. I take it that a poet writing a satire is very much in the privileged position of an advocate attacking a man in a law court." [1] Moreover, he goes on, " There may be a complete answer to the lawyer's . . . attack." [1]

There are in fact few rules in the game. If satirists have seemed to observe certain bounds, the self-restriction was more apparent than real. It was not because they were sticklers for the truth or lacked gall, but because they were practitioners of an art in which nothing succeeds like moderation. Indeed satirists completed the evolution of their art, not when they first became articulate haters or when they turned moralists or when they acquired skill in lying, but when they learned how to play " The smyler with the knyf under the cloke." [2] It was then that they discovered how to be the more damaging by being the more restrained, and how the more delicate methods of laughing contempt were far more telling, at least as the civility of their audience developed, than the more emphatic ones of straightforward abuse.

VIII

I remarked before that the satirist, unlike the generality of poets in other kinds, is always an orator or a talker, conscious of his audience, adjusting himself to them and looking for their applause. He speaks to them on topics which concern them and him as members of a community or group, or, more often, a group within the community, sharing the same beliefs, standards, and interests. He gibbets or lashes those who offend against either the moral sense, or the sense of fitness, of the community or the group. " We that have free souls," he seems to say, " it touches us not : let the galled jade wince, our withers are unwrung." [3]

But not only does he address his audience on their own terms and with explicit or implicit agreements, but the whole technique of his art demands an audience for its display. It is a verse rhetoric, of which every trick is called forth and perfected only

---

[1] *The Collected Satires of Lord Alfred Douglas*, 1926, p. iii.
[2] Chaucer, *The Knightes Tale*, 1141.
[3] Shakespeare, *Hamlet*, III, ii, 252-3.

by the presence of an audience. The satirist is like an actor who cannot perform in an empty theatre, an orator who cannot persuade in a deserted chamber, a conversationalist who cannot shine in a soliloquy. Wit, ridicule, irony, sarcasm, cynicism, the sardonic, and invective are the devices of satire ; and they are all, as it were, with the possible exception of the sardonic, by their very nature public and indeed impossible except when there is for each an audience for whose benefit and admiration they are exercised.

I have arranged the seven devices of satire in an order of rising intensity and decreasing charity. They are the seven colours of the satirical spectrum, the seven pigments of the satirist's palette which he lays on in subtle blends and shot effects. He is a practitioner of a kind of broken colour or pointillism (to transfer to the description of a stylistic variability in literature a term invented by the critics of impressionism and neo-impressionism in painting). He presents a surface brilliant, variegated, and iridescent, so as to keep up the interest in the details for lack of a larger interest of design, and to dazzle our judgment as to his matter by the sparkle of his manner. Hence the derivation of the word " satire " from *satura* (sc. *lanx*) a dish of many ingredients, an olla podrida, would be as much justified by the variety of manners as by the variety of matters.

IX

The satirist does not make any use of unadulterated humour, which is by definition the kindly, tolerant acceptance of human nature and the sympathetic presentation of its oddities and incongruities to all and sundry. The humourist, his subjects, and his audience are all recognised as partaking of the same humanity, are all reconciled by the same revelation.

One touch of nature makes the whole world kin.[1]

The satirist, on the other hand, does not accept : he rejects. He is at war with things as they are, not (except Swift) with the essential and permanent nature of man (which is the province of the true humourist), but with aberrations from what he and his audience regard as the standards of the good life and of good sense. The humorist when he is most typical is too much in

[1] Shakespeare, *Troilus and Cressida*, III, iii, 175.

love with humanity to want to alter it ; and even its weaknesses and absurdities are dear to him because in his eyes they are of the very being of man. Human nature is a mine of inexhaustible interest to the humourist or humanist as he might appropriately be called by a legitimate return to the etymological meaning of the word. The most adequate stages for him are the novel and the drama, where he can display such manifestations of the infinite variety of the species as fall within his generous scope, either quite objectively or, if with a commentary, only with such a one as reveals the idiosyncrasies to better advantage, not with any implied or expressed criticism of an adverse kind. If there are any tendencies of human nature which he does not pursue, then they might be described as slopes leading obliquely away from the broad highway, on the crown of whose causeway he himself stands, to defects and excesses, to perversities and inhumanities which run counter to the tide of human life. As soon as the humorist begins to take notice of these obliquities, the character of his work changes. A malicious acid begins to adulterate the purity of his humour ;

> And with a sudden vigour it doth posset
> And curd, like eager droppings into milk,[1]

the milk of his former human kindness. This lacing of humour with more or less liberal dashes of malice is very common. In fact it is perhaps characteristic of the practice of most humorists. For they seldom maintain intact for any length of time their unruffled geniality and their undisturbed tolerance, their observant sympathy and their sense of human kinship : they never travel far without noticing, however delicately, something they would wish away or would alter, without flicking somebody with a whip, without a slightly malicious and superior laughter. Thus humour as an element in satire is never quite pure ; and indeed since the admixture of malice makes it something else, it might almost be said not to co-exist with satire at all. In its pure state it is to the satiric spectrum what the ultra-violet waves are to light.

Wit, however, is an essential constituent of any satiric design. Perhaps in one degree or another it exists or can exist in any department of literature, especially those which are most closely related to the spoken word, like oratory which is an oral art, or the drama and the novel which imitate speech, or satire which

[1] Shakespeare, *Hamlet*, I, v, 68-9.

by convention implies an audience. It is not restricted to particular subjects, as may be seen from the diversity of its applications in Burton and Burke, Addison, Johnson, and Gilbert; and it combines readily with many temperamental states from the utmost triviality to the intensest passion—one need not go beyond the Metaphysicals to find every gradation—because it is neutrally toned, or rather because it is not a tone at all, but a value. It might be described as the sparkle in style. It is one aspect of the interest which a literary artist extracts from the medium in which he works; it is thus comparable to the phrasing of a composer or to the advantage taken respectively by a sculptor or by a painter of the intrinsic qualities of stone or of paint. It is, more obviously than these other artistic refinements, an appeal to a select and intelligent audience; it attempts to please quick-witted people by a series of agreeable surprises due to generating sparks through the skilful and economical manipulation of language. Sometimes it is a display of quite innocuous dexterity, merely showing with what ease, grace, and originality the possessor of it can move his ideas, but carrying no hostility against any one. But more often, and in satire nearly always, wit is a weapon of offence, to bewilder, to intimidate, or to wound a victim, and at the same time to win the admiration of those who can appreciate the skill of fence. In satire, wit engages the esteem of the audience, because it appears to prove the satirist's superiority to his victim, the particular superiority in the use of language being in their minds generalised and extended. For there is a deep-seated respect in man for what appears to be in any way superior to something else. Moreover, wit is the satirist's most effective dazzle-disguise of, or compensation for, the malignity of his satire. Just as the obscene can be indulged if it is sprung in the form of a witticism on an audience off its guard, so can be palmed off the rancorous and the ill-natured under the veil of wit, though undisguised and uncompensated it would give offence. It is, therefore, as necessary to the satirist as patter is to the conjuror.

Ridicule, the second colour of the satiric spectrum, is a gay malice, a laughing scorn. It proceeds mainly by belittlement to a kind of *reductio ad absurdum*, on the general principle that what is small is also contemptible. It is mainly concerned with the petty vices or the foibles, inanities, affectations, and stupidities of men and women. But it varies in tone between raillery which is a more or less playful teasing, and derision which is a mocking hate. It is a sort of incipient and as yet exoteric irony which invites as many as possible to enjoy it and join in. That is to say, its audience is made up of all who in their own opinion are immune.

The usual definition of irony is :—A mode of speech or writing, the meaning of which is contrary to the literal sense of the words. But this is an inadequate description ; for while irony may indeed mean the contrary of what it says, it may just as frequently both mean what it says and imply something over and above, the unsaid being more significant than the said. It is, therefore, as often the art of implication, insinuation, and omission, as the art of inversion. Irony is always an indulgence in the esoteric and the exclusive ; for the ironist's true audience is an inner circle of initiates, who are invited to enjoy the mystification of the presumedly uninitiated and unsuspecting victim. It is a rapier that can give a wound which its recipient does not feel, or which, with a refinement of contempt, he is presumed to be too dull to feel. Perhaps it is the most characteristic of all the satirist's weapons, at least in fully developed satire. Deprived of it he would be as much restricted as the symphonic composer without his first violins. By his mastery of its apparent detachment and surface moderation, more than by anything else, his status as a satirist is determined.

Sarcasm is akin to the irony of inversion, for it always means the opposite of what it says. But it is much cruder than irony. There is no real or pretended mystification about it ; it is intended to give pain as with the flick of a whip, and must therefore be intelligible to the victim as well as to the bystander. Its emotional accompaniment is a momentary exasperation. Thus, unlike irony, it is rarely sustained and is most effective when it is in the nature of a by-play or an aside. The satirist who has frequent recourse to it appears to be lacking in self-control.

Cynicism is psychologically the obverse of idealism. The philosophical cynic is an idealist *manqué* who has cut his losses and contemptuously accepted the bald, unpleasant facts of life as he sees them. Such also the satirical cynic affects to be, as a rule, however, less because his experience has really driven him to the position than because he wants to *épater* the conventionally respectable who are his audience and, to a certain extent, his victims, the victims of his shock tactics. But cynicism in satire is seldom thoroughgoing. It is so in Gulliver's fourth voyage in which Swift blackguards the physical and the moral nature of the whole human race. But by so doing he really defeats his own end as a satirist ; because, for one thing, he leaves no one outside the scope of his censure to form its audience ; and because, for another, systematic cynicism condemns the generality of men as vicious and implies that the righteous, if there are any at all, are negligible exceptions to a depressing rule, whereas satire normally condemns the exceptions and implies that the generality are righteous. In most satires, however, cynicism does no more than polarise the thought, as in *Don Juan*, or give the thought an occasional bias and fillip.

Just as irony is akin to sarcasm, so is the cynical to the sardonic, the sixth colour in the satiric spectrum. Like the cynic, the sardonic man has subsided into a pessimism which laughs, but which laughs grimly that it may not weep. Unlike the cynic, however, who finds the cause of his laughter outside in the world of men, he finds it within in his own intellectual or spiritual defeat. The laughter of the cynic is edged with contempt, but sardonic laughter is blunted with chagrin and mortification. The sardonic man chuckles hollowly to himself and all-but-forgets his audience, like Hamlet in the churchyard, and makes his bitter comments *sotto voce*.

Finally, there is invective, which constituted practically the only weapons in primitive satire but which has now been largely superseded by subtler instruments. Invective makes a direct but exaggerated accusation of major vices and serious abuses. It rejects indirection, moderation, and every note in the gamut of laughter. The audience for whom it is calculated are the virtuous and the serious-minded, the pillars of society. It purports to be the voice of the community's righteous indignation for which the satirist is only a mouthpiece. But it carries with it not only impersonal anger but personal hate, not only the passion of the patriot and the citizen but the malignity of the enemy and the avenger. When it can purge itself of these grosser alloys, it becomes the anathema of the prophet and passes out of the reach of the satirist proper. Thus if, as I suggested before, pure humour falls, like the ultra-violet waves in spectroscopy, above the satiric spectrum, the prophetic anathema falls, like the infra-red waves, below it.

D

A DEFENCE OF RHETORIC

OR

PLATO, PASCAL, AND PERSUASION

Eloquence . . . consists . . . in a correspondence which we seek to establish between the head and the heart of those to whom we speak on the one hand, and, on the other, between the thoughts and the expressions which we employ. This assumes that we have studied well the heart of man so as to know all its powers, and then to find the just proportions of the discourse which we wish to adapt to them. We must put ourselves in the place of those who are to hear us, and make trial on our own heart of the turn which we give to our discourse in order to see whether the one is made for the other, and whether we can assure ourselves that the hearer will be, as it were, forced to surrender.

Pascal's Pensées. Translated by W. F. Trotter, 1931, p. 6.

No analysis is subtle and delicate enough to represent adequately the state of mind under which we believe, or the subjects of belief, as they are presented to our thoughts. The end proposed is that of delineating, or, as it were, painting what the mind sees and feels : now let us consider what it is to portray duly in form and colour things material, and we shall surely understand the difficulty, or rather the impossibility, of representing the outline and character, the hues and shades, in which any intellectual view really exists in the mind. . . . It is probable that a given opinion, as held by several individuals . . . is as distinct from itself as are their faces.

J. H. Newman, *Implicit and Explicit Reason* in *Fifteen Sermons preached before the University of Oxford between A.D. 1826 and 1843,* 1872, p. 267.

I

THE word *rhetoric* has two chief meanings :—either, the attempt to produce an effect by spoken words—the rhetoric of the rostrum ; or, the body of rules which is taught as a means of acquiring verbal effectiveness—the rhetoric of the class-room and the text-books of composition. I have to admit that in common, as distinct from academic, use the word has certain scandalous or at least discreditable connotations, although most of the dictionary definitions are innocent enough.[1] For it connotes

[1] *Cf.* Johnson's, Webster's and the *New English* Dictionaries, and the *Encyclopædia Britannica, sub* Rhetoric.

in many contexts, as the kindred words *oratory* and *eloquence*
do not, a certain manipulation of the facts, a sophistication of
the arguments, and a more or less unscrupulous appeal to the
weaknesses, prejudices, and passions of an audience by verbal
artifice and insincere declamation.[1]   It calls up mental pictures
of Mark Antony swaying the mutable Roman mob in the Forum,
or Mirabeau declaiming under the arcade of the Palais Royale,
or Mussolini bellowing from the balcony of the Palazzo Venezia,
or Hitler booming in the Sportpalast.   It suggests passion,
violence, and crowd hysteria.   Perhaps the rhetoricians themselves all down the ages, by accusing their opponents of sophistry
and juggling, or by complimenting them on their seductive
eloquence, have done more than anyone to implant in the public
mind a suspicion of the art which both sides in every dispute
practise.   They have themselves been the worst filers of their
own nest.   For one of the readiest ways of securing faith in your
own sincerity is to decry your *vis-à-vis's*.   Thus Antony was a
plain blunt man compared with the more gifted Brutus :—

> but were I Brutus,
> And Brutus Antony, there were an Antony
> Would ruffle up your spirits, and put a tongue
> In every wound of Cæsar, that should move
> The stones of Rome to rise and mutiny.[2]

II

It is quite true that rhetoric was originally something spoken
to an audience, generally with a purpose of persuasion.   For it
was in the realm of the spoken word in an almost bookless world
that the Greeks first realised the need and the value of skilful
oral presentation ; and it was mainly with a view to persuade
an audience on a legal, legislative, or other public occasion that
rhetoric was first consciously employed.   A rhetor was a public
speaker, and rhetoric was his medium.   The special circumstances
of citizenship in a city-state laid such emphasis on the gift of
oratory[3] that Aristotle reckoned inability to defend oneself in
speech as even more disgraceful than physical incapacity, since

---

[1] *Cf.* Richard Whately, *Elements of Rhetoric*, 1850, p. v.
[2] Shakespeare, *Julius Cæsar*, III, ii, 230-4.
[3] *Cf.* P. S. Richards, *In Defence of Useless Knowledge* in *Hibbert Journal*,
October 1935, p. 69.

" speech is more characteristic of man than the use of the body." [1]
It is also true that the power of rhetoric was no sooner appreciated
than it was abused ; and the orators of Greece practised every
rhetorical device, legitimate or illegitimate, commonly employed
since. As it happened, the first rhetoricians displayed their
talents in Athens when Socrates, the first practitioner of the new
art of dialectic, was displaying his. And in three of the Platonic
dialogues, the *Protagoras*, the *Gorgias*, and the *Phædrus*, he is
made to prefer the method of convincing by logical, point-by-
point adjustment and the brief exchanges of question and answer
to the method of persuasion by long speeches, and to disparage
the latter as a bastard art which sought not good but pleasure,
and recked no more of the health of the soul than the cook
who serves up enticing but unwholesome dishes does of the health
of the body.[2]

This attack on rhetoric on moral grounds is analogous to the
impugning of other new ventures, as for example the execration
of Machiavelli for codifying an art of politics, or the denunciation
by Cobbett and Carlyle of the Utilitarians for their economic
abstractions. Indeed, just as the tendency of every study is to
abstract itself from the totality of life and pursue it without
qualifications, so it is the way of the intelligent layman to
protest against such specialism in the name of morality and
humanity.

I would remark in passing that the dialogue, of which Plato,
if not the inventor, was the earliest exponent, was not only a
powerful means of interesting the more thoughtful Athenians in
the new analytic philosophy of his master and himself—a solvent
both of pre-Socratic speculation and of the encyclopædic sciolism
of the sophists—but it was also an admirable field for the display
of the dialectical method itself. To some extent, indeed, Plato's
hostility is to be explained by the facts that in his day both
dialectic and rhetoric were new, that their true scope and function,
especially that of rhetoric, was not realised, and that the two
were rival arts of oral persuasion. Plato championed the new
kind of dialectical thinking, which had gone to his head, and
was so much in love with it that, like a boy with a new penknife,

---

[1] *The Rhetoric of Aristotle*, ed. J. E. C. Welldon, 1886, p. 8.

[2] Cf. *Gorgias* in *The Dialogues of Plato*, ed. Benjamin Jowett, 1875, ii,
p. 335. *Cf*. also Thucydides, iii, 38, 42-43, for the denunciation by Cleon,
and the defence by Diodotus, of debate.

he wanted to use it on all suitable and unsuitable occasions and subjects.

III

As the Platonic objection to rhetoric is the first recorded one (though perhaps Adam and Eve, as the first victims, may have also been the first critics, of the art), I should like to offer some considerations in mitigation of its apparent gravamen, or rather of its unmodified citation at the present day.

In the *Gorgias* Socrates avows himself to be " one of those who are very willing to be refuted if I say anything which is not true, and very willing to refute anyone else who says what is not true, and quite as ready to be refuted as to refute." [1]

In the first place, then, I would suggest that the Platonic dialogues are abused and their real value lost sight of or obscured when they are taken as dogma and *ipse dixits*. More than once Socrates remarks that he enters a discussion without knowing whither it will lead. And at least once in his search for truth he is led to an unpalatable conclusion. " Let this then be our excuse for expelling poetry, that the argument constrained us. . . . Notwithstanding this, let us assure our sweet friend and the sister arts of imitation, that if she will only prove her title to existence in a well-ordered State we shall be delighted to receive her, knowing that we ourselves are very susceptible of her charms ; but we may not on that account betray the truth. . . . Shall I propose, then, that she be allowed to return from exile, on this condition—that she is to make a defence of herself in lyrical or some other metre ? . . . And to those of her defenders who are lovers of poetry and yet not poets, I think that we may grant a further privilege—they shall be allowed to speak in prose on her behalf : let them show not only that she is pleasant but also useful to States and to human life and we will gladly listen, for if this can be proved we shall surely be the gainers, I mean, if there is a use in poetry as well as a delight." [2]   He had worked himself into a position in which he had no choice but to surrender to what seemed an imperative truth. " But," though you eliminate hypotheses until only one is left, " that does not mean it is *the*

---

[1] *Ed. cit.*, ii, p. 358.
[2] *The Republic* in *The Dialogues of Plato*, ed. cit., iii, p. 504.

truth.   It only means you can go no further " [1] at least along
that way and with your original prepossessions.

The real virtue and characteristic of the Platonic dialogues
is not, however, to establish any position of final stability, but,
in the Socratic metaphor, to serve as a sort of maieutics.
Phænerete, Socrates's mother, was a midwife ; and he himself,
he tells us, belonged to the same profession, for by skilful leading
questions he delivered souls of the truths with which they were
pregnant and which they could not themselves bring into clear
consciousness.[2] " Sometimes," says T. W. Rolleston, " no truth
appears at all, as in the *Theætetus* or the *Greater Hippias*—but
what of that ? We have been concerning ourselves about it, and
who knows when or how the moment of illumination may
appear ? " [3] Thus Plato is truly honoured and understood, not
by setting him up as an infallible pope, but by following his
example of thinking freshly and freely for ourselves. " A man,"
says Schopenhauer, " cannot turn over anything in his mind
unless he knows [*i.e.* has something to turn] ; he should, therefore,
learn something ; but it is only when he has turned it over that
he can be said to know it. . . . It is incredible what a different
effect is produced upon the mind by thinking for oneself, as
compared with reading . . . reading forces alien thoughts upon
the mind—thoughts which are as foreign to the drift and temper
in which it may be for the moment, as the seal is to the wax on
which it stamps its imprint. . . . The safest way of having no
thoughts of one's own is to take up a book every moment one
has nothing else to do. . . . The thought we read is related to
the thought which springs up in ourselves, as the fossil-impress
of some prehistoric plant to a plant as it buds forth in springtime." [4]
And, I may add, fossilised Plato is as dead as any other specimen.
Surely he of all authors is to be used as grist for the mills of
thought, not as borrowed grindstones ; or, to vary the metaphor,

---

[1] Edwin Muir, *Against being Convinced* in *Latitudes*, n.d., p. 234.

[2] *Theætetus* in *The Dialogues of Plato*, ed. cit., iv, pp. 293-6.   Cf. *Pascal's
Pensées*, ed. cit., p. 12 :—" There are some who speak well and write badly.
For the place and the audience warm them, and draw their minds more than
they think of without that warmth."

[3] *Selections from Plato, from the Translation of Sydenham and Taylor*,
ed. T. W. Rolleston, n.d., p. xx.   *Cf.* J. W. H. Atkins, *Literary Criticism in
Antiquity, A Sketch of its Development*, 1934, i, p. 36.

[4] *The Art of Literature*.   A Series of Essays by Arthur Schopenhauer,
ed. T. B. Saunders, 1891, pp. 59-61.

he is to be used like water in a dry pump to start the flow of
thought in us, not to canalise it. For Plato's eager longing for
the truth, " more than theirs who watch for the morning," [1]
is better than any conclusion he reached : his example of thinking
is more vivifying than his thought. Let us not, therefore, without
demur and under the rebuke of his genius accept as final his
objection to rhetoric any more than his rejection of poetry.

Even when in the *Gorgias*, if not elsewhere to the same extent,
he is arguing against the rhetoric of persuasion Plato, in a spirit
of mockery and caricature and under the show of dialectical
scrupulosity, descends to the artifice of putting the abuse of the
thing for its use.[2] But the abuse of anything taketh not away
the use thereof, even of rhetoric which, I admit, has been often
misapplied. But so have all other human arts and practices and
all earthly things. " If it is argued," says Aristotle, who wrote
the first extant, systematic treatise on the subject, " that the
unjust use of this rhetorical faculty would be exceedingly
mischievous to the world, this is a charge which may be brought
against all good things, save virtue only, and most of all against
the things of highest utility." [3] Yes, indeed : *corruptio optimi
pessima*. Strength, health, riches, and military skill, says
Aristotle, may be blessings in the hands of the just man and
curses in the hands of the unjust.[3] So may sculpture be
demoralised by Pompeian artists and draughtsmanship by
Aubrey Beardsley, music in the lascivious rhythms of Haarlem
and Broadway, and poetry in the scurrilities of Scarron and
Cotton. Surgery may set a limb and dissect an unwanted wife.
Your tongue, which can sing hymns, can wreck families. Your
pen, which can sign cheques for orphanages, can write libels and
defamations of saints. A building may be the House Beautiful
or a den of thieves. A book—aye, the same one—may be precious
or disastrous, a savour of life unto life or a savour of death unto
death ; for every book can be put to a wrong use, even the Bible
by those who pervert its texts to justify their evil or by the
immature who read it out of prurience ; and every book is written
for a fit audience, however few—as Coleridge says somewhere,
perhaps for one solitary individual. It is obvious that it is the

---

[1] *Psalms*, cxxx, 6.
[2] Cf. *The Gorgias of Plato*, ed. W. H. Thomson, 1871, p. iv ; Richard
Whately, *op. cit.*, pp. 7-8 ; and P. S. Richards, *op. cit.*, p. 70.
[3] *The Rhetoric of Aristotle*, ed. cit., p. 8.

human purpose which makes beneficent or evil; and as Aristotle said of rhetoric in particular, it is "not the faculty but the moral purpose which constitutes the sophistical character."[1] Like civilisation or justice, rhetoric is liable to be corrupted. But having once devised them man must carry them through to their earthly perfection. What we want is not abolition, but betterment. For in the moral world a kind of converse Gresham's Law operates and the good civilisation, justice, and rhetoric drive out the bad.

Plato had too little faith in humanity and too much fear of abuse. Hence his recourse to prohibitions and censorships, by which rulers of a certain habit of mind have always vetoed what they said was bad for their subjects—as often as not really because they feared that it was bad for themselves and their power. It is by this repression that dangerous complexes are set up in the mind politic. It is a far wiser policy to take all the risks of complete freedom of speech, in the faith that the truth will, because it must, triumph.

But truth must appear to as good advantage as its opposite. It would be unfair, as the Rev. Rowland Hill said, if the devil had all the good tunes.[2] Indeed, Plato in the *Phædrus* and the *Gorgias* admits that there is a true rhetoric, that of the philosopher who is able to make people wiser, juster, and so happier in themselves and to help them to embody wisdom in their laws.[3] But in this admission he has given his whole case away. To allure a man to wisdom and justice is as much the rhetoric of persuasion as is to influence him to violence and riot.

IV

Even if for the time being we restrict rhetoric to oral persuasion, I would point out that as such it is a counterpart, as Aristotle

---

[1] *The Rhetoric of Aristotle*, ed. cit., p. 9.

[2] Cf. *The Rhetoric of Aristotle*, ed. cit., pp. 6-7, 8 :—" truth and justice possess a natural superiority to their opposites, and therefore, if judgments are not given as they should be, it must be the speakers themselves who are responsible for the defeat ; and this is itself a state of things which is reprehensible " ; " whatever is true or expedient may be said generally to be always in its nature more easily susceptible of proof and more persuasive " ; and Richard Whately, *op. cit.*, pp, vii-viii, 8 (note 10), 9, 116.

[3] *Phædrus* in *The Dialogues of Plato*, ed. cit., ii, pp. 137-59, and *Gorgias*, *ibid.*, pp. 382-5.

said,[1] to dialectic, not its rival. Both are instrumental arts, and applicable to various kinds of subject-matter.[2] They are both methods for conducting probable reasoning (πιθανολογία) in the realm of opinion (δόξα) which covers all that lies beyond the scope of absolute certainty, and are therefore both contrasted with demonstrative reasoning (ἀπόδειξις) in the sphere of knowledge (ἐπιστήμη) which extends only to what experience forces upon us, or what can be deduced by indisputable means from what experience confirms.[3] They are both related to logic thus : Both divide and subdivide, inspect and analyse a topic to find out the various avenues by which it can be approached, defended, and attacked ; how to criticise these arguments is the province of logic—dialectic and rhetoric providing, and logic appraising, the argumentation—dialectic and rhetoric exercising the invention, and logic the judgment ; and the characteristic logical figures for dialectic and rhetoric are respectively the syllogism and the enthymeme. Whereas the proper home of dialectic is the retirement of the philosophic schools, the true abode of rhetoric is the law-courts and the deliberative assemblies of the world of affairs. The end of dialectic is a *point de départ* for more dialectic. The end of rhetoric is some sort of decision and action in a world which forces decision and action on us at every hand and at short notice. Dialectic is an art of leisure and slow approximation to truth, making its way by gradual trial and error, elimination, and repeated retroversion. Rhetoric is an art of urgency and impressionism, reaching its conclusions by short-cuts, suggestion, and momentum.

Dialectic, then, is admittedly the severer mode of probable reasoning, and rhetoric the more specious. But is any kind of human reasoning, even the demonstrative variety, and the more

[1] *Rhetoric*, ed. cit., p. 1.

[2] *Cf.* Richard Whately, *op. cit.*, p. 3. Aristotle (*Rhetoric*, ed. cit., p. 12) calls rhetoric and dialectic " mere faculties of supplying arguments." Both, he says (*ibid.*, p. 1) " are concerned with such subjects as fall in a sense within the cognizance of all men, and neither is limited to any definite science." He also says (*ibid.*, p. 15) that " the materials of Dialectic are such subjects as need discussion, and those of Rhetoric are the ordinary and recognized subjects of deliberation ; " and (*ibid.*, p. 21) that the more a man takes his special topics from his subject the more his discourse will be a science distinct from both rhetoric and dialectic.

[3] The distinction between opinion and knowledge is analogous to, but not identical with, that between the metaphysical (τὸ μεταφυσικόν) and the physical (τὸ φυσικόν).

stringent branch of the probable, so purely rational and so objectively intellectual in practice as many philosophers notionally assume it to be ?

V

In the later phases of the Renaissance, under the influence of the great scientific discoveries of the period, the spirit of rationalism was strong and confident of its capacity to prove all truth by its own light. It tried to put an end to any conception of double truth, such as follows from the general classical distinction between knowledge and opinion, already referred to, and the analogous classical distinction between the two provinces of the physical ($\tau\grave{o}$ $\phi\upsilon\sigma\iota\kappa\acute{o}\nu$) and the metaphysical ($\tau\grave{o}$ $\mu\epsilon\tau\alpha\phi\upsilon\sigma\iota\kappa\acute{o}\nu$), or from the medieval distinction between the provinces of faith and revelation on the one hand and of reason and dispute on the other. The attempt, however, was short-lived ; and in fact rationalism could not exclude itself from its own purview and inevitably turned in on itself in re-entrant criticism.

Pascal supplies a perfect illustration of rationalism realising its own inadequacy. He had begun, as his treatise *De l'Esprit Géométrique* shows, by believing, in the spirit of the most confident rationalism, that there were only rational approaches to the truth. Before he explains his geometrical method, he feels compelled to point out an even more excellent way. It consists principally of two rules :—" the one, to use no term whose meaning had not previously been clearly defined ; the other, to advance no proposition which could not be demonstrated by truths before ascertained : in one word, to define all our terms, and prove all our propositions." [1] Error could then be avoided by mentally substituting the definition for the thing defined and having " the former so present to the mind that . . . these two things shall be so inseparably blended in our thoughts, that when the one is expressed in word, the other is at once responded to by the mind." [2] This " beautiful process," [3] however, Pascal recognises to be utterly impracticable because no terms can be defined except by other simpler terms and no propositions can be proved except by other precedent propositions. The method, therefore, involves an infinite regress in which " we should never

---

[1] *The Miscellaneous Writings of Pascal*, ed. G. Pearce, 1849, pp. 74-5.
[2] *Ibid.*, p. 76. [3] *Ibid.*, p. 77.

arrive at any primary terms or propositions," [1] or it would take us back to an unscalable wall of " primitive words which cannot be defined, and principles so clear that no other plainer ones can be found to serve for their demonstrations." [1]   Though Pascal thereby accepts the logical conclusion of the incapacity of man to deal with any science whatever with absolute completeness, he will not admit that the search for all order and method along analogous lines must be abandoned.   There remains for him the estimable, if inferior, order and method of geometry, like the *ordo geometricus* of Spinoza.   It does not define every term or demonstrate every proposition.   But it defines everything except what is " plain and intelligible to all men " [2] and demonstrates all that is not " known to everyone." [2]   That is to say, it derives from an irreducible body of axioms and postulates.

When Pascal wrote *De l'Art de Persuader*, probably some years later and when he was already in the transitional stages of conversion, he modified the strict rationalism by which in *De l'Esprit Géométrique* he had proposed to extend the special procedure of geometry to the subjects of general reasoning.

" Everyone knows," he says, " that there are two principal channels through which opinions find their entrance into the mind—the understanding and the will.   That which would seem to be the most obvious of these is the understanding ; for we ought never to yield our assent to anything but demonstrated truths : yet the most common, although the one which is opposed to the proper order of things, is the will ; for the larger number of men have their belief impelled, not so much by external proofs, as by their own inclinations. This latter method, however, is ignoble and unworthy ; and is, therefore, disavowed by all. Everyone professes to believe, and even to admire, only such things as are deserving of belief and admiration." [3]

He immediately, however, excludes religious truths from the scope of the art of persuasion.   They enter the soul only through the power of God and in the way He wills—" into the understanding through the heart ; and not into the heart through the understanding." [3]   This order of entry " is intended to humble the pride of the reason, which is prone to set itself up as a judge of things which are agreeable to the will ; and to heal that infirmity of the will, which inclines us to indulge in unworthy

---

[1] *The Miscellaneous Writings of Pascal*, ed. G. Pearce, 1849, p. 77
[2] *Ibid.*, p. 78.   [3] *Ibid.*, p. 149

attachments. And thence it arises, that while, in human matters, we are accustomed to inculcate that ' we must *know* before we can love,' . . . Divine wisdom teaches, that, in regard to spiritual things, we must ' *love* in order to know them,' and that we can attain to truth only through the medium of charity, or love." [1] Unfortunately men have perversely extended this rule, proper only for religious truths, to secular matters. In fact they have come to believe little but what falls in with their own tastes —what comes into the understanding through the heart ; and not into the heart through the understanding, very different as this may be from the Divine truths which enter the soul in like manner. Hence, says Pascal, the great repugnance of mankind to receive Christian truths, because of their opposition to our natural inclinations.

Excluding, then, religious truths from the scope of persuasion, he finds that of the truths " of an inferior nature " [2] with which alone he is concerned few enter by the understanding, " while multitudes crowd in by the caprices of the will, without the correctives of reason." [2] Now in persuasion there are instruments of different qualities and powers, as it were, five categories. First, those derived from general principles and therefore acknowledged to be truths by necessary sequence are irresistible. Secondly, there are those which are likewise irresistible because they are closely bound up with objects of personal enjoyment. Thirdly, some which unite the unmistakable appeal to the understanding with the attraction of pleasure have a force which " nothing can exceed." [3] Fourthly, come those which, having no sympathy either with our judgment and understanding or with our tastes and inclination, appear to us to be alien, repulsive, and false. And lastly, we have the instances " in which the things proposed to our judgments, while firmly based upon admitted truths, are, at the same time, repugnant to our most sensible enjoyments." [3] It is in the cleavages of the last category " that the convictions of truth, and the instigations of sense, hold the man in suspense . . . [and] wage within him a conflict, of which the issue must ever be uncertain : for, to conjecture of its result, we ought to know all that passes in the very interior of his spirit, of which the man himself is scarcely conscious." [4] When, therefore, we have to persuade others, " we must have especial regard to their

[1] *The Miscellaneous Writings of Pascal*, ed. G. Pearce, 1849, pp. 149-50.
[2] *Ibid.*, p. 151.　　　[3] *Ibid.*, p. 152.　　　[4] *Ibid.*, p. 153.

individual peculiarities, their mental constitutions, and natural propensities,—the principles they acknowledge, and the objects in which they find satisfaction. And then it should be our aim, to conform and adjust the matters to be proposed to their judgment to these ascertained principles, and their favourite and cherished tastes." [1]

Although Pascal thus recognises, as had Aristotle long before, that the art of persuasion has two sides and consists as much in conciliating the will as in convincing the judgment, he attempts to lay down only rules for the intellectual appeal, since only its governing principles are fixed and definite. He does not mean thereby that the art of pleasing is not, " beyond comparison, more elaborate, more refined, more useful, and more interesting," [2] but he knows " no art by which to regulate the caprices of the will . . . it is beyond my power. To do it justice passes human skill; I believe it to be an impossibility." [2] The cause of this extreme difficulty, he continues, is that " the sources of pleasure are not fixed and permanent. They differ in different men; and even, in the same individual, they are so variable, that there are no two persons to be found equally different from each other, as the *same* man will be from himself at successive periods. The pleasures of the man, also, differ from the female's; those of the rich from the poor's; the tastes of the prince, of the warrior, of the merchant, citizen, peasant,—of the young, the old, the healthy, and the sick,—all differ; they are varied by the minutest accidents, and the most trivial circumstances." [3]

Pascal confines himself, therefore, to the exhibition of the connection of truths with their principles, both those that convince the understanding and those that please the taste, and of course those that do both, " provided the principles once avowed be firmly and consistently maintained." [4] For the purpose of effecting persuasion in this admittedly narrow field he proposes exactly the same method as in *De l'Esprit Géométrique* :—the clear definition of terms; the proposition of self-evident principles or axioms for proving the subject in question; and the mental substitution throughout the demonstration of the definition for the term defined. So far from admitting this method to have little utility outside the geometrical field, Pascal maintains that it is of the greatest and most general value and that it, not the

---

[1] *The Miscellaneous Writings of Pascal*, ed. G. Pearce, 1849, pp. 152-3.
[2] *Ibid.*, p. 154.   [3] *Ibid.*, pp. 154-5.   [4] *Ibid.*, p. 155.

useless and injurious method of logic, is the only way to true demonstrations.

Thus he began as a complete rationalist, recognising only one kind of truth and only one method of setting it forth, the geometric. Then he realised that the convincing of the reason is only one side of the complex problem of persuasion, and distinguished between the higher truths of the Divine order and the lower of the natural order to which alone he restricted his proposed method. Even with regard to these matters he had to admit that conviction entered the soul by two channels, a rational and a volitional. But his art of persuasion is in fact only concerned with the display of his third category of instruments, those which appeal both to the understanding and to personal enjoyment. It was meant to take the place of the scholastic logic with its barbarous jargon and unreal precision which still appeared to be strongly established in the universities; and as such a method of reasoning it is affiliated to the mathematical instrument of Galileo and its development in Descartes, and is likewise akin to their modifications in the new logics of Spinoza and Leibniz. But it is not really an art of persuasion at all, as we, not to mention Aristotle, understand the phrase. It is a method only of irrefragable demonstration, as far as this is possible. The art of persuasion in the true sense Pascal set aside as something too subtle and complex to be systematised.

VI

When, however, Pascal's interests and attention were turned by his conversion from the truths of the natural, to the truths of the spiritual, order, and he began to collect ideas and arguments for a great apologia for Christianity which should win over libertines, epicureans, sceptics, and indifferent men of the world, he had specially to concentrate on the last of his categories in *De l'Art de Persuader*, the cases in which men's judgments are in favour of a particular proposition but their wills in the interests of their sensible enjoyments are against it. His problem, as he saw it, was to re-edify the fabric of Christian apologetics against attacks from two sides—one from the epicurean scepticism of Montaigne and his pupils who virtually denied to human reason the power of knowing anything and who in any case were prejudiced against revelation and a spiritual interpretation of the universe ; the other from the rationalism of Descartes who in spite of his polite respect for Christianity regarded reason as the common centre of knowledge, life, science, morality, and religion, thus in effect denying, as Pascal himself had done, the existence of any but strictly rational truth.[1] He saw that he was now engaged in a task not only of the greatest importance and urgency but of a kind for which the method of inexpugnable demonstration was quite unsuitable. But in the world of men and fashionable life he had acquired a rich, empirical knowledge of human nature, and from that experience he understood how imperative it was in the sphere of his new interests to make propositions attractive as well as convincing and to work on the volitional as well as on the intellectual side of his pupils.

Indeed his *Provincial Letters*, written soon after his conversion, show him exhibiting in action what was for him a quite new conception of the art of persuasion. The *Letters* are frankly rhetoric, polemical and one-sided, addressed not to specialists but to the world in general. They are in short, a work of persuasion in the fullest sense, not indeed attempting to conciliate direct opponents but playing with the utmost skill on any who were uncommitted in the Jansenist - Jesuit quarrel.

The apologia for Christianity, of which the *Pensées* are the fragmentary raw material, was to have been of a higher kind intellectually and yet by no means a piece of frigid intellectualism. It was to be reasonable, and at the same time wooing :—" Come now, and let us reason together, saith the Lord." [2] Pascal did not, it is true, lay down the rules for managing the caprices and securing the assent of the will, which he had declared in his *De l'Art de Persuader* to be beyond human capacity. But there are many passages which theorise on, rather than practise, persuasion. Hence, for example, his distinction between *l'esprit de géométrie*, which had determined his earlier conceptions of persuasion, and *l'esprit de finesse*, which was to have its say in his apologetics ; and hence his parallel distinction between the mathematical and the intuitive types of mind.

In the mathematical type " the principles are palpable, but

[1] *Cf.* R. H. Soltau, *Pascal : the Man and the Message*, 1927, p. 135, and Émile Boutroux, *Descartes and Cartesianism* in *The Cambridge Modern History*, 1906, iv, pp. 796-8.
[2] *Isaiah*, i, 18.

removed from ordinary use ; so that for want of habit it is difficult
to turn one's mind in that direction : but if one turns it thither
ever so little, one sees the principles fully, and one must have a
quite inaccurate mind who reasons wrongly from principles so
plain that it is almost impossible they should escape notice.
But in the intuitive mind the principles are found in common
use, and are before the eyes of everybody. One has only to look,
and no effort is necessary ; it is only a question of good eyesight,
but it must be good, for the principles are so subtle and so
numerous, that it is almost impossible but that some escape
notice. Now the omission of one principle leads to error ; thus
one must have very clear sight to see all the principles, and in
the next place an accurate mind not to draw false deductions
from known principles." [1]

These two types rarely coalesce in the same person. And yet
in matters of the highest moment, in the field of religion and
values, the only effective pleaders are those who command both
esprits. Pascal fully appreciated the fact that Christianity was
not simply a theological system to be given assent to on strictly
rational grounds, or for that matter simply a religion with a
purely emotional appeal. It is a way of life, and its appeal must
penetrate past the reason and deeper than the senses down to
that source of personality which Pascal calls the heart. In the
ultimate analysis the heart is the individual's fortress and Capitol,
his court of final appeal, his cabinet, and his executive. It is
there that the absolute decisions are taken and thence that the
effective orders are issued. Until the Christian apologist has
taken that citadel he is baffled. He may convince a man of the
abstract validity of the faith without making him a Christian.
For do not "the devils also believe, and tremble "? [2] Contrariwise
the intellect may refuse its assent because it is under the domina-
tion of such powerful resistants as pride, self-interest, and love of
sensual pleasure. What the apologist must do is to beset his man
behind and before, to press forward his siege on every side, and
then to carry the fortress by a massed attack on every scarp and
rampart, the innermost defences of the central government.

Here are some of the most relevant *Pensées* :—

"All our reasoning reduces itself to yielding to feeling." [3]

---

[1] *Pascal's Pensées*, ed. cit., p. i.
[2] *The General Epistle of James*, ii, 19.
[3] *Ed. cit.*, p. 78.

" The heart has its reasons, which reason does not know. We feel it in a thousand things. I say that the heart naturally loves the Universal Being, and also itself naturally, according as it gives itself to them ; and it hardens itself against one or the other at its will. You have rejected the one, and kept the other. Is it by reason that you love yourself ? " [1]

" It is the heart which experiences God, and not the reason. This, then, is faith : God felt by the heart, not by the reason." [1]

" Faith is a gift of God ; do not believe that we said it was a gift of reasoning. Other religions do not say this of their faith. They only gave reasoning in order to arrive at it, and yet it does not bring them to it." [2]

" We know the truth, not only by the reason, but also by the heart, and it is in this last way that we know first principles ; and reason which has no part in it, tries in vain to impugn them. The sceptics, who have only this for their object, labour to no purpose. We know that we do not dream, and however impossible it is for us to prove it by reason, this inability demonstrates only the weakness of our reason, but not, as they affirm, the uncertainty of all our knowledge. For the knowledge of first principles, as space, time, motion, number, is as sure as any of those we get from reasoning. And reasoning must trust these intuitions of the heart, and must base on them every argument. (We have intuitive knowledge of the tri-dimensional nature of space, and of the infinity of number, and reason then shows that there are no two square numbers one of which is double of the other. Principles are intuited, propositions are inferred, all with certainty, though in different ways.) And it is as useless and absurd for reason to demand from the heart proofs of her first principles, before admitting them, as it would be for the heart to demand from reason an intuition of all demonstrated propositions before accepting them.

" This inability ought, then, to serve only to humble reason, which would judge all, but not to impugn our certainty, as if only reason were capable of instructing us. Would to God, on the contrary, that we had never need of it, and that we knew everything by instinct and intuition. On the contrary, she has given us but very little knowledge of this kind ; and all the rest can be acquired only by reasoning." [3]

[1] *Ed. cit.*, p. 78.   [2] *Ibid.*, p. 79.   [3] *Ibid.*, pp. 79-80.

E

VII

In a way, then, Pascal's method of countering the scepticism that prided itself on reason, was to oppose to it a deeper scepticism that doubted reason itself and that attained to belief by consulting the very nature of man.

He was, therefore, a precursor of Hume whose own scepticism was subordinate to a naturalistic theory of sensitive and satisfactory but comparatively alogical belief. We almost hear the voice of Pascal in these dicta from *A Treatise of Human Nature* :—" all probable reasoning is nothing but a species of sensation. 'Tis not solely in poetry and music, we must follow our taste and sentiment, but likewise in philosophy. When I am convinc'd of any principle, 'tis only an idea, which strikes more strongly upon me."[1] " Belief is more properly an act of the sensitive than of the cogitative part of our nature." [2]

VIII

That such a view is not inconsistent with the firmest conviction is sufficiently proved, if not by Hume's adherence, then by Pascal's own and that of another believer, Newman. For the fact is that we generally believe what we cannot demonstrate, if we believe it at all, with a far greater warmth than we have for the completely demonstrated.

It is perhaps Newman who has best described the activity and progress of the " reasoning " mind. " Reasoning," he says, " . . . is a living spontaneous energy within us, not an art,"[3] as the logicians suppose. One fact may serve as foundation for a whole theory, one principle may give rise to a whole system, and one minute clue may lead to a great discovery. " The mind ranges to and fro, and spreads out, and advances forward with a quickness which has become a proverb, with a subtlety and versatility which baffle investigation. It passes on from point to point, gaining one by some indication ; another on a probability ; then availing itself of an association ; then falling back on some received law ; next seizing on testimony ; then committing itself

---

[1] Ed. L. A. Selby-Bigge, 1888, p. 103.

[2] *Ibid.*, p. 183.

[3] *Implicit and Explicit Reason* in *Fifteen Sermons preached before the University of Oxford between A.D. 1826 and 1843*, 1872, p. 257.

to some popular impression, or some inward instinct, or some obscure memory; and thus it makes progress not unlike a clamberer on a steep cliff who, by quick eye, prompt hand, and sure foot, ascends how he knows not himself, by personal endowments and by practice, rather than by rule, leaving no track behind him, and unable to teach another." [1]

Such is human reasoning in practice, as distinct from theory. It is a complex interplay of knowledge, deduction, and induction, of syllogism, enthymeme, analogy, illustration, metaphor, and symbol, of feelings, passions, and prejudices, of memories, associations, and imagination. Thus the truth, as we proudly call our final position, has been reached " by processes which we cannot remember, or fail to analyse, or construe erroneously. Descartes's criterion of evidence, clear ideas with lucid chains between them of irresistible argument, breaks down, for it need not exist, although we are in possession of truth. Nay, very often, or always in concrete matters, it does not exist." [2]

Moreover, before any purposive reasoning at all can occur, we must have more or less of what William James called the will to believe. Every hypothesis either attracts the mind or leaves it uninterested. But why one hypothesis is alive for us and another dead is ultimately no more rational than our liking bacon and disliking beans. Once an attractive hypothesis, however, has been offered to the mind from a distance, as it were, the thought sets out to reach it by hook or by crook. That is to say, every conclusion of our thinking is first of all intuitively desired, for

> We must love it ere to us
> It will seem worthy of our love. [3]

The Delectable Mountains are seen afar off, and the glimpse of them gives us the resolution to find out the way. Sometimes the going is slow, like that of a frigate in a calm which makes way by tacking with every fugitive breeze, or by an oceanic current, or by its own momentum. Sometimes it is swift, like that of a monkey speeding through an equatorial jungle, now on stout branches, now on slender twigs, now on mere leafage. If the speed and the complexity of thought varies with the case, it

---

[1] Newman, *op. cit.*, p. 257.
[2] William Barry, *Newman*, 1904, pp. 183-4.
[3] *Cf.* Wordsworth, *A Poet's Epitaph*, 43-4.

varies just as much with the character of the individual—from the man (more often, if common opinion is reliable, the woman) who seeing the desired goal at a distance leaps to it in one bound, so dynamic is the desire for it and so uncritical the imagination, to the man who is so cautious that he tries every step ahead before he will move his weight from his right foot to his left; from the philosophers who make difficulties at the threshold of thought and perhaps stick at the very axioms and postulates of being and knowing, to the Baconians and the interpreters of the Great Pyramid who can pass from the centre to the circumference of any mystery and swallow more camels than there are gnats to strain at. But the sequence, even at its most scientific and logical, is always intermittent, proceeding by hops, skips, and jumps; and it is always psychological, passional, and æsthetic as well as logical. It involves a kind of self-persuasion and internal rhetoric to prick the sides of our intent. What we conclude to be true ideas are distinguished for us from what we reject as false by their " superior *firmness*, or *solidity*, or *force*, or *vivacity*," in the phraseology of Hume ;[1] and belief " consists merely in a certain feeling or sentiment ; in something that depends not on the will. . . . When we are convinc'd of any matter of fact, we do nothing but conceive it, along with a certain feeling, different from what attends the mere *reveries* of the imagination."[2]

IX

I am afraid that I have not yet done with Plato and must return to him on another side. He was a born aristocrat of the mind, contemptuous of the obvious deterioration of the Athenian democracy in the fourth century before Christ and so of the means of persuading men in the mass, and also a root-and-branch reformer with the utopian's usual impatience at the essential nature of man. Such thinkers as Plato, Calvin, Rousseau, Godwin, Bentham, Karl Marx, and Mr Shaw, who plan brave new worlds, are soon so irritated by the complexity which the

[1] *A Treatise of Human Nature*, ed. cit., p. 106. *Cf.* Walter Bagehot (*On the Emotion of Conviction* in *The Works and Life of Walter Bagehot*, ed. Mrs Russell Barrington, 1915, v, pp. 103-4) who holds that the emotional accompaniment of conviction is determined by the clarity, intensity, constancy, and interestingness (*i.e.* " the power of the idea to gratify some wish or want of the mind ") of the proposition.

[2] *A Treatise of Human Nature*, ed. cit., p. 624.

nature of man introduces into their problems that in the end they ignore his claims to be considered in any scheme for the reform of his own world and substitute for him in their speculations a political, or ecclesiastical, or social, or economic monster-ideal —" By this good light . . . a very shallow monster " [1]—which has for their purposes the merit of being a known and constant, not an unknown and inconstant, factor. But is this fair ?

> Why should a man desire in any way
> To vary from the kindly race of men ? [2]

Or rather what is the practical use of speculation which poses and solves a problem so vastly different from the problems of this work-a-day life and this incalculable humanity, set as it is,

> Not in Utopia, subterraneous Fields,
> Or some secreted Island, Heaven knows where,
> But in this very world which is the world
> Of all of us, the place in which, in the end,
> We find our happiness, or not at all ? [3]

It is true that " we know what we are, but know not what we may be " [4] when reformers and doctrinaires have done their best for us. But they must *begin* with us as we are and take us forward step by step, and proposition by proposition. They must keep in touch with present fact and draw us (by rhetoric, I suppose) to its gradual betterment ; they,

> as a bird each fond endearment tries
> To tempt its new-fledg'd offspring to the skies,
> Must try each art, reprove each dull delay,
> Allure to brighter worlds, and lead the way. [5]

Meanwhile the world, sad and bad and mad as it is, must continue while the philosophers make up their minds. As the constitutional maxim says, His Majesty's Government must go on. As the poet brutally puts it, " wretches hang that jury-men may dine." [6] In parliaments and international conferences, in law courts and town councils, decisions must be reached on

---

[1] Shakespeare, *The Tempest*, II, ii, 147-8.
[2] Tennyson, *Tithonus*, 28-9.
[3] Wordsworth, *The Prelude* (1805-6), x, 724-8.
[4] Shakespeare, *Hamlet*, IV, v, 42-3..
[5] Goldsmith, *The Deserted Village*, 167-70.
[6] Pope, *The Rape of the Lock*, iii, 22.

peace or war, on life and death, on tram-fares and bus-routes ; and debate is the imperfect means by which as many facets of a question as possible are ventilated, often before an audience, not of experts in the subject, but of average, uninstructed men and women.[1] In debate the worth of an opinion is not prejudged, but is presented by its advocate as well as he can, for so (abstractly speaking) the opinion has a right to be treated, as Johnson explained when Boswell had misgivings as to the honesty of advocacy :—Boswell, " But what do you think of supporting a cause which you know to be bad ? " Johnson, " Sir, you do not know it to be good or bad till the Judge determines it . . . you are not to be confident in your own opinion that a cause is bad, but to say all you can for your client, and then hear the Judge's opinion." [2] If an audience will heed only one side, that is not the fault of debate, which should be an equal contest between opinions all canvassed to stimulate the auditors' interest and decision ; nor is it the fault of rhetoric, except in so far as the speaker on the defeated side has let it down by his inadequacy. A good cause well presented will not, however, always triumph and a bad cause on the other hand frequently will. Let the blame in such circumstances rest on the human factors, the human beings who by their dullness or their unfairness blunt their own instruments and undermine their own intelligence.

We cannot hold up every item of the world's business till we have reached inexpugnable truth ; for even if the delay did not, as indeed it would, cause anything from a traffic jam to international bankruptcy according to the gravity of the issue, yet we should have no absolute guarantee in the end that all our logicians and dialecticians would ever come to a conclusion both unanimous and certain. If a surgeon hesitated to operate till he had consulted every colleague, and examined every surgical text-book and theory, not to mention every social, economic, religious, and metaphysical implication and contingency of the case, the patient would die in his agony and the surgeon himself in his ignorance. If before trying to hit a golf-ball, you gave your days and nights to the study of the dynamics and ballistics, tensions and torsions of golf, and then to its value for the

[1] Cf. *The Rhetoric of Aristotle*, ed. cit., pp. 7, 15, 21, and Richard Whately, *op. cit.*, p. 3.

[2] *Boswell's Life of Johnson*, ed. G. B. Hill and L. F. Powell, 1934–, ii, p. 47.

community and for the individual as a husband, a father, and a
friend, for his body and soul in this world and the next, you
would never play golf this side of the Elysian links.

I am not impugning the immense value of deliberation : I
merely assert that by the very nature of man and of the universe,
it has no finality and that life has. In every problem of life
there is a time-factor :—

> at my back I always hear
> Time's winged chariot hurrying near. [1]

While we think, we must also live and act, and not " propter vitam
vivendi perdere causas " ; [2] we must keep as well as we can a
balance between thought and deed.

That the wrong side has often carried its motion by the
rhetoric of words is true, as I have admitted. But wrong has
as often prevailed in the slow deliberation of philosophers, in the
scrupulous exactitude of scientists, in the arbitrament of war—
ultima ratio regum—and in every human issue. For man is a
fallible being in an infinite maze, " a Creature Moving about in
worlds not realised." [3]

If wrong has prevailed, it has not always prevailed ; and
anyhow we must take the risk after we have sought such counsel
as the urgency and importance of the issue permits. " In all
important transactions of life," says Sir James Fitzjames
Stephen, " we have to take a leap in the dark. . . . If we decide
to leave the riddles unanswered, that is a choice ; if we waver in
our answer, that, too, is a choice ; but whatever choice we make,
we make it at our own peril. . . . Each must act as he thinks
best ; and if he is wrong, so much the worse for him. We stand
on a mountain pass in the midst of whirling snow and blinding
mist, through which we get glimpses now and then of paths
which may be deceptive. If we stand still we shall be frozen to
death. If we take the wrong road we shall be dashed to pieces." [4]

X

We should be the less intimidated by Plato from the very fact
that where his Socrates speaks most disparagingly of rhetoric

---

[1] Andrew Marvell, *To his Coy Mistress*, 21-2.
[2] Juvenal, viii, 84.
[3] Wordsworth, *Intimations of Immortality*, 144-5.
[4] *Liberty, Equality, Fraternity*, 1874, p. 353.

he uses devices as open to criticism on the score of disingenuous-
ness as any in the subtlest rhetorician's bag of tricks. His art
of dialectic may have been maieutic, but not infrequently he
used it for illegal operations. Two of his favourite and most
successful sleights are first, juggling with the ambiguity of such
vague terms as the good, pleasure, justice, and the like, and
secondly, what Sir Thomas Browne in a different reference calls
" concluding metaphors from realities, and from conceptions
metaphorical inferring realities again." [1] Again, though he
proposes to be convinced only by strict logic and sound reason,
his argumentation is often a sort of dialectical fiction by which
(no doubt on the principle that the end justifies the means) he
leads to the conclusions he desires by short-cuts and across thin
ice as hazardous as any in the most daring rhetorician's route.
One feels compelled to ask if sophistry under a show of dialectical
precision and philosophic candour is any better than, or in any
way different from, sophistry in rhetoric, and if the end justifies
the dialectical, but not the rhetorical, means.

Moreover, the author of the dialogues, as distinct from their
protagonist, can be as fairly charged with similar recourse to the
armoury of rhetoric. Thus though they purport to be records
of actual conversations in which topics arose spontaneously (a
perfectly legitimate, but really rhetorical device to give veri-
similitude and dramatic interest), they were in fact invented
dialogues over which a single mind presided. Plato knew before
he put pen to paper how he was to proceed and what final
impression he was to leave ; and though he employed the
dialogue, which has obvious advantages for critical enquiry by
presenting a question from several angles, he can scarcely be
said to be fair to any side but one. He realised that the solution
of a problem which he had reached only by long, roundabout
reflection could be and indeed had to be presented to his pupils
by the shortest route that was consistent with their understanding
it and with all the ramblings and wrong turnings of his pioneering
thought omitted ; just as any man who in his ignorance has
taken a devious path from A to B will ever after go by a directer
way. But surely such action and arrangement, such adjustment
and calculation, such economy and the presentation of *multum*

---

[1] *Pseudodoxia Epidemica* in *The Works of Sir Thomas Browne*, ed.
Simon Wilkins, 1852, i, p. 88. *Cf.* Benjamin Jowett in *The Dialogues of Plato*,
ed. cit., ii, pp. 294-5.

in parvo, whether you chose to use the medium of an imaginary dialogue or not, is rhetoric. In the later works Plato even abandoned the question-and-answer method altogether in favour of continuous exposition,[1] partly perhaps from a failure of dramatic power, but partly, too, from a recognition that the dialectical dialogue was slow and even cumbrous ; and with the harangue he was compelled by the nature of things to submit still more obviously to the practice of rhetoric. But early and late he could not have helped realising that the communication of ideas is an art which every man, woman, and child must practise ; a rhetorical art, not new but as old as man, by which as in the other arts all that can be transferred from mind to mind is only a symbol of an idea, not the idea itself, in the hope that the symbol will evoke something like the idea it stands for ; just as a happy or sad musician by a sequence of notes which is not happiness or sadness produces happiness or sadness in his audience. In all the arts there is a double translation :—of idea into symbol by the artist, of symbol into idea by the recipient ; and the double process admits the possibility of strange divergence between the original idea and the received one. Plato, too, must have known that because language is essentially elliptical, it is a very imperfect means of correspondence, a kind of short-hand, and that only by enlarging its scope through the use of tropes and figures of all kinds which give oblique glimpses of the intended meaning or make indirect stabs in its direction can fairly adequate communication be established. But these extensions of the resources of language (metaphors and similes, paradox and hyperbole, allegory and myth, analogy, pun, antithesis, and so on) are rhetorical devices. " We are all," says Aristotle, " in a sense dialecticians and rhetoricians ; for everybody essays up to a certain point the criticism and support of a thesis, defence and accusation." [2] We are all at any rate emphatically rhetoricians, even the traducers of rhetoric, for the other reason that we all must use language, and that even its humblest use is the exercise of an art.

XI

So far I have accepted the ancient definition of rhetoric as the art of oral persuasion, because such was its main function in

---

[1] *Cf.* Richard Whately, *op. cit.*, pp. 3-4, 23.
[2] *The Rhetoric of Aristotle*, ed. cit., p. 1.

its beginnings, and because Plato evidently regarded it as having no other.

But I should now like to redefine it and to submit a more adequate conception of its scope and purpose. Aristotle himself with characteristic precision gave a slight modification of the contemporary definition by saying that its end was " not to persuade, but to discover the available means of persuasion in any subject " ; just as in medicine the function is not " to restore a patient to perfect health, but only to bring him to as high a point of health as possible ; for even people who can never possibly recover their health may still be scientifically treated." [1] Thus, I suppose that he means, rhetoric will make the best of a case even when it is hopeless. But surely I may extend this principle from forensic and deliberative oratory, the oratory respectively of the law-court and of the public assembly (to which alone in the passage I have just quoted Aristotle was referring), to cover as well epideictic or ceremonial oratory, which is the last of his three categories. For in such speeches as that of Pericles on the Athenian dead, or Burke's on declining the poll, or His Majesty's at the opening or the proroguing of Parliament, or in other speeches less certainly epideictic, as, for example, a judicial summing-up or a state criminal's oration before his execution, there is no attempt at persuasion at all, that is to say, at persuasion as generally understood.

If rhetoric's only function were oral persuasion, then it would be of all forms of composition the most ephemeral.[2] For it could fit only one audience, one situation, and one occasion. It would be, like music, existent only when it was being delivered. But, unlike music, it could never be the same again—" Never, never, never, never, never ; " [3] for the audience would never be the same again on a different occasion, even an audience of the same individuals being no longer a *tabula rasa* but a sheet already scribbled over.

But the rhetoric of the orator need not be ephemeral. The speeches of Burke (which, by the way, were not always persuasive of the audience addressed) are as magnificent as ever ; and the splendid pleas and the tremendous denunciations of Cicero and Demosthenes can still command us two thousand years after their

---

[1] *The Rhetoric of Aristotle*, ed. cit., p. 9 ; *cf.* p. 10.
[2] *Cf.* Richard Whately, *op. cit.*, p. 20.
[3] Shakespeare, *King Lear*, V, iii, 308.

delivery. Are their speeches the less, and (let us say) Gladstone's once so effective and now so unreadable harangues the more, truly rhetoric, because theirs and not his both fitted and survived their occasions ? No, indeed : their power of survival is part and parcel of their excellence as rhetoric. They may not persuade us as they did their original auditors, but they do not cease to hold, to interest, and to delight. We may in imagination even be persuaded by them of causes long dead, no more to us than Hecuba to Hamlet's player, and warmed by loyalties long since cold, though the glamour of the orator's personality and the music of his voice have departed for ever. And if the words of a dead advocate pleading for a dead client in a dead language can still enchant us ; if a statesman who gave to the problems of a day and to a party the genius that was meant for mankind can still hold us and expand our views ; so also can a great preacher being dead yet speak on issues which concern us in all our generations—nay, he can speak with a strange power even to those who reject his theology and deny his creed, as St Paul deeply moved George Moore and as Bossuet perturbed Anatole France.

XII

It will have been seen from these remarks that I propose to extend rhetoric to include the written, as well as the spoken, word. As early as Aristotle rhetoric was recognised as covering the art of composition in all the prose, and even the verse, varieties, since rules for success in speaking and in writing are largely the same. Thus he included rules for composition other than oral,[1] and the later professors of the art concerned themselves more and more with the general power of expression in literature to be read. Indeed, as political life dwindled and died under the Empire, so that public oratory ceased to have any reality or any influence on public affairs, the word *eloquence* gradually changed its meaning and came to bear the same sense as the word *literature* has for us. The invention of printing by extending still further the sphere of the operation of the writer has gradually displaced the speaker, or at least, if he still retains his position in the law-courts, in parliament, and in the church, has raised up so many rivals whose medium is the printing press that to-day oral composition is of comparatively little account

[1] *Cf.* Richard Whately, *op. cit.*, p. 1.

and influence. We have now indeed almost lost the faculty of taking things in by the ear. (The workman who, when offered a paper and a pencil to take notes of a lecture, asked Dean Inge " What's my sanguinary ear for ? " was something of an exception.) And our writers have in general lost the gift of speaking. For even what is meant to be spoken, as, for example, radio talks and the majority of sermons and lectures, is nearly always merely written prose to be delivered orally, but otherwise in style and structure the same as prose meant only to be read. Thus whereas in classical times the rhetoric of speech largely determined the rhetoric of writing, to-day written composition rules even our so-called oratory. Moreover, whereas classical rhetoric was concerned mainly with affairs, to a much smaller extent with instruction, and still less with imaginative composition, modern literature is primarily devoted to imaginative composition, secondly to instruction, and only thirdly to affairs ; and the literatures of instruction and of affairs tend to adopt the graces, and even sometimes the creative liberty, of the literature of the imagination.

Not only has the speaker given place to the writer, but the latter has evolved more and more new literary orders, families, genera and species, hybrids, and sports. The novel and the short story, the essay and the article are by far the most comprehensive and richly diverse classes. But there are many other new kinds or surprising modifications of old ones in biography, autobiography, and memoir ; in history and romance ; in epistle, dialogue, and prose satire ; in allegory, fantasy, and fable ; in treatise and tract (to keep within the bounds of prose).

In a sense the relation of author to reader is fundamentally the same as that of speaker to auditor. For the reader is the *raison d'être* of literature as the auditor is of oratory, since without a reading or a listening public there would be no reason or reward for literature or for oratory ; and the man who writes in his study is obliged to consider his unknown and invisible readers, though, unlike the orator, he cannot see step by step how they are taking his work and cannot make adjustments accordingly.

But if without a reading public there would be no literature, without a rhetoric in written composition most assuredly there would be no reading public, any more than there would be patrons at a restaurant if the edibles left the kitchen for the table as raw, crude, and unappetising as they came in at the back door.

Therefore I suggest that the most elementary function of rhetoric is, not to persuade, but to select and arrange. First of all there must be the private selection and arrangement, primordial and antecedent to any purpose, which the author for his own sake has to impose on the flux of his own mind,

> a dark
> Illimitable Ocean without bound,
> Without dimension, where length, breadth, and highth,
> And time and place are lost ; where eldest Night
> And Chaos, Ancestors of Nature, hold
> Eternal Anarchie, amidst the noise
> Of endless warrs, and by confusion stand.[1]

For all thinking, whether reasoning, remembering, or imagining, is like the act of creation, a selective ordering, a finding of a thinkable form by the mind which abhors the inchoate and amorphous (as I can feelingly avouch, for often have I rushed out of doors in the hope that a walk might reduce my jarring, whirling, buzzing ideas to some sort of order, till they were

> founded, then conglob'd
> Like things to like, the rest to several place
> Disparted).[2]

It is an artistic attempt to reduce the indiscriminate to rule, order, and category. And indeed it is not without significance that in one language at least, Latin, one word *forma* stands for both *order* and *beauty*. But such preliminary shaping is rarely more than a working model or sketch for the final selection and arrangement to be offered to the reader. That final result itself is not achieved by a straightforward and undeviating procedure, but by a process of gradual and blundering approximation (as I have often painfully realised in the five-, six-, seven-, or more-times-, repeated composition, decomposition, and re-composition of my material). Indeed, the heaping up of things to say is much the easiest part of authorship. To discover the appropriate organisation for them and to appreciate the relation of part to part and of part to whole, is by far the most difficult, whether in a scientific text-book or in a novel, in an argument or in the description of a purely imaginary scene.

[1] Milton, *Paradise Lost*, ii, 891-7.   [2] *Ibid.*, vii, 239-41.

Selection and arrangement are common to all kinds of composition, oral and written, and to all kinds of purposes.[1] Even in the most matter-of-fact presentation of a bald and unalluring fact, the whole bald and unalluring fact, the presenter has still to choose from a multitude of possible arrangements that which does the least injury and the most justice to his subject-matter. Thus, to give an obvious example from Euclid, the Pythagoras problem would be entirely unconvincing if presented to someone ignorant of geometry before, instead of after, all the preceding axioms, postulates, and propositions. Or again, a logical sorites exists only in virtue of a particular order. But if selection and arrangement mean so much in these sciences of abstract ratiocination, they play no less vital a part in the communication of anything else that man would say to man. For if of two men who want to state the same matter (be it an incident true or invented, a medical opinion, a legal case, a critical theory, or an election address) the one is muddled and the other orderly, the difference between them is one of selection and arrangement, in short a rhetorical difference. Yes; " a thousand excellent, strenuous words can leave us quite cold or put us to sleep, whereas a bare half-hundred words breathed upon by some man in his agony, or in his exaltation, or in his idleness, ten generations ago, can still lead whole nations into and out of captivity, can open to us the doors of the three worlds, or stir us so intolerably that we can scarcely abide to look at our own souls." [2] Not that the one has no rhetoric and the other has, but that the one has bad rhetoric, a badly planned, wasteful,

---

[1] Which, though many, may be classified under the two chief offices of literature, according to De Quincey's division. These, he says (*The Poetry of Pope* in *The Collected Writings of Thomas De Quincey*, ed. David Masson, 1890, xi, 54-5), " may blend and often *do* so, but [are] capable, severally, of a severe insulation, and naturally fitted for reciprocal repulsion. There is, first, the literature of *knowledge* ; and, secondly, the literature of *power*. The function of the first is—to *teach* ; the function of the second is—to *move* : the first is a rudder ; the second, an oar or a sail. The first speaks to the *mere* discursive understanding ; the second speaks ultimately, it may happen, to the higher understanding or reason, but always *through* affections of pleasure and sympathy. Remotely, it may travel towards an object seated in what Lord Bacon calls *dry* light ; but, proximately, it does and must operate, else it ceases to be a literature of *power*, on and through that *humid* light which clothes itself in the mists and glittering *iris* of human passions, desires, and genial emotions."

[2] Rudyard Kipling, *A Book of Words*, 1928, p. 8.

and dull design, and the other has a good rhetoric which gives strength with grace, power with beauty. The difference is the command of what Coleridge calls the awful power of words [1] and of that potent magic which out of the infinite number of possible arrangements summons the absolutely best.

It is quite true, as I have implied, that in selecting and arranging the writer or speaker has an end in view—to make his readers know through the literature of knowledge or feel through the literature of power something which without him they would not, to accept such-and-such facts or appreciate such-and-such a point of view on the one hand or to follow imaginatively a story or undergo sympathetically an experience on the other. This process may be regarded as a kind of persuasion. But whether in *belles lettres* or in didactic literature or, for that matter, in legal and deliberative oratory, persuasion in any sense can only be a secondary aim. The primary end of every writer and every speaker is and always was to *interest*, and unless they do so there can be no persuasion of any kind because there can be no communication. Rhetoric before all else is an instrument to win and hold the attention—first to allure as the flower spreads its corolla to summon the bee, and then to detain as the flower keeps the bee by its honey. As Pascal remarks, " Eloquence is the art of saying things in such a way, first that our hearers can understand them without trouble, and with pleasure ; secondly, that they feel themselves to be so concerned that a sense of duty to themselves induces them the more willingly to reflect on the things said." [2] As he says elsewhere, " We either carry our audience with us, or irritate them." [3] But if we irritate them, they will not remain our audience for long—the exasperated hearers can always begin talking or shouting themselves or can walk away : the bored readers can shut the book and read no more that day, or any other.

Thus rhetoric is primarily the architecture of communication, its structure and ordonnance ; and each of the different literary

---

[1] *Coleridge's Essays and Lectures on Shakespeare and some other Old Poets and Dramatists* (Everyman's Library), 1909, p. 11.

[2] Cf. *Pensées, Opuscules, et Lettres de Blaise Pascal, publiés dans leur texte authentique*, 1873, ii. p. 60 ; and *Pascal's Pensées*, ed. cit., p. 6.

[3] Cf. *Pensées, Opuscules, et Lettres*, ed. cit., ii, 13 ; and *Pascal's Pensées*, ed. cit., p. 8.

kinds, in fact every separate piece of literature, has an archi-tectural design, which reconciles as well as may be all the factors in the situation—the author, the reader, the matter, the space available, and so on ; just as the design for a building has to reconcile the architect's ideas, the customer's wishes and purse, municipal regulations, and the lie of the land.[1] A satisfactory design, moreover, is not applied from without, but is organic. That is bad rhetoric, or rather is not rhetoric at all, which is like the whigmaleeries and curliewurlies of the man who said in defence of an ugly building that the architecture was to be put on later ; for rhetoric and architecture are integral parts of their several composures.[2]

So much is this so that the statement made in and by one selection and arrangement of words would not be the same in a different selection and arrangement, but another statement more or less similar according to the degree of divergence in expression. For just as there are no exactly synonymous words, so *a fortiori* there are no exactly synonymous sentences. In the ultimate analysis, one thought can be said only in one way. " Let no one say," said Pascal, " that I have said nothing new ; the arrangement of the subject is new. When we play tennis, we both play with the same ball, but one of us places it better. I had as soon it was said that I used words employed before. And in the same way if the same thoughts in a different arrangement do not form a different discourse, no more do the same words in their different arrangement form different thoughts. . . . Words differently arranged have different effects." [3]

Quite possibly half-a-dozen different approximations to the same archetypal statement may all be worth making and have a rhetorical, if not any other, value. A man need not forbear, says Dr Johnson, " till he has discovered some truth unknown before ; he may be sufficiently useful, by only diversifying the surface of knowledge, and luring the mind by a new appearance to a second view of those beauties which it had passed over in-attentively before. Every writer may find intellects correspondent to his own, to whom his expressions are familiar, and his thoughts congenial ; and, perhaps, truth is often more successfully pro-pagated by men of moderate abilities, who, adopting the opinions of others, have no care but to explain them clearly, than by subtle

---

[1] Cf. *Pascal's Pensées*, ed. cit., p. 6.   [2] Cf. *ibid.*, p. 6.
[3] *Ibid.*, pp. 1-2.

speculatists and curious searchers, who exact from their readers powers equal to their own, and if their fabricks of science be strong, take no care to render them accessible." [1]

The value of a building is not in its materials, however costly (witness the expense of demolishing), but in the skill and design of the architecture. So in literature it is the manner in which the ideas are fitted into a symmetry and harmony, as well as their adornment and embellishment, quite as much as the ideas themselves which constitute the work. In the same way a diamond is nothing till it is cut.

I claim, then, that rhetoric is inherent in, indwelling in, all expression through words, oral or written, even as the skeleton is in the body ; and that on its structure in the larger elements and down to the smallest details depends the effectiveness of all thought. It gives the form on which the expression of all philosophy and speculation, science and history, poetry and imagination must be erected and without which they cannot be displayed.

And now that I have come to the great partnership and dependence of rhetoric and literature, I feel that I might have saved you and myself all the arguments for the utility of rhetoric by celebrating only its glory. In short, instead of a laboured defence, I might have recited a short and uncompromising panegyric :—

> Many can rule and more can fight,
> But few give myriad hearts delight. [2]

---

[1] *The Adventurer*, No. 137, in *The Works of Samuel Johnson*, 1792, iii, pp. 290-1.

[2] *Selections from Walter Savage Landor*, ed. Sidney Colvin, 1890, p. 195.

F

POETRY AND VERSE

That Verses stood by sense without either Colour's or accent, which yett other tymes he denied.

> Ben Jonson's Conversations with William Drummond of Hawthornden in *Ben Jonson*. Edited by C. H. Herford and Percy Simpson, 1925, i, p. 143.

Sounds as well as thoughts have relation both between each other and towards that which they represent, and a perception of the order of those relations has always been found connected with a perception of the order of the relations of thought. Hence the language of poets has ever affected a sort of uniform and harmonious recurrence of sound, without which it were not poetry, and which is scarcely less indispensable to the communication of its influence, than the words themselves, without reference to that peculiar order.

> Shelley, *A Defence of Poetry* in *The Prose Works of Percy Bysshe Shelley*. Reprinted from the Original Editions and Edited by Richard Herne Shepherd, 1912, ii, p. 7.

We must not insist on knowing where verse ends and prose (or verseless composition) begins, for they pass into one another.

> G. M. Hopkins, *The Note-Books and Papers*. Edited with Notes and a Preface by Humphry House, 1937, p. 221.

I

So far as I know, it was Aristotle who first explicitly stated that verse was one of the accidents of poetry and that μίμησις was its quiddity, whether in prose or in verse.[1]

The question has been repeatedly raised since, and the majority of critics have sided with Aristotle. Curiously enough, however, in so enthusiastic an Aristotelian, the elder Scaliger took the view diametrically opposed to his master :—" Poetæ igitur nomen non a fingendo, ut putarunt, quia fictis uteretur ; sed initio a faciendo versu ductum est." [2] This seems to be an echo of the strong voice of Dante, who, poet and critic both,

---

[1] *Aristotle on the Art of Poetry*, ed. Ingram Bywater, 1909, pp. 5, 27. From his contrasting Homer as a poet with Empedocles as a versifier of physics, it would appear as if he had in mind a similar dictum on Homer and Empedocles in Plato (*Theætetus* in *The Dialogues of Plato*, ed. Benjamin Jowett, 1875, iv, p. 298).

[2] *Julii Cæsaris Scaligeri Poetices libri septem*, 1561, p. 3.

had uncompromisingly proclaimed the essentiality of verse :—
" recolimus nos eos qui vulgariter versificantur plerumque vocasse
poetas : quod procul dubio rationabiliter eructare presumpsimus,
quia prorsus poete sunt, si poesim recte consideremus, que nichil
aliud est quam fictio rethorica musicaque posita." [1] Later poets,
on the other hand, have generally agreed that the essence of their
art was something other than the versification. Thus Ronsard
declared :—" Tous ceux qui escrivent en carmes, tant doctes
puisent-ils estre, ne sont pas poëtes. Il y a autant de différence
entre un poëte et un versificateur qu'entre un bidet et un genereux
coursier de Naples." [2] And Sidney seems to echo him with a
characteristic turn of phrase :—" verse [is] but an ornament and
no cause to Poetry, sith there haue beene many most excellent
Poets that neuer versified, and now swarme many versifiers
that neede neuer answere to the name of Poets." [3] Shelley
maintained not only that " The distinction between poets
and prose-writers is a vulgar error," [4] but that Plato, Bacon,
Herodotus, Plutarch, Livy, and others were poets without verse—
apparently for no better reason than that they had beauty of style
and imagery and striking thoughts, or in short, because Shelley
admired them to a degree of emotional uplift. He does not say,
as Sidney did of Plato,[5] that such writers were poets by virtue
of anything mimetic in them. Coleridge, too, by finding " un-
deniable proofs " in Plato, Jeremy Taylor and Thomas Burnet
" that poetry of the highest kind may exist without metre, and
even without the contradistinguishing objects of a poem," [6]
appears to have had a conception of poetry which depended on
something other than $\mu i\mu\eta\sigma\iota s$, though not one which omitted
passion and imagination.[7] On the other hand, Coleridge distinguishes, as had become customary since at least the third century

---

[1] *De Vulgari Eloquentia*, II, iv, 2 ; cf. *Il Convivio*, II, vi, 4.

[2] *La Franciade : Au Lecteur Apprentif* in *Ronsard : Œuvres Complètes*,
ed. Gustave Cohen, 1938, ii, p. 1021.

[3] *An Apology for Poetry* in *Elizabethan Critical Essays*, ed. G. Gregory
Smith, 1904, i, pp. 159-60.

[4] *A Defence of Poetry* in *The Prose Works of Percy Bysshe Shelley*, ed.
R. H. Shepherd, 1912, ii, p. 7.

[5] *An Apology for Poetry*, ed. cit., p. 152.

[6] *Biographia Literaria*, ed. J. Shawcross, 1907, ii, p. 11.

[7] Cf. *Lectures*, 1818, in R. P. Cowl, *The Theory of Poetry in England*,
1914, p. 234 :—" poetry . . . does not rest in metre . . . it is not poetry,
if it makes no appeal to our passions or imagination."

B.C.,[1] between poetry (ποίησις) and poem (ποίημα). There is some ambiguity about his view of the latter. Or rather in one or two passages of the *Biographia Literaria* [2] he is entirely inconsistent both with the general tenour of his poetic in the *Biographia* and with his remarks elsewhere on the nature of a poem. In the passages in question, probably for the sake of an *ad hoc* argument, metre is reduced to an accidental factor, something superadded, and the connection between metre and poetic expression is regarded as purely mechanical. In general, however, all that Coleridge postulates of a poem can be supplied best, and perhaps only, when metre is a contributory cause.[3] Coleridge's fellow-logician, Whately, puts the case for metre very uncompromisingly, but with less than his usual subtlety :—
" Notwithstanding all that has been advanced . . . to prove that a work, not in metre, may be a Poem . . . universal opinion has always given a contrary decision. Any composition in *verse* (and none that is not) is always called, whether good or bad, a Poem, by all who have no favourite hypothesis to maintain." [4] G. H. Lewes is more eloquent and not less un-compromising :—" Verse is the form of poetry ; not the form as a thing *arbitrary*, but as a thing vital and essential ; it is the incarnation of poetry. To call it the *dress*, and to consider it apart as a thing distinct, is folly, except in technical instruction. Rhythm is not a thing invented by man, but a thing *evolved* from him, and it is not merely the accidental form, but the only possible form of poetry : for there is a rhythm of feeling correspondent in the human soul. ' Melody,' said Beethoven, ' is the sensual life of poetry. Do not the spiritual contents of a poem become sensual feeling through melody ? ' Verse is the type of the soul within." [5]

[1] In Neoptolemus of Parium. *Cf.* J. W. H. Atkins, *Literary Criticism in Antiquity. A Sketch of its Development*, 1934, i, pp. 170-2.

[2] *Ed. cit.*, ii, pp. 52, 53.

[3] *Cf.* e.g. *Coleridge's Essays and Lectures on Shakespeare and some other Old Poets and Dramatists* (Everyman's Library), 1909, pp. 9-12 ; and *Biographia Literaria*, ed. cit., ii, pp. 10-11, 49-51.

[4] *Elements of Rhetoric*, 1850, p. 216. *Cf.* Johnson, *Lives of the Poets : Milton* in *The Works of Samuel Johnson*, 1792, ix, pp. 180-1 :—" perhaps, of poetry as a mental operation, metre or musick is no necessary adjunct ; it is, however, by the musick of metre that poetry has been discriminated in all languages."

[5] *The Inner Life of Art* in *The Principles of Success in Literature*, ed. T. S. Knowlson, 1898, pp. 193-4.

II

Unfortunately the issue has been much confused. It is true, of course, that metre alone does not make poetry. But the question is, Can we have poetry without it ? Metre can be used with advantage for any matter so long as, and only so long as, it has helped towards the author's end. Thus it has been frequently and successfully adopted for all sorts of mnemonics and *jeux d'esprit*, which are not and were never meant to be poetry. It has been employed to make easily memorable long genealogies, tribal histories, sacred scriptures, and other matters, which were likewise quite unpoetical. In all these examples it was an aid to expression, and the only sound objection to it would be that it has given no such help. It would be a sheer nuisance in, for example, an act of parliament or a chemistry text-book.

On the other hand, just because poetry has been so long and so regularly couched in verse, verse has been taken by poetasters as an abracadabra or Open Sesame, as an infallible formula for the achievement of poems. They try to proceed from metre, which they can mechanically master, to poetry, which they cannot. But this does not mean that metre is not of the highest value in genuine poetry. It may still be, for all its possible misuses and utilitarian debasement, such a valuable receptacle for retaining better the volatile spirit of poetry and such a powerful vehicle for giving it momentum that poets forgo it only at their own risk. It is " not metres, but a metre-making argument, that makes a poem," says Emerson, " a thought so passionate and alive, that, like the spirit of a plant or an animal, it has an architecture of its own, and adorns nature with a new thing. The thought and the form are equal in the order of time, but in the order of genesis the thought is prior to the form." [1]

Another source of confusion in discussions on the propriety of metre in poetry is due to taking metre as limited to the established verses and stanzas. But, as Shelley says, so long as harmony is achieved, the traditional forms may be dropped or altered ; " every great poet must inevitably innovate upon the example of his predecessors in the exact structure of his peculiar versification." [2] Indeed, the innovators have not always been

[1] *The Poet* in *The Complete Works of Ralph Waldo Emerson*, ed. G. T. B., n.d., pp. 93-4.
[2] *A Defence of Poetry*, ed. cit., ii, p. 7.

themselves great poets. But certainly the corpus of recognised measures and stanzas has been steadily augmented either by deliberate experiment or by sound impulse. Nor is the process likely to stop, any more than the process by which composers have been continually extending the range of permissible harmonies in music. And what can be done in any art cannot be prophesied : it can only be recognised as right when it has actually been done.

It may, however, be recognised as wrong ; for, despite many tacit assumptions to the contrary in the writings of the more revolutionary critics, it is not true that in art whatever is, can be, or shall be, is right. It may be that an artist inadvisedly or perversely tries to do that which the essential nature of his art forbids, or which overstates something secondary at the expense of something primary, or which loses the substance for the sake of the shadow.

III

Now those who with Aristotle regarded metre as one of the accidents of poetry did not, until recent times, recommend poets to write in any other mode. While poetry might be in prose and some prose was claimed as poetry, metre was on all hands admitted, at least tacitly, to be the preferable vehicle. But other vehicles which are neither prose nor metre are now on the market, free verse, *vers libéré*, *prose cadencée*, and the like.

The *raisons d'être* of all of them—especially of free verse, to which as a rival to metre I shall confine myself—are two interdependent but not very well-worked-out propositions, namely :— (1) that poetry must be free of metre or at least that it loses nothing vital by being thus unbound, because metre is an artificial and external restriction ; and (2) that the old metrical forms are exhausted.

The second of these propositions seems to admit that once upon a time the forms were unexhausted. But I will not press that. I should, however, like to know what is meant by exhaustion of forms. Is the form of the human face exhausted or exhaustible ? Do we grow tired of the shape of a wheel ? And in any case, are there no new metrical forms which will give such advantages as metre can and which will yet be like a new bottle to contain the strong wine of the new poetry ?

The first proposition is traceable to the æsthetics of Shaftesbury with its distinction between dead or external and inward or organic form. This is not, I believe, a false distinction. But it is, I contend, out of the struggle between external form and organic that artistic beauty is born. That is just the difference between art and non-art. The latter has only organic form. The former has both ; it makes the organic, which is free and infinitely various and incalculable, submit to the external, which is stable and harmoniously repetitive and predictable. Thus the natural is brought within the scope of the artificial—within the kingdom of man and his reason. The expressive faculties of man are twofold : his senses demand rhythmical variability, his mind rhythmic consistency. Out of the perfect union of these two, under the influence of imaginative excitement is great poetry born. Creative life combines absolute regularity with intense diversity.

IV

What exactly is the difference between metre and rhythm ? As the word implies, metre is a measure, marking off lengths of so many syllables, quantities, or accents. It has no direct relation to the contents of these lengths. Rhythm, on the other hand, is a regular movement and speed generated by the contents of its phrases. It is, therefore, not merely a regular movement in time, as it has sometimes been briefly defined. It is a co-ordination of movements in time which accords sympathetically with the feelings of the author and appeals sympathetically to the feelings of his audience.

Now prose admits of rhythm ; and verse, metrical or free, demands it. A great deal of prose has none at all, or at the best one quite as accidental as the rattle of a lorry over cobbles. It may be that good prose should be rhythmical. But no prose ceases to be prose merely because it is arhythmical. In fact it is not declassed even if it is also ungrammatical and incoherent. In metrical poetry the rhythm is given continuity by the metre to which it is accommodated, just as in music the rhythm is steadied by the tempo. The poet's art, however, is to vary the expected rhythm in an appropriate accord with the sentiments and yet without disappointing the expectation. Prose avoids rhythms already associated with some metre or other, partly because they are so associated, but more because they are naturally too positive for its purpose. It prefers constantly shifting rhythms, rhythms not so strong that a change in them or a breach of them to suit the sense will be resented by the reader. Its rhythms are most acceptable when they appear to be accidental or spontaneous. Whenever a prose rhythm begins to overrule the sense and to try to perpetuate itself over a passage of some length, it is well on the way to becoming not prose but poor metre, as in Dickens's lapses into a kind of blank verse. And this facility is distasteful to the reader, because the rhythm has become a mere automatism, or rather has become a metre without relation to the sense. The same thing can happen in metrical poetry, as in Longfellow's *Hiawatha*. But so long as the metrical poetry is of some musical interest, the metre will not become stereotyped and the rhythm will not ignore the sense. Rather between them they will produce an essential friction, like that of a bow on the strings of a violin ; and the rhythms, which ought to have an emotional origin and propriety, will be kept by the metre, which has a formal origin and purpose, within an artistic unity of tone.

V

Somewhere in between the two modes of prose and metre comes free verse, which is supposed by its champions to partake of the virtues of both of the others. By freedom they do not mean formlessness, but rhythmical adaptability on a common-speech basis. Thus free verse might be described as a kind of composition in which the lines are made not of " arbitrary " lengths as in metre, but of phrases determined by the sense and yet agreeably modulated. These phrases are not all complete, separable statements, though they may be. They each, however, consist of such a group of words as grammar, sense, and feeling mark off for utterance in one breath or without a major pause. " Each line or phrase has (*ex hypothesi*) to show convincing propriety of diction and rhythm, together with other proprieties of relative length, sonority, and poetic value." [1] The lengths are presumably unlimited in theory : they will in fact be limited by grammar, sense, feeling, or breath. These may be said to be the positive characteristics of free verse. Negatively—and here we may hint that the free-verse lines are not so free as the name implies—they must reject all the rhythms of metre and its formal pauses and groupings.

[1] Bridges, *Humdrum and Harum-Scarum : A Lecture on Free Verse* in *Collected Essays, Papers, etc.*, 1928, p. 49.

Free verse is supposed by its practitioners to partake of the virtues of both prose and metre. But in reality it may prove to be a weaker, because less reliable, instrument than either. It is not a spontaneous mode, like prose which one can speak all one's life without realising it, or like metre into which man's emotions have run from time immemorial, but a highly sophisticated and precarious compromise which can maintain itself only by a disabling protest. Indeed composition according to the positive or negative prescriptions of free verse will almost inevitably tend either to the more predictable and repetitive rhythms of metre or to the looser, intermittent, and irregular rhythms of prose.

Where free verse " is most successful," says Bridges, whose love of rhythmical experiment will free him from any suspicion of prejudice, " its cadences provoke too much of the expectancy of verse to appear so wholly free from restraint as the best prose can : and it is right enough to call it verse rather than prose. And if it is quite satisfactory—as in short poems it very well may be—it is so by virtue of the poet's sensibility to rhythmical form, and by his mastery of it ; and he will so combine his rhythms that they do create expectancy as they proceed : indeed I do not doubt that a free-verse poet would regard the pleasure which accompanies this satisfied expectancy, as a note of his success." [1]

But what is this if not the way-back to the metrical fold ? As Bridges says, in so far as the rhythms of free verse produce expectancy in the reader, they can be analysed and reduced to rule. For that matter even the less predictable rhythms of pure prose have been systematically classified. To quote Bridges again :—" What generally satisfies the ear does so by some principle or law ; and the simplest, the commonest, and most pervading conditions will soon be recognized ; and they would be the simplest elements of any possible reduction of all verse rhythms to one system. The writer of free verse cannot escape from this : indeed his rejection of metre is based on the recognition of rhythms. . . . He has cast off his visible chains but has not escaped into liberty. If he is a law unto himself, he is so only by unconscious obligation to a wider law to which he has appealed. . . . [O]f what nature are these effects which he is aiming at, and on which he relies ? That he can rely on them implies that they are what other ears are prepared to accept, and such effects can only be the primary movements of rhythm upon which all

[1] Bridges, *op. cit.*, p. 45.

verse has always depended, and which, on his own assumption, poets have elaborated into the perfected metrical forms which he repudiates. . . . I think that free verse is good and theoretically defensible only in so far as it can create expectancy without the old metrical devices. If it fails to effect this, it seems to me but a broken jerky sort of bad prose." [1]

What it comes to, then, is this : when free verse is agreeably modulated, its rhythms will either approximate to rhythms perfectly feasible in metre but perhaps disguised to look new, or else will be new but not beyond the reach of metrical experiment ; and when free verse fails of even the effect that it ought to achieve, it will be found to be a kind of *prose tranchée*, and none the better for the slicing.

VI

Not only do I believe that poetry will lose if it is not in verse, but I am convinced that the only fitting verse for it is metrical. One sound reason for these opinions is the conservative one that poetry in all languages has nearly always been metrical. And if we can answer the question, Why has this been so ? we shall have gone near to solving our original problem.

A comprehensive, half-way answer to this second question might be, Because the first poets could not help it and their followers recognised the value of metre even when they used it deliberately, and because the hearers or readers are more responsive as a result of it and in any case like it. But such a condensed answer may be elaborated with, I hope, some little interest.

VII

Mr T. S. Omond believes that in states of strong emotion it is more natural to dance than to walk, to sing than to speak, to use measured language than to adopt the uncadenced falls of ordinary utterance. " Emotion," he says, " seeks rhythmical expression ; the two are inseparably connected. Mere excitement, indeed, prompts to shout rather than to sing. But high, heart-felt emotion—and is not this the very *essentia* of poetry ?— has always urged men to cadenced speech long before David

[1] Bridges, *op. cit.*, pp. 45-7.

elegized Saul and Jonathan or cried in his anguish, ' O Absalom, my son, my son ! ' " [1]

But is Mr Omond not confusing two states of mind which are no doubt similar but which are never identical, the primary emotion of experience and the secondary emotion of expressing the experience ? I think it is scarcely accurate to say that the primary emotions themselves seek rhythmical expression. So long as these emotions are operating in full force on the primary level and in immediate response to the stimuli which produced them, the accompanying words, if indeed there are any words at all, tend to be broken and incoherent, and not expressive. There is always a pause, however momentary, between experience and expression—a psychological interval in which the subjective becomes in a measure objective and that which is naturally inarticulate becomes voluble, so voluble perhaps as to be an overflowing and impetuous stream of words and images without bounds or control. At this stage there may be a kind of proto-rhythm. But it is only when the emotion is, in Wordsworth's profound phrase, " recollected in tranquillity," [2] that a true and recognisable rhythm supervenes, that is to say, a rhythm which is begotten of a reasserted control by the poet and which begets an expectancy in the audience by a co-ordination appealing to the feelings. David's elegy for Saul and Jonathan, like Mr Shandy's eloquence on the loss of his firstborn, was not an *immediate* response to events.

Wordsworth puts his views on the antecedents of poetical composition thus : " the emotion is contemplated till, by a species of re-action, the tranquillity gradually disappears, and an emotion, kindred to that which was before the subject of contemplation, is gradually produced, and does itself actually exist in the mind. In this mood successful composition generally begins, and in a mood similar to this it is carried on." [3]

I should be inclined to explain the process by which the broken rhythms of the original emotions give place to more regular ones rather differently. I suggest that by the mere lapse of time, which may be longer or shorter according to the degree

[1] *Some Thoughts about Verse*, English Association Pamphlet, No. 55, p. 3.
[2] *Preface to the Second Edition of . . . " Lyrical Ballads "* in *The Poetical Works of William Wordsworth*, ed. E. de Selincourt, 1944, ii, p. 400.
[3] *Op. cit.*, ii, pp. 400-1.

or cause or circumstances of the emotion, its oscillations and reverberations will diminish to a point, a focus as it were of negative repose and, in Wordsworth's terms, of " contemplation " and " tranquillity."   Thereafter the emotion will echo on the far side of the focus, producing an emotion akin to the original, but with its erratic throb regulated, by the reassertion of the primary physical pulsations of heart and breath and by the control of the conscious mind, into more or less disciplined rhythms or metre.[1]

The substitution of articulate expression for inarticulate feeling, as in Cicero's sorrow for Tullia or the aforesaid Mr Shandy's for Bobby, and the essentially similar substitution of regular for broken rhythms, as in Beethoven's increasing control of the violent, sweeping surges at the opening of the *Appassionata* sonata, produce separately, and still more in their conjunction in poetry, a feeling of relief and satisfaction which is pleasurable even when the original emotions were painful. For the very utterance of despair in words and rhythm is a triumph over it and a kind of moral victory and consolation. The new world of art has been called in to redress the balance of the old world of fact. As Coleridge says, the great poet provides " a more than usual state of emotion with more than usual order." [2]

Something like this is, I think, the process in poets, early or late, who express their own authentic passions and write because they must, not because they would.

But poetry as often as not is the expression of passions imagined and presented either subjectively or objectively. For a poet can be not only " a man pleased with his own passion and volitions," but one " delighting to contemplate similar volitions and passions as manifested in the goings-on of the Universe and habitually compelled to create them where he does not find them. To these qualities he has added a disposition to be affected more than other men by absent things as if they were present and ability of conjuring up in himself passions, which are indeed far from being the same as those produced by real events, yet . .

[1] *Cf.* Coleridge, *Biographia Literaria*, ed. cit., ii, pp. 49-50.

[2] *Coleridge's Essays and Lectures on Shakespeare and some other Old Poets and Dramatists*, p. 12. Cf. *Biographia Literaria*, ed. cit., i, p. 4 :— " I learnt from [the Rev. James Boyer], that Poetry, even that of the loftiest and, seemingly, that of the wildest odes, had a logic of its own, as severe as that of science ; and more difficult, because more subtle, more complex, and dependent on more, and more fugitive causes."

do more nearly resemble the passions produced by real events, than anything which, from the motions of their own minds merely, other men are accustomed to feel in themselves." [1]

VIII

When a poet expresses an observed or imagined emotion, the process is still the metamorphosis of something undisciplined into something disciplined ; and it produces, as does the expression of primary emotion, a pleasurable satisfaction.

So much for the poet. But what of the reader ? I cannot agree with Coleridge that for any poetic purpose metre is like yeast, which, though worthless and disagreeable in itself, gives vivacity and spirit to a liquor.[2] For I believe metre to have not only an instrumental, but an intrinsic, value, as indeed Coleridge himself admits elsewhere.[3]

Just as rhythm or, still more, metre marks the triumph of the poet's control over the naturally wayward vibrations of feeling, and just as the substitution of regular for broken rhythm and of articulate expression for inarticulate emotion gives a deep satisfaction to the poet himself, so a parallel satisfaction is provided for the reader—the profound æsthetic satisfaction of a feeling in harmony with regularity, of a feeling which by the consummation of art has been freed from frustration and incompleteness. The true poet and his gratified audience are both delightfully conscious and unconscious of the pattern. Rhythm is the reverberation of passion ; but the faculties of men are so constituted that he realizes and rejoices in its natural variations most when they subtly advertise themselves upon a ground of uniformity.

From a slightly different angle Wordsworth argues to very much the same effect. " The end of Poetry," he postulates, " is to produce excitement in co-existence with an overbalance of pleasure." [4] But there is some danger that the excitement, which is after all an unusual and irregular state of the mind, may

---

[1] Wordsworth, *op. cit.*, ii, p. 393.

[2] Cf. *Biographia Literaria*, ed. cit., ii, p. 52.

[3] *Ibid.*, ii, p. 9 :—" a particular pleasure is found in anticipating the recurrence of sounds and quantities " ; *cf.* ii, pp. 49-50, 261-2, and *Anima Poetae*, ed. E. H. Coleridge, 1895, 153.

[4] *Op. cit.*, ii, p. 399.

exceed the proper bounds. In this danger lies metre's justification and opportunity. For " the co-presence of something regular, something to which the mind has been accustomed in various moods and in a less excited state, cannot but have great efficacy in tempering and restraining the passion by an intertexture of ordinary feeling, and of feeling not strictly or necessarily connected with the passion." [1] It operates also by a number of different ways to produce what Wordsworth calls " a complex feeling of delight," [2] which is of great importance in moderating the element of pain always intermingled with powerful representations of the stronger passions. These are :—the sheer music of harmonious language in metre ; the sense given to the reader of difficulty overcome ; the remembrance from previous occasions of the pleasure due to other works in rhyme or metre ; and the perception that metre, while it allows language to approximate to that of real life, nevertheless divests language of some of its reality and throws " a sort of half-consciousness of unsubstantial existence over the whole composition." [3] Hence the more pathetic or painful situations and sentiments are made more endurable by metre, especially rhymed metre, than they would be in prose, and therefore much more pleasurable to the reader.

This agrees with the Aristotelian view that " the Melody is the greatest of the pleasurable accessories of Tragedy." [4] But it goes farther than Aristotle, and, I believe, rightly though one might question some of the wording. For whereas Aristotle probably regarded tragedy in its totality as a channel by which the feelings could be released along the right lines and within just limits, tragedy being as it were both an outlet for, and an instruction of, the feelings ; Wordsworth assigns such a function to the metre itself. Elsewhere there is abundant evidence to show that he regarded good poetry in its matter and apart from its form not only as " the spontaneous overflow of powerful feelings," [5] but as the product of " habits of meditation," [6] prompting and regulating these feelings and so conferring on the poetry which results a worthy purpose. And by good poetry

---

[1] *Biographia Literaria*, ii, p. 399. (The 1802 text is given. It differs slightly from the 1800.)

[2] *Op. cit.*, ii, p. 401.

[3] *Ibid.*, ii, p. 399.

[4] *Aristotle on the Art of Poetry*, ed. cit., pp. 21-3.

[5] *Op. cit.*, ii, p. 387.

' the understanding of the Reader must necessarily be in some degree enlightened, and his affections strengthened and purified." [1] Nevertheless, in the passage quoted in the last paragraph, Wordsworth rightly emphasised the regulative effect of metre in itself which had not been sufficiently recognised before.

Incidentally I should note that of course not all poetry deals with the stronger passions or with passions at all. Much of it is concerned with or appeals to comparatively neutral states of the mind or the wits. Nevertheless, much of what has been said about the pleasure due to metre holds good of these lower degrees of poetry as well.

There is another reason for the pleasure which metre gives. I say " another reason " ; but it may be the same in other words. For when we get down to fundamental levels in æsthetics, we are apt to find that one explanation fades into another and that, while everything may have a cause, the cause of anything is everything.

In any case, it would seem as if a passion for symmetry is one of the innate desires of the mind. Just because we are creatures with two complementary hands and feet, eyes, and ears, we instinctively create an answering symmetry in our works of art and of use. Discord, oddity, and asymmetry are *per se* as displeasing as concord, balance, and symmetry are pleasing, whether in music, sculpture, painting, architecture, and poetry, or indeed in any article of which the function does not entirely dictate the shape. Not that an obvious symmetry is the most pleasing, but rather that which, though real, has to be discovered. For we are so made as to be pleased æsthetically by the perception of likeness in unlikeness, and also, on a secondary level, by the converse. The perception is inseparable from our recognition of the beautiful. Wordsworth, indeed, would find in it " the great spring of the activity of our minds, and their chief feeder. From this principle the direction of the sexual appetite, and all the passions connected with it, take their origin : it is the life of our ordinary conversation ; and upon the accuracy with which similitude in dissimilitude, and dissimilitude in similitude are perceived, depend our taste and our moral feelings." [2]

So far as metre is concerned, this kind of pleasure comes in the first place from the perception of a metrical norm underlying departures from, and approximations to it. It resides, to put the

[1] *Op. cit.*, ii, p. 388.   [2] *Op. cit.*, ii, p. 400.

same thing by means of a musical metaphor, in the recognition of a theme on which every line plays variations that please by a half-revealed, half-concealed recurrence or by an occasional contrast between expectation and fulfilment, between suspension and resolution. "[T]he essence of verse," says Dr Johnson, " is regularity, and its ornament is variety " : [1] it realises that last idea of beauty itself, which includes the charm of diversity within the flowing round of habit and ease.

In the second place, coincidently with the pleasure given by the metrical modulations, there is a pleasure-giving perception of quite another likeness in unlikeness, namely, the likeness of the diction to that of ordinary life by reason of the use of the same basic language, and the unlikeness due to the necessity of accommodating the diction to the metre. This is a subtler matter and not so much metrical as syntactical and verbal. But the cause of the variations on normal usage is metrical, just as in the miming ballet the cause of the variations on the physical movements of everyday life is the necessity of moving in accord with a musical tempo.

This pleasure, due to the presence of something regular controlling the irregular, or (for it may be the same thing) to the perception of likeness in unlikeness and *vice versa*, can be considerable only if the verse is metrical. The more thoroughly free verse lives up to its name, the more will its irregularity and variety prevail over its regularity and uniformity, such as they may be, and the more intermittent and sketchy will be the reader's perception of likeness in unlikeness and of the converse. Moreover, just because free verse tries to make the line-units approximate to common-speech units, its lines will tend to a greater monotony of grammatical form than will the lines of metrical verse, which can, if the poet pleases, cut across the grammar without destroying it and produce endless counterpoint, so to say, between grammar and metre. " The grammatical forms of sentences in English are few, and must repeat themselves again and again ; and each form has its proper and natural inflexion of voice which, however overlaid, will impose its typical intonation on the sentence. Now if the grammatical forms are made co-incident with the lines of the verse, they must impose the recurrence of their similar intonations upon the lines." [2]

[1] *Lives of the Poets : Dryden* in *The Works of Samuel Johnson*, ed. cit., ix. p. 443.
[2] Bridges, *op. cit.*, p. 51.

So much for the pleasure which metre gives to the reader. It has also the rather more utilitarian function of heightening the reader's responsiveness. This it does in, I think, two chief ways.

In the first place, the metre produces and sustains the mood ; at least the metre and the rhythm together do so. The rhythm of a good poem in metre—

> The ocean-like enchantment of strong sound,
> Which flows intenser, keener, deeper yet
> Under the ground and through the windless air [1]—

is perhaps the most potent single element in it. For poetical expression includes sound as well as meaning, and poetry unlike prose must be listened to even by the silent reader. The rhythm of poetry, like the rhythm of music, has some secret and mysterious power over our feelings and imaginations. It can both confirm what the words do and effect that which words alone cannot do. Indeed metre, rhythm, and all that belongs to the mode of expression rather than to the substance of it are the natural results and spontaneous signs of the poet's emotion. And as regards the reader they are both a measure of the poetic intensity and the means by which a similar emotional warmth is produced in him and by which he partakes of the passion, as well as of the imaginative perception, of the theme. So intimate is the connection between emotional stimulus and rhythm, between feeling and cadence, that by the mere run of the lines the poet, in a process the exact opposite of that which had operated on himself, produces in the reader the first stirrings of an emotion which the contents of the poem express more articulately and make good. That is to say, the poet by his metre and rhythm produces a conditioned reflex : instead of the emotion begetting in the reader the rhythm as it had done in the poet himself, the appropriate rhythm prepares the reader for the emotion to come and maintains him in the right mood. Thus " rhythmus," says De Quincey—and we may take this to include all the metrical and musical side of a poem—" is both a cause of impassioned feeling, an ally of such feeling, and a natural effect of it." [2]

Hence the reader experiences an unpleasant jar and a certain emotional confusion when, as sometimes happens, the poet has

[1] Shelley, *Prometheus Unbound*, iv, 203-5.
[2] *Style* in *The Collected Writings of Thomas De Quincey*, ed. David Masson, 1890, x, p. 172.

G

been injudicious in his choice of metre, as for example Cowper in *The Poplar Field* and the *Verses supposed to be written by Alexander Selkirk*. In such cases the meaning of the words has to work its effect unaided by the metre or rather actually running counter to it.

On the other hand, " if the Poet's words should be incommensurate with the passion, and inadequate to raise the Reader to a height of desirable excitement, then (unless the Poet's choice of his metre has been grossly injudicious) in the feelings of pleasure which the Reader has been accustomed to connect with metre in general, and in the feeling, whether cheerful or melancholy, which he has been accustomed to connect with that particular movement of metre, there will be found something which will greatly contribute to impart passion to the words, and to effect the complex end which the Poet proposes to himself." [1]

But there is still another and not less important way in which metre integrates and sustains a poem. As Coleridge justly says, " a poem of any length neither can be, [n]or ought to be all poetry " [2]—that is, poetically imaginative and poetically impassioned all through. There are bound to be matters which are stubbornly matter-of-fact, and passages which are purely connective or explanatory. " Yet," to resume the quotation from Coleridge, " if an harmonious whole is to be produced, the remaining parts must be preserved *in keeping* with the poetry ; and this can be no otherwise effected than by such a studied selection and artificial arrangement, as will partake of *one*, though not a *peculiar*, property of poetry." [3] Coleridge was seeking to justify the use of a poetic *diction*. But his words will apply just as well to metre which is also " a studied selection and artificial arrangement." And I submit that it is by metre more than by diction that poets poetise the prosaic along with the poetic, the commonplace transitions and explanations along with the imaginative. The metre carries the vessel over the shallows. It is the lack of this carrying power which makes free-versifiers either flat when they tackle the unpoetic subordinate matter honestly, or obscurely inconsequent when they abruptly skip over it, or distressingly self-conscious when they try to disguise it. But " the old metrical system was designed to

[1] Wordsworth, *op. cit.*, ii, p. 400.
[2] *Biographia Literaria*, ed. cit., ii, p. 11.
[3] *Ibid., ed. cit.*, ii, p. 11.

obviate [this], for therein the poet did not choose his form to suit every special turn and item of his matter, but adapted his matter to the exigencies of a prescribed form; and in doing this he found a further reward, because the changes of his matter provoked and justified all the varieties of rhythm that his metre allowed, so that their desirable irregularities came spontaneously, and his metrical form, harmonising whatever he had to deal with, offered him endless opportunities for unexpected beauties." [1]

In the second place, metre itself, quite apart from its share in producing a rhythm appropriate to the dominating mood of the poem, has the effect of stimulating the reader's susceptibility and his attention. Coleridge believed that the increased alertness of the feelings and the increased awareness of the attention were due to " the continued excitement of surprise and . . . the quick reciprocations of curiosity still gratified and still re-excited, which are too slight indeed to be at any moments objects of distinct consciousness, yet become considerable in their aggregate influence. As a medicated atmosphere, or as wine during animated conversation; they act powerfully, though themselves unnoticed." [2] I have no doubt that this alternating systole and diastole of excitation and gratification plays with some effect on the reader. But a more satisfactory explanation of the heightening of awareness by metre is offered by Sir Philip Hartog's theory that metre, if it is not so obvious as to be a mere jog-trot, absorbs more of the residual or marginal attention which is always liable to lure the mind away from its focus. " I suggest," says Sir Philip, " that for steady concentration it is an immense advantage to have that marginal attention taken up by some regular recurrence and stimulus for which the mind waits, and which is both sufficient to exclude other extraneous circumstances, and yet insufficient to come into the centre of the field." [3] Moreover—and this, I think, is more important—the regularities of metre are slightly hypnotic, inducing a suggestible state in the reader; whereas the irregularities of it are mildly exciting and tend to keep the mind alert. Now " one of the characteristics of poetry is to re-awaken within us that inner life with which will and logic are not directly concerned; . . . the power of the

---

[1] Bridges, *op. cit.*, pp. 49-50.
[2] *Biographia Literaria*, ed. cit., ii, p. 51.
[3] *On the Relation of Poetry to Verse*, English Association Pamphlet, No. 64, p. 12.

poet lies partly in the command which he exercises over this
' sub-conscious ' side of our life ; a command which we do not
feel as a command or resist ; in which, indeed, we have the sense
of being active and not passive, so that the poet's work lives in
us again. We reach the ' moment of judgment and contemplation ' of which Croce speaks, ' in which our spirit is one with
that of the poet, and we are one single thing.' " [1]   In short,
metre is a kind of spell cast over our resistance, a kind of hypnosis
by which the poet at the same time as he soothes our dispersed
restlessness makes us more intensely and æsthetically aware and
releases the mind from its routine associations and unimaginative
habits. It leads the mind off its habitual track and releases it
from the inhibitions that tie it down to the familiar, the commonplace, and the matter-of-fact.

IX

But here I would enter a caveat. It is the usual practice to
dismiss bad poetry as not poetry at all—to deny it the essence,
because it is deficient in the excellence, of its kind. However
excusable this may be in the somewhat rhetorical criticism of
assessment, it is not permissible in the criticism of analysis. To
the critical analyst even bad poetry is poetry, for it at least tried
to give the οἰκεία ἡδονή of poetry ; just as to the anatomist an
imbecile is a man. " Poetry is not distinguished from Prose by
superior Beauty of thought or of expression, but is a distinct
kind of composition ; and they produce, when each is excellent
in its kind, distinct kinds of pleasure." [2]   " Poetry . . . is not
the antithesis to prose, neither is animal the antithesis to plant ;
but a generic difference exists, which it is always fatal to overlook.
Verse is not synonymous with poetry, but is the incarnation of
it ; and prose may be emotive—poetical, but never poetry." [3]

X

That difference manifests itself in many respects. But the one
of most consequence in this context is the effect on the medium
of words. As I have tried to point out elsewhere, prose structure
is a utilitarian convenience, but structure in poetry is an æsthetic

[1] Sir Philip Hartog, *op. cit.*, p. 13.   [2] Whately, *op. cit.*, p. 216.
[3] G. H. Lewes, *op. cit.*, p. 194.

end. Ideally prose tries to *state* an idea without drawing attention to its medium, whereas poetry tries to draw attention to its medium in order to work an æsthetic effect by its ideas.

The distinction can be admirably illustrated by analogy from Adam Smith's *Essay on the Imitative Arts*, in which he contrasts dancing and walking, singing and speaking. In what I might call the prosaic or non-artistic activities of walking and speaking, a person may show grace in the one and an agreeable tone of voice in the other. Yet " if he betrays the least intention of showing either, he is sure of offending more or less, and we never fail to accuse him of some degree of vanity and affectation."[1] But in the poetic or artistic activities of dancing and singing the display of grace or the production of beauty of tone " is, in reality, the proper purpose of the action ; and there can never be any disagreeable vanity or affectation in following out the proper purpose of any action. When we say of any particular person, that he gives himself many affected airs and graces in Dancing, we mean either that he gives himself airs and graces which are unsuitable to the nature of the Dance, or that he executes awkwardly, perhaps exaggerates too much . . . the airs and graces which are suitable to it. Every Dance is, in reality, a succession of airs and graces of some kind or other, and of airs and graces which, if I may say so, profess themselves to be such."[2] Similarly, singing has its legitimate and proper deliberations.

As Whately remarks, this passage from Adam Smith can be applied *mutatis mutandis* to poetry and prose.[3] It is of the nature of poetry to call attention to itself. Its medium is not transparent. Its purpose is not to give information and be itself then forgotten, but to give pleasure, and to be read and re-read and remembered for a repetition of the pleasure.

Hence " the Senate of Poets hath chosen verse as their fittest rayment, meaning, as in matter they passed all in all, so in maner to goe beyond them : not speaking (table talke fashion or like men in a dreame) words as they chanceably fall from the mouth, but peyzing each sillable of each worde by iust proportion according to the dignitie of the subiect. . . . For if *Oratio* next to *Ratio*, Speech next to Reason, bee the greatest gyft bestowed vpon mortalitie, that can not be praiselesse which dooth most pollish that blessing of speech, which considers each word, not only

---

[1] *Essays*, 1869, p. 435.   [2] *Ibid.*, pp. 435-6.   [3] *Op. cit.*, p. 218.

. . . by his forcible qualitie but by his best measured quantitie, carrying euen in themselues a Harmonie." [1] For metre, apart from its other uses and aids, gives an interest to diction which would be affected in prose ; it is comparable to the interest of surface with which the sculptor enhances his medium, or to the interest of quality with which a painter or a composer diversifies passages in paint or music. Common words become new merely by appearing in metre ; rare words are justified ; weak words are made strong ; and vague words are defined. Then again metre is more rhetorically effective for its purpose than prose or free verse would be for the same purpose. It can be briefer and more compendious by its power of compacting and by verbal ellipses, as can be well seen by contrasting with it the verbosity of free verse—the mere number of words it takes to say its say and the loose articulation of the words—or, for that matter, with the natural wordiness of prose. Metre, on the other hand, can be more elaborate and cumulative than is feasible in a diction which has a common-speech basis, by reason of its freer admission of amplification, repetition, parallelism, balance, anaphora, and the like. Indeed metre both allows the poet to introduce, and reconciles with the reader's sense of fitness, all kinds of figures of speech and tropes in addition to those already named, from apostrophe and vision, interrogation and exclamation to metaphor, personification, and hyperbole. In their very nature these rhetorical modes are passionate : they originated, as did metre and rhythm, in the passionate utterance of man, and their most natural place is still the language of passion. If some of them have been naturalised in prose—and not all of them have been— it has been because the prose was attempting to achieve its end by a short-cut, not by statement but by suggestion, not by communicating a cause in order to work its own effect by direct means but by transmitting something of an effect in order to suggest a cause by indirection. It has come to recognise the power of the coefficients of passion for purposes other than their own origination. (Similarly, though more unconsciously, incipient metres tend to develop in oratory and the more eloquent kinds of prose.) Nevertheless these tropical and figurative stigmata of passion would appear unnatural and affected if they were as freely admitted to prose as to verse. For verse is a means of

---

[1] Sidney, *An Apology for Poetry*, ed. cit., pp. 160, 182. *Cf.* Puttenham, *The Art of English Poesy*, *ibid.*, ii, p. 8.

harmonising them, and they seem no more than natural when the metre has attuned and prepared the mind for them.

XI

Moreover, there is a special kind of rhetorical effect which metre favours, that of emphasis. Metre can be more emphatic in a simple way by making the beat fall on significant syllables, and more emphatic in a subtle way by the play of rhetorical emphasis in and about the beats or across them. There is, too, a special kind of emphasis which is peculiar to metre. It has the power of fixing the subordinate or indeterminate accentuations and of putting them into a significant relation. Bridges explains the matter thus :—" A poem in metre has a predetermined organic normal scheme for its lines, and whatever their varieties of rhythm no line can be constructed without reference to its form ; hence the same syllabic rhythms acquire different values according to their place in the line." [1] The delicacy of this mechanism is extraordinary, as can be hinted by a single illustration. Thus if

> High on a Throne of Royal State, which far
> Outshon the wealth of *Ormus* and of *Ind*.[2]

be written as the free-versifiers would write it in rhythmical phrases instead of decasyllables,

> High on a Throne of Royal State,
> Which far outshon the wealth of *Ormus* and of *Ind*,

the value of " far " is lost. " [T]he word cannot in itself determine for itself any special value ; in the free verse it is flat and dull, and one does not know what to do with it, for if it be unaccented it is useless, and if accented it is foolish. Indeed, no accentuation can restore to it what it has lost." [3] At the end of the line the word obtains, by virtue of that place, such a sensitive value as makes a beauty of it. And, I would add, it is not only " far " which loses quality, but the whole balance of each phrase which is impaired, the first being now too abrupt and the second now too dragging. Nor is this loss of delicate nuances surprising. In metrical verse the position of every word and its relation to its neighbours are far more important than they are *ex hypothesi* in prose or free verse.

[1] *Op. cit.*, p. 52.   [2] *Paradise Lost*, ii, 1-2.   [3] Bridges, *op. cit.*, pp. 52-3.

It is also because of its rhetorical superiority, its subtlety of emphasis, and its more highly organised structure by which word is dovetailed to word in a recognisable measure that metre is more easily memorised than is prose or free verse. On first entering the mind the impact of such a formal unity leaves a deeper impression. And this depth of the original impression is in itself favourable to memorising. But in addition the memory on subsequent occasions is relieved from some of its inhibiting doubt by yielding to the swing of the rhythm and by anticipating the recurrence of sounds and quantities, and thus word recalls word in a more fluent association.

XII

For all these reasons, then, I would maintain that since the end which poetry would achieve is pleasure, not only rhythm but also metre is essential to it. As soon as the general superiority of metre over prose and free verse for the purposes peculiar to poetry is recognised in the abstract, metre becomes normally obligatory as well as advisable. Otherwise the poetry would be content to be less agreeable and less effective than was in its power to be. " For this Art undertaking to gratify all those desires and expectations of pleasure, that can be reasonably entertained by us, and there being a capacity in language, the instrument it works by, of pleasing us very highly, not only by the sense and imagery it conveys, but by the structure of words, and still more by the harmonious arrangement of them in metrical sounds or numbers, and lastly there being no reason in the nature of the thing itself why these pleasures should not be united, it follows that poetry will not be that which it professes to be, that is, will not accomplish its own purpose, unless it delight the ear with numbers, or, in other words, unless it be cloathed in VERSE." [1] This, however, is in my opinion a conditional obligation, and does not impose metre when prose or free verse can be *shown* to be preferable. But the *onus probandi* is on poets who choose a vehicle other than metre, and they must give better reasons than personal whim or boredom or the technical difficulties of it. I cannot think that there will be many cases in which they will be able to do so.

[1] Richard Hurd, *On the Idea of Universal Poetry*, in *Q. Horatii Flacci Epistolae ad Pisones, et Augustum*, 1776, ii, p. 144.

MILTON AND THE RENAISSANCE REVOLT
AGAINST RHYME

The Measure is *English* Heroic Verse without Rime, as that of *Homer* in *Greek*, and of *Virgil* in *Latin*; Rime being no necessary Adjunct or true Ornament of Poem or good Verse, in longer Works especially, but the Invention of a barbarous Age, to set off wretched matter and lame Meeter; grac't indeed since by the use of some famous modern Poets, carried away by Custom, but much to their own vexation, hindrance, and constraint to express many things otherwise, and for the most part worse than else they would have exprest them. Not without cause therefore some both *Italian* and *Spanish* Poets of prime note have rejected Rime both in longer and shorter Works, as have also long since our best *English* Tragedies, as a thing of it self, to all judicious eares, triveal and of no true musical delight; which consists only in apt Numbers, fit quantity of Syllables, and the sense variously drawn out from one Verse into another, not in the jingling sound of like endings, a fault avoyded by the learned Ancients both in Poetry and all good Oratory. This neglect then of Rime so little is to be taken for a defect, though it may seem so to vulgar Readers, that it rather is to be esteem'd an example set, the first in *English*, of ancient liberty recover'd to Heroic Poem from the troublesom and modern bondage of Rimeing.

John Milton, The Verse of Paradise Lost, 1668.

I

MILTON'S revolt against rhyme, announced in a note on *The Verse* prefixed to *Paradise Lost* (1668), was not an isolated phenomenon. It had both an immediate topical reason and a wider, more general one, both of which I should like to discuss in this essay.

II

The topical reason was a Commonwealth debate on the propriety of rhyme in the epic that continued on into the Restoration and expanded to include the question of rhyme in the drama as well, especially in the heroic play. Milton does not mention, even in order to record his disapproval, either the recent rhymed epics or the contemporary rhymed dramas. But he does approve of the rejection of rhyme " long since [by] our best

English tragedies." This may be regarded as a vague allusion
to the question at issue—all the negative notice that he was
prepared to take of the sons of Belial and their works. But we
can assume with reason that he was fully aware of the deliberate
choice of rhyme for the two most notable of recent epics,
Davenant's *Gondibert* (1650) and Dryden's *Annus Mirabilis*
(1667) and of what they [1] and Hobbes [2] had to say in recommendation of the heroic quatrain as an epic vehicle, and we can
be as sure that he knew Dryden to be the leading practitioner
of rhyme in the drama and the champion of its dramatic use in
several critical essays. [3] For one thing, there is on record the
Miltonic dictum (undated, it is true, but recorded by his widow
and presumably uttered in the late sixteen-sixties or early sixteen-
seventies) to the effect that Dryden was " a rhymist but
no poet." [4] More contemptuous are the lines by Marvell which
Milton admitted to the second edition (1668) of *Paradise Lost* :—

> Well mightst thou scorn thy Readers to allure
> With tinkling Rhime, of thy own sense secure ;
> While the *Town-Bayes* writes all the while and spells,
> And like a Pack-horse tires without his Bells. [5]

And it was to this edition that Milton added the already cited
preface.

III

But in stating his case against rhyme, Milton linked the
Commonwealth Restoration discussion, which was local and

---

[1] Davenant in a dedicatory preface addressed to Hobbes ; and Dryden
in a dedicatory preface to Sir Robert Howard. Several other epics or pseudo-
epics, such as Cowley's *Davideis* (1656, 1668 and 1668-9) and Chamberlayne's
Pharronida (1659), were published without any discussion of their
vehicles.

[2] In a reply to Davenant, published along with *Gondibert*.

[3] *The Epistle Dedicatory* of *The Rival Ladies* (1664), *An Essay of Dramatic
Poesy* (1668), and probably *A Defence of An Essay of Dramatic Poesy*, prefixed to the second edition of *The Indian Emperor* (1668). Dryden in *An
Essay of Dramatic Poesy* (in *The Essays of John Dryden*, ed. W. P. Ker,
1900, i, p. 101) pronounced blank verse as " acknowledged to be too low for a
poem [*i.e.* an epic], nay more, for a paper of verses ; but if too low for an
ordinary sonnet, how much more for Tragedy . . . ? "

[4] David Masson, *The Life of John Milton*, 1859-94, vi, p. 682.

[5] 45-8.

soon over, with another, which was European and prolonged. For he repeated with characteristic differences a pedantic disapproval of rhyme which began in earnest in Italy a hundred and fifty years before [1] and spread in due course to England, France, Spain, and Germany in that order. It was one manifestation of a too superstitious acceptance of the classical and of a too sweeping rejection of the unclassical at the Renaissance, which led to much futile theorising and to ill-advised imitation of the mechanics of classical poetry, without the recognition that certain features were the natural outcome of languages with different characteristics and histories, and that they had nothing to do with the essentials of poetry but only with its appearance in Latin or Greek.

IV

Though there had been earlier experiments in unrhymed Italian verse, anything like a concerted movement for the abolition of rhyme began only in the second decade of the sixteenth century. As one might expect, *versi sciolti* in the shape of rhymeless hendecasyllables were first used for a drama as an equivalent to the classical iambic trimeter. The play was Trissino's *Sofonisba* (1515), which despite its total lack of poetry and passion marks an era in the Italian theatre and began the not infrequent and still continuing use of unrhymed verse for serious occasions. It was almost certainly Trissino's use of unrhymed hendecasyllables for tragedy which suggested to Ariosto *versi sdruccioli*, twelve-syllabled lines with the last accents on the antepenultimates, for comedy. He used such would-be Plautine verses first in *Il Negromante* (1520) and thereafter for his new comedies and for revisions of his earlier prose ones. Within ten years of *Sofonisba*, either in Trissino's operatic epic *L'Italia Liberata dai Goti* (begun in 1525, but not published till 1547-48) or in Rucellai's more agreeable georgic *Le Api* (1525), *versi sciolti* had found their way into non-dramatic

---

[1] Unrhymed verses had appeared in Italy much earlier, especially at the beginning of the thirteenth century, as in St Francis's irregular ode or canticle and in the anonymous, regular *Mare Amoroso*. In the fifteenth century there were even attempts at unrhymed classical metres. See Dante, *De Vulgari Eloquentia*, II, xiii, 2 and 4, for stanzas with one or more or all the lines rhyming only to lines in other stanzas.

poetry. In non-dramatic poetry, however, the new verse made little headway. Apart from Alamanni and from Tasso in his declining years, it attracted no practitioners " of prime note " ; [1] and Alamanni's *La Coltivazione* (1546) and Tasso's own *Le sette Giornate* (1592) are dull and uninspired. It is perhaps needless to say that the still more thoroughgoing classicists, who advocated not merely the rejection of rhyme but the adoption of quantitative metres, met with still less support. The leaders in this ill-advised enthusiasm were Claudio Tolomei whose *Versi e Regole della nuova Poesia Toscana* (1539) found some favour among his fellow-members of the Accademia della nuova Poesia, and Felice Figliucci who attacked rhyme and exemplified the virtues of quantity in his commentary on Aristotle's *Ethics* (1551). But the Renaissance revolt against rhyme failed ; except for some dramas rhyme remained in undisputed possession of the Italian Parnassus till the nineteenth century when Leopardi and Carducci, under the influence both of their classical devotion and of German examples and æsthetic treatises, experimented with the Italian equivalent of blank verse and with unrhymed lyrical measures as well. But their undoubted successes are exceptional and highly individual ; and they have not sufficed to divert many of their Italian followers from the charms of rhyme.

V

That the introduction of unrhymed verses or *versos sueltos* into Spanish literature was due to the poets in the first half of the sixteenth century who wrote *al itálico modo* is generally taken for granted. But unrhymed lines alternating with full rhymes or with assonances were long established in the *romance* or ballad, one of the oldest and to this day one of the most popular varieties of Spanish poetry. The *romance* is a short poem of a narrative-lyrical kind, consisting of octosyllabic lines, usually

[1] As Johnson says in his *Life of Milton* (in *The Works of Samuel Johnson*, ed. 1792, ix, p. 181) " Of the Italian writers without rhyme, whom Milton alledges as precedents, not one is popular." Daniel in his *Defence of Rhyme* (in *Elizabethan Critical Essays*, ed. G. Gregory Smith, ii, pp. 368-9) denies Milton's assertion by long anticipation :—" Nor could this very same innouation . . . but die in the attempt, and was buried as soone as it came borne, neglected as a prodigious and vnnaturall issue amongst them."

alternately unrhymed and rhymed or, more often, assonating. (Metrically, then, to say nothing of the matter in this context, it is not unlike the ballad of *Kinmont Willie* :—

> Then shoulder high, with shout and cry,
>   We bore him down the ladder lang ;
> At every stride Red Rowan made,
>   I wot the Kinmont's airns play'd clang ! [1]

This stanza is in our so-called long measure with rhymes only on the even lines. Our ballad metre or common measure of alternate octosyllables and hexasyllables also frequently has only every other line rhymed.) The explanation generally offered for the alternation of rhymeless with rhymed or assonantal lines in Spanish is that each octosyllable is only a hemistich of the sixteen-syllabled epic line which rhymed in couplets. This is confirmed by the common persistence of one assonance throughout an entire poem, in correspondence with the unity of assonance within one epic *laisse*. (One could plausibly argue that in the English common and long measures also the line really consists of fourteen and sixteen syllables respectively.) Another metrical scheme which allowed lines to be occasionally unrhymed was the *silva*, though the best versifiers permitted no such escapes. It will be seen, therefore, that rhymelessness was nothing new in Spain and long antedated the Italianising school of Boscán and Garcilaso. Perhaps, too, the custom of assonating, which can be regarded as intermediate between rhyming and not rhyming, prepared the way for *versos sueltos*.

It will not be surprising, then, that *versos sueltos*, in hendecasyllables or in hendecasyllables interspersed with seven-syllabled lines, were not at first, and have not been by any means since, completely dissociated from rhyme and assonance. These latter accidents, for so they seem to be rather than deliberate graces, in *verso suelto*, are governed by no sort of rule though they tend to appear more frequently at the ends of the main divisions of a poem. Such is the verse of Boscán's long *Historia de Leandro y Hero* (written between 1526 and 1534, and published in 1543), of Garcilaso's single *epistola* to Boscán (written before 1536, and published in 1543), of Acuña's *La contienda de Ayax Telamonio y de Ulises* (c. 1550, and published in 1591), of

[1] 153-6.

Gonsalo Perez's partial translation of the *Odyssey* (1552),[1] and lastly of Figueroa's *Tirsi* (*c.* 1560, and published in 1625) which is the first composition in Spanish entirely unrhymed and unassonated. It would seem, therefore, as if the Spanish poets were loath to part with their traditional rhymes and chimes. And certainly *versos sueltos* never took deep root. Even the drama rhymed or assonated when it was not in prose; and later attempts to displace from non-dramatic verse both rhyme and assonance have met with as little encouragement as success. Of quantitative experiments in Spanish I can find no trace.

VI

Contrary to the usual order of the transmission of literary fashions and ideas in the Renaissance, unrhymed verse had reached England before it had appeared in France. Its appearance there was of short duration indeed. Though the poets of *La Pléiade* were fanatical in devotion to their classical masters and precedents, there was one habit of medievalism from which they could not and would not break, the habit of rhyme. Ronsard tried unrhymed verses once, but once only, in the ode (1544) beginning thus :—

> En quel bois le plus separé
> Du populaire, et en quel antre
> Prens-tu plaisir de me guider,
> O Muse ma douce folie,
> A fin qu'ardent de ta fureur,
> Et du tout hors de moy, je chante
> L'honneur de ce royal enfant
> Qui doit commander à la France ? [2]

Curiously enough he was in England in 1539-40, about the time when Surrey was at work on his translation from Virgil. Whether he knew anything about the translation or not, he was not much predisposed in favour of the unrhymed ; and, as Lanson says, " Il n'essaya jamais la chimère des vers métriques." [3] In fact

---

[1] Ascham, who was a correspondent of Perez, praises him along with Surrey for avoiding " the fault of Ryming, yet neither of them hath fullie hitte perfite and trew versifying " (*The Schoolmaster*, in *Elizabethan Critical Essays*, ed. G. Gregory Smith, i, p. 32).

[2] *Sur la naissance de François, Dauphin de France, Fils du Roi Henry II* in *Oeuvres Complètes*, ed. Gustave Cohen, 1938, i, pp. 503-4.

[3] *Histoire de la littérature française*, 1903, p. 276.

Ronsard and Du Bellay, the two leaders of the brotherhood, regarded rhyme as practically essential to French versification.[1] In his *Déffence et Illustration de la Langue Françoyse* (1549), the manifesto of the school, Du Bellay says :—" le vers Francoys lié, et enchainé, est contraint de ce rendre en cete etroite prison de Rhythme, soubz la garde le plus souvent d'vne couppe feminine, facheux, et rude Gëolier, et incongneu des autres vulgaires." [2] So far is he from wishing to escape from the prison that he insists on the strictest fetters. For he will have no licences, no facile or forced or merely approximate rhymes such as the less exacting *École Marotique* might pass. To please him rhyme must be true and "riche," "voluntaire, non forcée : receue, non appellée : propre, non aliene : naturelle, non adoptiue : bref, elle sera telle, que le vers tumbant en icelle ne contentera moins l'oreille, qu'vne bien armonieuse Musique tumbante et vn bon, et parfait accord." [3] Rather than tolerate defective rhymes, he would much prefer none at all, after the style of some of Petrarch and of Alamanni's *Coltivazione* (1546), with the proviso that " ces Vers non rymez, feussent bien charnuz, et neru_eux : afin de compenser par ce moyen le default de la Rythme." [4] Ronsard made similar conditions, not for an easy and slipshod method, but for one in which " la belle invention " [5] and the natural order and proper pronunciation of the words were not sacrificed for the sake of the rhyme, " laquelle vient assez aisément d'elle mesme apres quelque peu d'exercice et labeur," [5] while at the same time the rhyme was to observe strict rules as to the elision of mute e within the line, the avoidance of the hiatus and of arbitrary enjambement, the preservation of the caesura, and the management of masculine and feminine rhymes. The notion, then, was that the poet should transmute his rhyming fetters to golden ornaments and carry them with an effortless grace— " ludentis speciem dabit." [6]

But though rhyme was thus highly esteemed by the *Pléiade*,

---

[1] *Cf.* Estienne Pasquier, *Les Recherches de la France*, 1643, p. 594 :— The poetry of France is " tout d'vne autre façon que celle des Grecs & Romains," but like that common "aussi . . . à toutes les nations qui se meslent de Poëtiser."

[2] Ed. Émile Person, 1892, p. 131.

[3] *Ibid.*, p. 131.

[4] *Ibid.*, p. 132.

[5] *Abbregé de l'art poétique françois* in *Oeuvres complètes*, ed. cit., ii, p. 1004.

[6] Horace, *Epistles*, ii, 2, 124.

as also by the rival *École Marotique*, it has to be admitted that
Jodelle, another member of the *Pléiade*, and certain poets outside
that charmed circle experimented in rhymeless verse some years
after the middle of the sixteenth century.   The very first essay
was an elegiac distich, " vrayement vn petit chef d'oeuure," [1]
by Jodelle for the poetical works of Olivier de Magny in 1553.
This was followed two years later by a longer piece in hendecasyllabics by the Comte d'Alcinois for the second impression of
Pasquier's *Monophile* and a year later still by Pasquier's own
elegiacs, " autant fluides que les Latins," [2] made at the request
of Petrus Ramus, " personnage . . . grandement desireux de
nouueautez." [2]   Later still Jean de la Taille recommended
quantitative measures in his *Manière de faire des vers en français
comme en grec et en latin* (written in 1562, and published in 1573).
La Taille, Baïf who was of *La Pléiade*, Passerat, Nicolas Rapin,
and other lesser lights experimented along these lines.   Baïf,
the most pedantic of his school, " Docte, doctieur, doctime " as
Du Bellay ironically called him,[3] was the most persevering.[4]   He
elaborated his own system for regulating French verse quantita-
tively, as well as for a reformed spelling,[5] in his *Étrènes de poézie
fransoèze au vers mezurés* (1574).

The French were thus several years later than the English in
resorting to unrhymed verse and more than a decade later in
venturing on *vers métriques* or " classical versifying."   But
neither kind was more than a curiosity.   Baïf proved to be " si
mauvais parrain que non seulement il ne fut suiuy d'aucun :
mais au contraire descouragea vn chacun de s'y employer.
D'autant que tout ce qu'il en fit estoit tant despourueu de cette
naïfueté, qui doit accompagner nos oeuures, qu'aussi tost que
cette sienne Poësie veit la lumiere, elle mourut comme vn

[1] Pasquier, *op. cit.*, p. 650.

[2] *Ibid.*, p. 651.

[3] In a sonnet addressed to Baïf.

[4] Pasquier, *op. cit.*, p. 652, says that Baïf, disappointed by the failure of his
Amours, about 1565 or 1566, " fit voeu de ne faire de là en auant que des vers
mesurez."

[5] This is practically the same as Petrus Ramus's in his *Gramere* (1562).
The question of reformed spelling was also raised in Italy and in England as a
result of the quantitative experiments ; see especially the Spenser-Harvey
correspondence, Stanyhurst's dedication and preface to *The First Foure Bookes
of Virgil's Aeneis*, and Campion's *Observations in the Art of English Poesy* in
Elizabethan Critical Essays, ed. G. Gregory Smith, 1904, i, pp. 87-122, 135-47 ;
ii, pp. 351-5.

auorton." [1] The status of rhyme was not in any way questioned or threatened even by the metrical experimenters,[2] and Milton could have found no backing among those " of prime note " in France, least of all in his once-admired Du Bartas. Boileau in *L'Art Poétique* (1674), the most authoritative document in French neo-classicism, takes rhyme for granted, and in his second *Satire* (1664) shows by his generous recognition of the superiority of Molière's rhymes to his own that he had no doubt of the value of the device, even while he regretted his own rhyming sluggishness. Thereafter apart from Fénelon who with his strong classical predilection threw out in his *Lettre à l'Académie* (1716) [3] some ill-considered criticisms of French versification, nothing of consequence against the propriety of rhyme appeared in France for over two hundred years. Théodore de Banville's *Petit Traité de Poésie Française* (1872) with its insistence on the essentiality of rhyme in French poetry may be taken as expressing the orthodox opinion. Such attempts as have been made by Claudel and others within the last thirty years to give to French poetry a looser robe owe nothing to the experimenters of the sixteenth century who in fact did not want metrical freedom but classical restraint. The modern movement which would substitute cadence and functional or organic rhythm without rhyme for rhymed syllabic verse derives directly or indirectly from Walt Whitman.

VII

In German-speaking countries prosody began to receive attention in the sixteenth century for very much the same reason as in England, the irregularity of the current poetic rhythms and the uncertainty of the accentuation. Very much, too, as in England, scholarly critics and poets looked to the classics or to contemporary foreign literature for guidance. The process of disciplining proceeded along two lines—attempts to substitute more regular accents, and experiments in pseudo-quantitative verse.

The former was the earlier in beginning and was to prove

---

[1] Pasquier, *op. cit.*, p. 652.

[2] Rhyme was so customary that it began to invade *vers mesurés* in Marc-Claude de Buttet, Pasquier, and Jean Passerat. Ronsard, Passerat, and Nicolas Rapin wrote rhymed Sapphics " sans pieds." *Cf.* Pasquier, *op. cit.*, pp. 652-4.

[3] He referred to rhyme also in his correspondence with Fontenelle.

the main line of development from Paul Rebhuhn's *Susanna*
(1535) onwards. But as it did not alter the position of rhyme, I
need not pursue it in detail. The principles for German quantitative verse were first formulated by Johan Clajus with specimens
in his *Grammatica Germanicae Linguae* (1578). A few other
sporadic exercises of the same kind followed in the next half-
century. And in 1615 Johannes Rhenanus made the first
attempt to introduce blank verse, known to him from its use in
English plays. But all these innovations were discouraged by
Martin Opitz. His *Buch von der deutschen Poeterey* (1624)
codified the rules of the accentual reformers during the previous
eighty or ninety years and put German verse into a strait waist-
coat of which rhyme was one of the straps.

Later in the seventeenth century a reaction against the
Opitzian rigour and in favour of older models and folk-poetry
prepared the way for the metrical experiments and the freer
handling of existing measures of the middle and end of the
eighteenth century. One seventeenth-century experiment, however, falls to be noticed here. This is von Berge's translation in
blank verse of *Paradise Lost* (1682), an event of more prophetic importance than was the earlier blank verse of Johannes Rhenanus.

The fact is that so far as German is concerned *Reimlosigkeit*
becomes significant much later than in other countries and only
after English poets, especially Milton and Shakespeare, became
popular. That popularising might be said to have begun in
Zurich with J. J. Bodmer and J. J. Breitinger who were already
weary of Opitzian regularity and ready for the banishment of
rhyme. In Addison, whose *Spectator* inspired their periodical
Die Diskurse der Mahlern (1721-3), they found exactly what
they wanted, his papers on *Paradise Lost* and on the Pleasures
of the Imagination. By the first set they were convinced of the
greatness of an English poet who had rejected rhyme ; and from
the second they learned that genius and the imagination should
not be hampered by artificial rules. Bodmer in his Miltonic
enthusiasm translated *Paradise Lost* into prose (1732) and
experimented in blank verse ; and both he and Breitinger, his
junior partner, formulated their theories in critical treatises.

They began to win support in the seventeen-thirties, at first
in a very unexpected quarter. For J. J. Gottsched, who as the
apostle of French neo-classicism and the principles of Boileau
later fell foul of Bodmer and Breitinger on these wider issues,

was not opposed to the various rhymeless metres including blank verse, and indeed recommended and practised them in his *Oersuch eines kritischen Dichtkunst für die Deutschen* (1730). He believed that if Opitz had left to Germany such an example as Milton had given to England it would have been frequently and unhesitatingly followed. It is obvious, however, that, unlike Bodmer and Breitinger, Gottsched, though he was prepared on occasions to drop rhyme, wanted more rather than less metrical regularity. Not so the young poets who in the dozen years from 1737 practised many kinds of unrhymed verse :—J. I. Pyra, S. G. Lange, J. P. Uz, J. N. Götz, J. W. L. Gleim, K. W. Ramler, J. E. Schlegel, and Ewald von Kleist. So far as they shared in a general tendency, it was towards greater metrical flexibility and " decontrol."

A more important adherent of the new movement than any of those I have named was F. G. Klopstock, the first instalment of whose *Messias* (1748) inaugurated the great period of German eighteenth-century literature. His use of the unrhymed hexameter, already well enough known, established that verse as the classical epic line. For his *Oden* (written from 1754 on, and published in 1771) he required still greater freedom. He realised how opposed was the Opitzian versification to his conception of lyrical poetry as the outpouring of heart and soul and the expression of intuition and ecstasy, the ethereal and the intangible. He did not want a versification of too great precision, but one as free from restrictions as possible, especially rhyme. Sometimes he used with success unrhymed strophes which give the effect of the Alcaic and Asclepiadean metres. At other times he tried modifications of classical strophes or invented ones of his own with less success. And for certain subjects he struck out free rhythms, a non-metrical mode with no set schemes and regulated by nothing but the promptings of his own feelings.

These free rhythms, which were on the borderline of verse and prose, were just what the age wanted. They were very popular with the *Sturm und Drang* poets to whom the repudiation of all fetters profoundly appealed, especially to Herder and to the Ossianic or " bardic" school of H. W. von Gerstenberg, K. F. Kretschmann, and Michael Denis, the translator of Macpherson (1768-9). Goethe also used them with masterly power as in his *Prometheus* (1774), though he approached closer to more regular rhythmical, if not metrical, patterning. They even found their way into the drama with J. M. R. Lenz's *Der Hofmeister* (1774) and *Die Soldaten* (1776) and F. M. von Klinger's *Die Zwillinge* (1775) and *Sturm und Drang* (1776). Free rhythms continued to play an important part in German poetry. Of their later exponents Heine is the greatest. It was from him that Matthew Arnold derived the rhythm of *The Strayed Reveller* (1849), and, less directly because through Arnold, Henley the rhythm of *A Song of Speed* (1903).

The German parallel to blank verse was fairly well established by the fourth decade of the eighteenth century, among other unrhymed measures, for non-dramatic purposes. Wieland first brought it on the German stage in his *Johanna Gray* (1758). From the same year onwards it was extensively employed, for long ambitious poems, especially by Lessing, Klopstock, J. W. von Browe, C. F. Weisse, F. W. Gotter, and others, Herder in his *Fragmente* (1768) laying down conditions for its use in place of the Alexandrine. Lessing's *Nathan der Weise* (1779) made it thenceforward the chief vehicle of the poetic drama, its place in non-dramatic poetry being already secure.

The practice of the already accepted unrhymed verses and rhythms was carried on by Goethe and Schiller, and they experimented freely in others. So did their contemporaries, and their nineteenth- and indeed twentieth-century followers from Platen and Heine onwards, including the alliterative revivalists who begin with Zacharias Werner, the forerunner by many years of Wagner.

VIII

Undoubtedly the Earl of Surrey, who was the first Englishman to write regular blank verse, as he did in a translation of books ii and iv of the *Aeneid* a few years before his death in 1547, had Italian models in *versi sciolti* before him. These were Niccolò Liburnio's version of book iv (1534) and Cardinal Ippolito de' Medici's of book ii (1539 and again in 1541 with translations of books i, iii, iv,[1] v, and vi by other hands).[2]

---

[1] By Alessandro Piccolomini. According to Professor F. M. Padelford (to whose edition of *The Poems of Henry Howard, Earl of Surrey*, 1928, pp. 233-4, I am indebted for these facts) it is doubtful if Surrey knew Piccolomini's translation. The debts to Gavin Douglas's Middle Scots *Aeneid* and Octavien de Saint Gelais's French translation (see *ibid.*, pp. 233-4) are not relevant to my purpose.

[2] A version of the complete *Aeneid* by F. M. Molza appeared in 1541.

There is no evidence [1] that Surrey was ever in Italy ; and while he was sufficiently acquainted with recent Italian experiments to want to imitate them in English, he might have been pre-disposed thereto by certain native literature. Not only did there exist in English, as Saintsbury points out, a large body of well-known unrhymed verse in *Piers Plowman* and other alliterative pieces, some of which " was not very much farther from actual metrical arrangement, even in decasyllable, than some of the rhymed verse " [2] of the period between Chaucer and Surrey ; but there are also inexplicable fragments of what is really a kind of blank verse in the prose tales of Chaucer. The " third and strongest argument," says Saintsbury, " for an at least partly independent experiment, which may have been encouraged by Italian, but did not necessarily start from it, is to be found in the vast, if rather vague, contemporary striving to get rid of rhyme altogether as a barbarous mediævalism, and to fall back upon unassisted metrical arrangement in the manner of the ancients " [3] (*i.e.* quantitative metre).

Surrey found a few non-dramatic imitators of his innovation in Nicholas Grimoald, George Gascoigne, and others. But by tacit consent blank verse fairly soon came to be regarded as most appropriate to drama of every kind, not merely " our best English tragedies." On the other hand its conquest of the drama coincided with its almost complete exclusion from all the other poetic kinds. Practically no specimens of non-dramatic blank verse or indeed of any unrhymed accentual verse appeared in Britain between Campion's in *Observations in the Art of English Poesy* (1602) and Milton's in *Paradise Lost* (1667).

IX

All unrhymed verse, however, was not accentual. Or at any rate attempts at classicised verse and critical pleas for the complete reform of English versification on classical lines began at least as early as 1544 when Ascham wrote *Toxophilus* with its accentual hexameters, the first in English. About the same

[1] Nashe's story of the love of Surrey and Geraldine in *The Unfortunate Traveller* (1594) is, like what the soldier said, not evidence.
[2] *A History of English Prosody*, 1906, i, p. 315.
[3] *Ibid.*, i, p. 315.

time, presumably, Thomas Watson was trying his hand,[1] and it could not have been much later that Thomas Drant drew up a body of rules, one of the first results of which was Thomas Blenerhasset's hexameter *Complaint of Cadwallader* [2] (1578). Ascham in *The Schoolmaster* (written in 1563-8, and published in 1570) declares that " Ryming . . . hath bene long misliked of many, and that of men of greatest learnyng and deepest iudgement." [3]   Indeed one of the regular topics of the Elizabethan critics was classical versifying which several misguided devotees hoped to see supplanting

> shifting rime, that easie flatterer,
> Whose witchcraft can the ruder eares beguile.[4]

Ascham's scorn for " our rude beggerly ryming " [5] and his preference for the " trew versifying" [6] of the Greeks and Latins were most emphatically reiterated by William Webbe in his *Discourse of English Poetry* (1586), who believed that it only needed " any one, of sound iudgment and learning, [to] putt foorth some famous worke, contayning dyuers formes of true verses" [7] and so to expel for good and all " the other barbarous custome " [8] of rhyming.   So convinced was he of the hoped-for benefits of the revolution that, despite his enthusiasm for Spenser, or because of it, he " with simple skyll " [9] and disarming modesty ventured to translate the lovely " laye of fayre Elisa " [10]—which begins with this gracious invitation :—

> Ye dayntye Nymphs, that in this blessed Brooke
>   doe bathe your brest,
> Forsake your watry bowres, and hether looke,
>   at my request :

---

[1] Ascham quotes two often-requoted lines in *The Schoolmaster*, ed. Edward Arber, 1913, p. 73, as made " a good while ago."

[2] In the 1578 edition of part of *The Mirror for Magistrates*.

[3] *Ed. cit.*, i, pp. 31-2. In his preface to *Paradise Lost* Milton seems to echo some of Ascham's phrases in *The Schoolmaster* (*ed. cit.*, i, pp. 29-34). Among the learned and judicious men who disliked rhyme Ascham would have numbered Sir John Cheke, Bishop Thomas Watson, and the elusive Thomas Drant who appears to have been the first to lay down rules for classical versifying in English.

[4] Thomas Campion, *Observations in the Art of English Poesy*, ed. cit., ii, p. 335.

[5] *The Schoolmaster*, ed. cit., i, p. 29.   [6] *Ibid.*, p. 30.

[7] *A Discourse of English Poetry* in *Elizabethan Critical Essays*, ed. G. Gregory Smith, i, 279.   [8] *Ibid.*, p. 278.   [9] *Ibid.*, p. 279.

[10] *The Shepheards Calender*, April, 33-4.

> And eke you Virgins, that on *Parnasse* dwell,
> Whence floweth *Helicon* the learned well,
>   Helpe me to blaze
>   Her worthy praise,
> Which in her sexe doth all excell— [1]

thus into what the critic believed to be the verse of the future :

> O ye Nymphes most fine, who resort to this brooke,
> For to bathe there your pretty breasts at all times,
> Leaue the watrish bowres, hyther and to me come
>   at my request nowe.

> And ye Virgins trymme, who resort to *Parnass*,
> Whence the learned well *Helicon* beginneth,
> Helpe to blase her worthy deserts, that all els
>   mounteth aboue farre.[2]

Absurd as this is, it is no more so than Spenser's falling for a season " more in loue wyth my Englishe Versifying than with Ryming " [3] and writing some peculiarly cacophonous examples to prove it (1579). Spenser's excuse is that both at Cambridge and in London he had fallen into the company of men whom he respected and whose opinions he was too ready to believe were his own. When " the twoo worthy Gentlemen, Master SIDNEY and Master DYER . . . proclaimed in their ἀρείῳ πάγῳ a generall surceasing and silence of balde Rymers," [3] and when the masterful Gabriel Harvey came down heavily on the same side, who was Spenser to oppose them, even if he had not convinced himself that they were right ? Still another of Spenser's friends, the E.K. of *The Shepheards Calendar* (1579), forcefully rejected " *the rakehellye route of our ragged rymers*," [4] without, however, meaning to include the good with the bad in his clean sweep and without proposing to discipline the rout by quantity. Whether any of Sir Edward Dyer's quantitative experiments (*c.* 1579) are now extant I cannot say. But they were probably rather feebler than Sidney's (*c.* 1579) which themselves will not bear comparison with Sidney's rhymes, and decidedly better than Harvey's (1579) than which they could

---

[1] *The Shepheards Calendar*, April, 37-45.
[2] *A Discourse of English Poetry*, ed. cit., i, p. 287.
[3] Letters of Edmund Spenser to Gabriel Harvey, *ed. cit.*, i, 89.
[4] Dedication of *The Shepheards Calendar* in *The Poetical Works of Edmund Spenser*, ed. J. C. Smith and E. de Selincourt, 1912, p. 417.

hardly be worse. Yet in fact worse even than Harvey's are Richard Stanyhurst's hideous hexameters (1582), as remarkable for the schematic fritters they make of English orthography as for their butchery of Virgil :—

> But the Queene in meane while carks quandare deepe anguisht,
> Her wound fed by Venus, with firebayt smoldred is hooked :
> Thee wights doughtye manhood, leagd with gentilytye nobil,
> His woords fitlye placed, with his hevnly phisnomye pleasing,
> March throgh her hert mustring, al in her breste deepelye she printeth.[1]

Nothing that Stanyhurst could say by way of introducing these monstrosities could take off their ugliness. The fact is that none of the Elizabethans who tried classical versifying [2]—and there are a few scattered examples in one or two writers whom I have not mentioned to add to the total—met with much success, except Campion in two or three not unpleasing lyrics (1602).

No reasoned defence of rhyme was made till Daniel in his admirably tempered and emancipated *Defence of Rhyme* (1603) seemed to give the *coup de grâce* both to the fashion and to its latest champion and most skilful exponent Campion. The following facts, however, are evidence of the tentativeness of the whole movement. Ascham, no poet himself to begin with, at least realised that the hexameter " doth rather trotte and hoble than runne smothly in our English tong "[3] and apparently concluded that only iambic verse—he mentions no other—was possible for his countrymen. When he wrote, there was little enough musical verse in accent and rhyme to recommend them to him. The secret of Chaucer's scansion had been lost ; Skelton was doggerel ; and even Wyatt and Surrey were not much more regular in their rhythms than were the contemporary experimenters in quantity. Besides Surrey in his most ambitious work had at least abandoned rhyme. The wonder in some ways, then, is that Ascham was not more decided in his advocacy of the new verse. Spenser abandoned classical versifying almost

---

[1] *The First Four Books of Virgil's Aeneis*, ed. Edward Arber, 1880, p. 94 (cf. *Aeneid*, iv, 1-5).

[2] Though Joseph Hall in his postscript to *Virgidemiarum. Six Books* (1597-8) spoke with contempt of rhyme, he had the good sense to stoop to the vulgar taste.

[3] *The Schoolmaster*, ed. cit., i, p. 30. But he does give several specimens of his own manufacture, trotting and hobbling in all conscience, in *Toxophilus* (1545).

as soon as he had tried it, as if he knew that he was but " ill
at these numbers." [1]   Harvey was simply a critical weathercock :
the names of Sidney and Dyer were enough to enlist him on the
same side.   And in fact his later writings show, negatively if
not positively, that he forgot his recommendation of quantitative
verse to Spenser as completely as he also forgot his sneaping
reception of the unpublished *Faerie Queene*.[2]   The wise Sidney in
practice regarded anything but rhyme and accent as purely
experimental, and even in theory declined in *An Apology for
Poetry* (written about 1583, and published in 1595) to pronounce
between the rival systems.[3]   Webbe, for all his quantitative ardour,
also esteemed rhyme " as a thing the perfection whereof is very
commendable," [4] and devotes a large part of his book to its
display and illustration.   So, too, does Puttenham (1589).   In
fact what he has to say for " our scholastical toyes, that is of the
Grammaticall versifying of the Greeks and Latines " [5] is obviously
only for the sake of completeness.   He believes in the sanctity
of usage and in respect for the spirit of the language.   Besides
he is a devout lover of rhyme, not merely in the commonly
accepted stanzas, but in hypothetical stanzas and in geometrical
figures and the like, such as " The Lozange, called Rombus,"
" The Fuzie or spindle, called Romboides," " The Tricquet
reuerst " and " The egge displayed." [6]   And " therefore," says
he, " I intend not to proceed any further in this curiositie then
to shew some small subtillitie that any other hath not yet done,
and not by imitation but by obseruation, nor to th' intent to haue
it put in execution in our vulgar Poesie, but to be pleasantly
scanned vpon, as are all nouelties so friuolous and ridiculous
as it." [7]   Even Webbe shows a divided loyalty ; though he will
not recognise rhyme as a true ornament and pronounces it too
easy, barbarous, and hostile to qualities more excellent, he admits
it deserves praise when it is well done and cannot " vtterly dis-
alowe it, least I should seeme to call in question the iudgement
of all our famous wryters, which haue wonne eternall prayse by
theyr memorable workes compyled in " rhyme. [8]   Lastly, Campion

[1] Shakespeare, *Hamlet*, II, ii, 120.
[2] Letters to Spenser, *ed. cit.*, i, pp. 115-6.
[3] *Elizabethan Critical Essays*, ed. G. Gregory Smith, i, pp. 204-5.
[4] *A Discourse of English Poetry*, ed. cit., i, p. 267.
[5] *The Art of English Poesy* in *Elizabethan Critical Essays*, ed. G. Gregory
Smith, ii, p. 116.   [6] *Ibid.*, pp. 96-7.   [7] *Ibid.*, p. 124.
[8] *A Discourse of English Poetry*, ed. cit., i, p. 266.

had not the courage of his declared convictions, and yielded to accent and rhyme in his later work.

X

Between Daniel and Davenant there were no more than echoes and reverberations of the Elizabethan debate. Needless to say Ben Jonson had to engage even in this dispute which had been settled theoretically, as far as literary disputes can ever be said to be settled, by Daniel, and practically by the triumphant successes of the Elizabethan rhymers. Jonson's contribution is not extant, but it probably dates from the beginning of James I's reign. For he boasted to Drummond (1619) of having " written a discourse of Poesie both against Campion & Daniel especially this Last, wher he proves couplets to be the bravest sort of Verses . . . and that crosse Rimes and Stanzaes . . . were all forced." [1] This is as ambiguous an attitude to rhyme as that of any of Jonson's predecessors. But it is no more so than his characteristic *Fit of Rhyme against Rhyme* (probably written after 1616, but not published till 1640), which chooses a more complicated stanza than his favourite decasyllabic couplet and is practically a jocose epitome of all that had been urged against

> Rime the rack of finest wits,
> That expresseth but by fits,
>   True Concept.
> Spoyling Senses of their Treasure,
> Cosening Judgement with a measure,
>   But false weight.
>
> Wresting words, from their true calling ;
> Propping Verse, for feare of falling
>   To the ground.
> Joynting Syllabes, drowning Letters,
> Fastning Vowells, as with fetters
>   They were bound !
>
> Soone as lazie thou wert knowne,
> All good Poëtrie hence was flowne,
>   And are banish'd.
> For a thousand yeares together,
> All *Pernassus* Greene did wither,
>   And wit vanish'd.

---

[1] Conversations with William Drummond of Hawthornden in *Ben Jonson*, ed. C. H. Herford and Percy Simpson, 1925-, i, p. 132. Daniel in *A Defence of Rhyme*, ed. cit., ii, p. 382, had deprecated the use of couplets in long poems.

Pegasus did flie away,
At the Wells no Muse did stay,
　　　But bewail'd,
So to see the Fountaine drie,
And *Apollo's* musique die,
　　　All light failed !

Starveling rimes did fill the Stage,
Not a Poët in an Age,
　　　Worth crowning.
Not a worke deserving Baies,
Not a lyne deserving praise,
　　　Pallas frowning ;

Greeke was free from Rimes infection,
Happy Greeke by this protection !
　　　Was not spoyled.
Whilst the Latin, Queene of Tongues,
Is not yet free from Rimes wrongs,
　　　But rests foiled.

Scarce the hill againe doth flourish,
Scarce the world a Wit doth nourish,
　　　To restore,
Phœbus to his Crowne againe ;
And the Muses to their braine ;
　　　As before.

Vulgar Languages that want
Words, and sweetnesse, and be scant
　　　Of true measure,
Tyran Rime hath so abused,
That they long since have refused,
　　　Other ceasure ;

He that first invented thee,
May his joynts tormented bee,
　　　Cramp'd for ever ;
Still may Syllabes jarre with time,
Still may reason warre with rime,
　　　Resting never.

May his sense, when it would meet,
The cold tumour in his feet,
　　　Grow unsounder.
And his Title be long foole,
That in rearing such a Schoole,
　　　Was the founder. [1]

[1] *Underwoods*, xxix.

Probably between Jonson's last discourse which put both Campion and Daniel in their places and the just-quoted poem came Bacon's judicial descent in *The Advancement of Learning* (1605) on the side of modern verse for modern poets. It is more in the spirit of his revolt from classical authority in philosophy than of his distrust of modern languages which he believed " will at one time or another play the bankrupts with books." [1] In poesy, he says, " though men in learned tongues do tie them-selves to the ancient measures, yet in modern languages it seemeth to me as free to make new measures of verses as of dances ; for a dance is a measured pace, as a verse is a measured speech. In these things the sense is better judge than the art. . . . And of the servile expressing antiquity in an unlike and an unfit subject, it is well said, *Quod tempore antiquum videtur, id incongruitate est maxime novum*." [2] He is somewhat more emphatic in his disapproval of misguided revivers of antique measures in the Latin of the *De Augmentis Scientiarum* (1623). The modern poets, he says, have not been wanting in wisdom in following the ancient practice of appropriating different measures for different purposes. But, he goes on, " Illud reprehendendum, quod quidam antiquitatis nimium studiosi linguas modernas ad mensuras antiquas (heroïcas, elegiacas, sapphicas, &c.) traducere conati sunt ; quas ipsarum linguarum fabrica respuit, nec minus aures exhorrent. In hujusmodi rebus sensus judicium artis praeceptis praeponendum. . . . Neque vero ars est, sed artis abusus, cum illa naturam non perficiat sed pevertat." [3]

At an unspecified date, between 1603 and 1625 but most likely at the beginning of James I's reign, Sir John Beaumont wrote a poem of thanks *To his Late Majesty* [4] (1629). The poem is in couplets and praises that measure which men like Beaumont himself and George Sandys and, somewhat later, Denham and Waller, the reformers of our numbers, were to establish as the pre-eminent favourite of the Restoration and the eighteenth century. I quote it to show not only the tendency towards the

[1] To Toby Matthew in *The Works of Francis Bacon*, ed. Basil Montagu, 1825-34, iii, p. xxi.

[2] *The Advancement of Learning* in *The Works of Francis Bacon*, ed. James Spedding, R. L. Ellis, and D. D. Heath, 1870-2, iii, pp. 401-2.

[3] *De Augmentis Scientiarum, ed. eadem*, i, pp. 656-7.

[4] For James's *Schort Treatise conteining some Revlis and Cautelis to be obseruit and eschewit in Scottis Poesie* (1584).

couplet but the complete acceptance of rhyme as natural and necessary :—

> In ev'ry language now in Europe spoke
> By Nations which the Roman Empire broke,
> The relish of the Muse consists in rime,
> One verse must meete another like a chime.
> Our Saxon shortnesse hath peculiar grace
> In choise of words, fit for the ending place :
> Which leave impression in the mind as well
> As closing sounds, of some delightfull bell :
> These must not be with disproportion lame,
> Nor should an eccho still repeate the same.
> In many changes these may be exprest :
> But those that coyne most simply, run the best :
> Their forme surpassing farre the fettr'd staves,
> Vaine care, and needlesse repetition saves.[1]

XI

Davenant, Hobbes, and Dryden, therefore, in approving of rhyme for the modern epic were in full accord with the feeling of the day ; and the only question was whether to fix on the couplet, the quatrain, or some other stanza. Indeed so complete was the triumph of rhyme that, largely because of the example of the French Alexandrine,[2] it took up its abode for some twenty years in the drama, including tragedy, in which even Daniel had disliked it.[3] Thus Milton was running counter to the times in his caustic objection to rhyme. Just as in his general theory of " that sublime art which in *Aristotles poetics*, in *Horace*, and the *Italian* commentaries of *Castelvetro*, *Tasso*, *Mazzoni*, and others, teaches what the laws are of a true *Epic* poem, what of a *Dramatic*, what of a *Lyric*, what decorum is, which is the grand master peece to observe " [4] he went back behind the French critical authorities of his own day to the Italians who had inspired Sidney and the Elizabethans, so in his metrics he belongs to the school of Campion and Webbe.

[1] 35-48.

[2] Dryden in the *Epistle Dedicatory of The Rival Ladies* in *The Essays of John Dryden*, ed. W. P. Ker, 1900, i, pp. 5-7, would give some credit, if not it all, to English dramatists.

[3] " [S]auing in the *Chorus*, or where a sentence shall require a couplet " (*A Defence of Rhyme*, ed. cit., ii, p. 382).

[4] *Of Education* in *Critical Essays of the Seventeenth Century*, ed. J. E. Spingarn, 1908-9, i, p. 206.

XII

But though the taste of his day was for rhyme, Milton's practice and his theory were not without influence. It might indeed be possible to take as the first sign of that influence Buckingham's lively skit on the rhymed heroic plays, *The Rehearsal* (performed in 1671, and published in 1672).[1] Contrary to the common opinion, *The Rehearsal* so far from exploding the heroic drama served at first as a kind of advertisement for it ; and only gradually did Buckingham's ridicule and the gravitational pull of Shakespeare back to blank verse begin to tell. As late as 1698 Crowne's *Caligula* had many scenes in rhyme, and the spirit of the heroic play, if not its rhymed couplets, persisted well into the eighteenth century. For several years after 1671 Dryden continued to rhyme his dramas in defiance of *The Rehearsal* and its repeated revisions. But he was always susceptible to changes in public taste, sooner rather than later. His veering with the breath of popular favour can be said to begin with *Aureng-zebe* (probably performed in 1675, and published in 1676), his last play wholly in rhyme. In the prologue he confesses himself to be " weary of his long-loved mistress," and in fact the marked tendency of the couplets in the play itself towards *enjambement* was symptomatic, as Saintsbury says.[2] *All for Love* (1678),[3] Dryden's next play and the first by anybody in tolerably good blank verse for more than thirty years, led the way for Otway, Lee, and others back to Shakespeare. Thereafter, like the Elizabethans, Dryden resorted to dramatic rhyme only for special purposes. Thus as Mulgrave, not an enemy to rhyme apart from the drama, bluntly puts it in his *Essay upon Poetry* (1682) :—

> Dances, Flutes, *Italian* Songs, and rime
> May keep up sinking Nonsence for a time ;
> But that will fail which now so much o're rules,
> And sence no longer will submit to fools.[4]

---

[1] The play owes much of its wit to Butler, Sprat, and Martin Clifford, Master of the Charterhouse.   [2] *Dryden*, 1902, p. 57.

[3] In this same year Thomas Rymer promised to send to Fleetwood Shepheard, to whom *The Tragedies of the Last Age* is addressed, " some reflections on that *Paradise Lost* of *Miltons* which some are pleas'd to call a Poem, and [to] assert *Rime* against the slender Sophistry wherewith he attacques it " (*Critical Essays of the Seventeenth Century*, ed. J. E. Spingarn, 1908-9, ii, 208). But if he did so, the reflections are lost.

[4] 305-8.

Mulgrave, however, also says that in the non-dramatic kinds

> Number, and Rime, and that harmonious sound,
> Which never does the Ear with harshness wound,
> Are necessary, yet but vulgar Arts.[1]

This is hardly a rebuttal of Milton and does not of itself even imply a knowledge of his views. However these lines, coupled with a later assertion that the world has brought forth only two " Gigantick souls " [2] capable of an epic, namely Homer and Virgil, and that a would-be emulator of them

> Must above *Cowley*, nay, and *Milton* too prevail,
> Succeed where great *Torquato*, and our greater *Spencer* fail,[3]

called forth the first critical agreement with the preface to *Paradise Lost*. This was in Roscommon's *Essay on Translated Verse* (1684). He had already translated *Horace's Art of Poesy* (1680) into blank verse, the first non-dramatic use of it since Milton's. But in the *Essay* he deliberately attacks rhyme (by means of rhyme) in a passage which echoes Milton's preface :—

> Of many faults *Rhyme* is perhaps the *Cause* ;
> Too *strict* to *Rhyme*, *We* slight more *useful* Laws ;
> For *That* in *Greece* or *Rome* was never *known*,
> Till, by *Barbarian* Deluges *o'reflown*,
> *Subdu'd*, *Undone*, They did at last *Obey*,
> And change their *Own* for their *Invaders* way.
>   I grant that from some *Mossie Idol Oak*,
> In *Double Rhymes* our *Thor* and *Woden* Spoke ;
> And by Succession of unlearned Times,
> As *Bards began*, so *Monks Rung on* the *Chimes*.
>   But now that *Phœbus* and the *sacred Nine*
> With all their Beams on our blest Island shine,
> Why should not *We* their *ancient Rites restore*,
> And *be*, What *Rome* or *Athens* were *Before* ?
>   O may I live to hail the Glorious day,
> And sing loud *Pæans* through the crowded way,
> When in Triumphant State the *British* Muse,
> True to herself, shall barb'rous aid Refuse,
> And in the *Roman* Majesty appear,
> Which none know better, and none come so near.[4]

---

[1] 15-17.   [2] 321.

[3] 349-50. In later versions Mulgrave thus significantly altered the lines :—
> Must above Tasso's lofty flights prevail,
> Succeed where Spenser, and ev'n Milton, fail.

[4] 363-82.

To make it quite clear that he was referring to *Paradise Lost*, he inserted in the 1685 edition of his poem before the last paragraph of the above quotation " An Essay on [*sc.* in] blanc verse " which is a summary of Milton's sixth book and begins

> *Have we forgot how* Raphaels *Num'rous Prose*
> *Led our exalted souls through heavenly Camps ?* [1]

XIII

But Roscommon's recommendation of blank verse converted few of the critics and no more of the greater poets. Dryden, Addison,[2] Prior,[3] Pope, Parnell, Gay, Savage, Johnson, Gray, Collins,[4] Churchill, Goldsmith were faithful to rhyme for poems long and short, narrative, didactic, satirical, occasional, and lyrical as well as for translation and paraphrase. Most people, whether poets or critics or readers only, would have agreed with Edward Bysshe, whose *Art of English Poetry* (1702) was a résumé of Restoration opinion on prosody and a code of metrical law for the eighteenth century, when he pronounced " *Rhyme . . . the chief Ornament of Versification in any of the*

---

[1] Dryden was the first critic to avow his admiration of *Paradise Lost*, implicitly by his *State of Innocence* (written before 1674, and published in 1677) and explicitly in his preface thereto. Then came Mulgrave's qualified approval in 1680, Roscommon's enthusiastic praise in 1684-5, and Somers's support for the 1688 edition of *Paradise Lost* containing Dryden's lines *Under Mr Milton's Picture*. By 1690 " All the educated Englishmen " known to Minutoli extolled *Paradise Lost* to the skies " as the *non plus ultra* of the human spirit " (Minutoli to Bayle in *Choix de Correspondance inédite de Pierre Bayle*, ed. Emil Gigas, 1890, p. 579). Professor J. E. Spingarn says (in *Critical Essays of the Seventeenth Century*, 1908-9, iii, pp. 321-2) that he has noted between thirty and forty tributes to Milton before Addison's *Spectator* papers (1712), including I. I.'s letter *To Mr T.S. in Vindication of Mr Milton's Paradise Lost* (in *Miscellaneous Letters and Essays on several Subjects*, ed. Charles Gildon, 1694) and John Dennis's *Advancement and Reformation of Modern Poetry* (1701) and *The Grounds of Criticism in Poetry* (1704).

[2] His *Milton's Style Imitated in a Translation of a Story out of the Third Aeneid* (1704) is no proof of his liking for blank verse.

[3] His remark that " he that writes in rhymes, dances in fetters " occurs in his preface to his rhymed *Solomon* (1718; in *The Poetical Works of Matthew Prior*, ed. R. B. Johnson, 1892, ii, p. 84). His practice showed he preferred rhyme, though he realised the possibility of monotony and the potentiality (in other hands) of blank verse.

[4] His unrhymed *Ode to Evening* (1747) is a solitary experiment in the style of Milton's *Fifth Ode of Horace, Lib. I* (1673).

Modern Languages." [1] Addison's authority was probably of greater weight with the general public in his own lifetime and for several generations thereafter. In his greener days he had one evening " made it his whole business to run down blank verse," [2] apparently more to puff his own *Campaign* (1704) and to put down Philips [3] than for any better reason. But in *The Spectator* he took up a middle position. Condemning among the varieties of false wit a number of trick arrangements and derangements which involve rhymes,[4] he has no objections to rhyme as such. It is true that he thinks blank verse a much more suitable medium for the drama, especially (I infer) the tragic ; indeed he is most emphatic against the rhyming play, particularly the play that varies between blank verse and rhyme in different scenes or dignifies odd similes with rhyme in the middle of blank verse. But he has no objection to terminating the whole tragedy or every act (he may even mean rather more, the conclusion of every scene or long speech) with two or three couplets in order to give the actor a graceful exit and to relieve the ear. Addison refers to non-dramatic blank verse only in discussing Milton, and it is quite obvious from his words that he considered Milton's medium only as particularly, not as generally, desirable :— " Rhyme, without any other assistance, throws the language off from prose [which difference was achieved in Greek, according to Aristotle, by the use of a tactful proportion of words and phrases departing in one way or another from common usage [5]], and very often makes an indifferent phrase pass unregarded ; but where the verse is not built upon rhymes, there pomp of sound, and energy of expression, are indispensably necessary to support the style, and keep it from falling into the flatness of prose." [6]

---

[1] Ed. 1718, ii, sig. N 5 verso. He dismissed at the outset as a " Design . . . now wholly exploded " (*ibid.*, i, p. 1) the attempt of the Elizabethan quantitative reformers.

[2] Joseph Spence, *Anecdotes, Observations, and Characters, of Books and Men*, ed. S. W. Singer, 1858, p. 261. Addison was himself put down by Jacob Tonson's declaring *Paradise Lost* to have been for him the most profitable of all poems.

[3] John (1676-1709) or Ambrose (? 1675-1749) ?

[4] *The Spectator*, nos. 58-63, in *The Works of Joseph Addison*, ed. Richard Hurd, 1854, ii, 342-66.

[5] *Poetics*, xxii ; cf. *Rhetoric*, iii, *passim*.

[6] *The Spectator*, no. 285, *ed. cit.*, iii, p. 194.

I

XIV

Even when blank verse was adopted for non-dramatic purposes, it was not always for reasons which Milton would have relished. John Philips's *Splendid Shilling* (1703) is a parody " To degrade the sounding words and stately construction of Milton, by an application to the lowest and most trivial things." [1] So also is his *Cerealia* (1706) ; and his *Cider* (1706) in " verse Nor skill'd, nor studious " [2] is an application not much more dignified of the Miltonic line and style. It is true that Philips thought he was serious in the blank-verse *Blenheim* (1705) and John Dennis may be said actually to have been so in a blank-verse paraphrase from Habakkuk in his *Grounds of Criticism in Poetry* (1704), perhaps the first respectful use of the vehicle since Roscommon's. But several later poems in blank verse down to and not excluding Cowper's *Task* (1785) were more or less parodic and jocose. I have to admit of course that blank verse was also well established by the end of the third decade of the eighteenth century for poems of a more solid, not to say heavy, kind.

XV

Before I come to them, however, I have to record two emphatic votes against rhyme and for Milton.[3] The first, itself in rhyme, is Edmund Smith's *Poem to the Memory of Mr John Philips*

---

[1] Johnson, *Life of J. Philips* in *The Works of Samuel Johnson*, ed. 1792, ix, p. 299.

[2] i, 4-5. Philips's epitaph at Westminster enlarges on his dispensing with rhyme, " uni in hoc laudis genere Miltono secundus, primoque poene par."

[3] A third but more incidental protest against " that monstrous ornament which we call rhyme " is found in Shaftesbury's *Miscellaneous Reflections* (1711 ; see *Characteristics of Men, Manners, Opinions, Times, etc.*, ed. J. M. Robertson, 1900, ii, 320). Our British poets' search for rhymes made them neglect " other ornaments and real graces " (*ibid.*, ii, 321). " However . . . in some parts of poetry (especially in the dramatic) we have been so happy as to triumph over this barbarous taste. . . . 'Tis a shame to our authors that in their elegant style and metred prose, there should not be found a peculiar grace and harmony resulting from a more natural and easy disengagement of their periods, and from a careful avoiding the encounter of the shocking consonants and jarring sounds to which our language is so unfortunately subject " (*ibid.*, ii, 321-2).

(1710) in which the author regrets his inability to manage
" *Miltonian* Verse " [1] :—

> with the meaner Tribe I'm forc'd to chime,
> And wanting Strength to rise, descend to Rhyme.[1]

Even without the mention of Roscommon,[2] one could have
guessed that Smith knew his *Essay*. In a passage of some
length he prophesies the emancipation both of English poets
and thus of " *Tuscan* Bards " [3] whose predecessors laid " The
dull Constraint of monkish Rhyme " [4] upon us, denounces the
tyranny, the encumbrance, and the like of which it is commonly
accused, and rebuts in passing those who, like Dryden, [5]

> say this Chain the doubtful Sense decides,
> Confines the Fancy, and the Judgment guides.[6]

The second attack on rhyme to which I have referred occurs
in Charles Gildon's long-winded *Laws of Poetry* (1721), a running
commentary on Mulgrave's and Roscommon's *Essays* and on
Lansdowne's *Essay upon Unnatural Flights in Poetry* (1701).
He will not even allow that rhyme is necessary for short poems.
From two paraphrases from Habakkuk, one in John Dennis's
blank verse (1704) [7] and the other in Mrs Rowe's Pindarics
(1696), he would prove the " meanness " of rhyme, its weakening
effect, and the padding which it necessitates. And from examples
in Waller and Dryden he tries to show how rhyme cramps the
sense and spoils the diction even in the best poets. Therefore
he asserts it to be only one of the " *vulgar arts*, mean and low
accomplishments, and mere superficial parts, that have no share
in the essence of poetry," [8] whatever "most, if not all of our taking
and popular versifiers " [8] and the author (*i.e.* Bysshe) of " a
book too scandalously mean to name " [8] may have supposed to
the contrary. Much later in his treatise Gildon returns to the
charge in the same strain, on this occasion to refute a certain
physician (? Garth or Blackmore) for maintaining that " rhyme

---

[1] 19, 21-22. An anonymous admirer wrote an elegy *On the Death of
Mr Edmund Smith* (1712) " In Miltonic Verse."
[2] 67.   [3] 81.   [4] 68.
[5] *The Epistle Dedicatory of The Rival Ladies*, 1664, *ed. cit.*, i, p. 8.
[6] 88-9.
[7] From *The Grounds of Criticism in Poetry*.
[8] *The Laws of Poetry*, 1721, p. 72.

is no more a constraint to the *English* poet than *quantity* is to those of *Greece* and *Rome*." [1]   But as he takes English accent and quantity to be two names for the same thing, what he has to say is not very convincing or clear.

XVI

Gildon's Miltonic views on rhyme obtained no immediate support from the critics. But the force of Milton's example, as distinct from his precept and his supporters', is shown by the frequent adoption of blank verse from James Thomson's *Seasons* (1726-30) onwards for certain fairly well-defined poetic purposes, namely long or longish poems, sometimes narrative with possible digressions of a discursive kind,[2] but more often a mixture in varying proportions of description, disquisition, reflection, and philosophising with possible digressions into illustrative narrative.[3] Most of these poems are grave enough, at least in intention. But Somerville, who belonged to an older generation, carries on the facetious manner of *The Splendid Shilling*. He, too, was exceptional in proclaiming his theoretical respect for blank verse in prose, not " ashamed to follow the example of Milton, Philips, Thomson, and all our best tragic writers," [4] and referring those who " think no poem truly musical but what is in rhyme " [4] to Milton's preface, Fénelon's letter to Fontenelle, and Edmund Smith's elegy for Philips. Another poet who gave in prose a reason for the faith that was in him as regards blank verse was Edward Young, even though he was so habitual a rhymer that his blank lines constantly have the run of couplets. In his *Conjectures on Original Composition* (1759) he deplores Pope's

---

[1] *The Laws of Poetry*, p. 341.

[2] *E.g.* Lyttleton's *Blenheim* (1727), Glover's *Leonidas* (1737-70) and *The Athenaid* (posthumously in 1787), and Mallet's *Amyntor and Theodora* (1747).

[3] *E.g.* Mallet's *Excursion* (1728), Thomson's *Britannia* (1729) and *Liberty* (1735-3), Somerville's *Chase* (1735), *Hobbinol, or The Rural Games* (1740), and *Field Sports* (1742), Dyer's *Ruins of Rome* (1740) and *The Fleece* (1757), Young's *Night Thoughts* (1742), Blair's *Grave* (1743), Armstrong's *Art of Preserving Health* (1744), Akenside's *Pleasures of the Imagination* (1744), Joseph Warton's *Enthusiast: or the Lover of Nature* (1744), Thomas Warton's *Pleasures of Melancholy* (1747), Grainger's *Sugarcane* (1764), Jago's *Edge-hill* (1767), Mason's *English Garden* (1772-81), and Cowper's *Task* (1785).

[4] Preface to *The Chase*.

failure in translating Homer to take advantage of Milton's freedom from " childish shackles and tinkling sounds," and his succumbing to " the temptation of that *Gothic* dæmon, which modern poesy tasting, became mortal." [1] But he is prepared to tolerate rhyme as a necessary evil in " our lesser poetry," [2] which is pretty much the position also of Joseph Warton in his *Essay on the Writings and Genius of Pope* (part 1, 1756; part 2, 1782).

XVII

Two of the minor poets of the eighteenth century deserve more than passing mention for championing in rhyme the rhyme in which they were themselves skilled. They were John Byrom and Robert Lloyd.

Byrom was interested both as a student of metrics [3] and as a technician. His astonishing facility in rhyming, often in intractable matter and in oddly inappropriate measures, inclined him to defend it, and Miltonism even in versification probably repelled his High-Church and Jacobite sympathies. [4] In his opinion rhyme was the " sweetest grace of English verse," [5] and

> men (I measure by myself) sometimes,
> Averse to reas'ning, may be taught by rhymes. [6]

About 1750-3 one Roger Comberbach testified in prose in favour of unrhymed verse and added an ode to prove that " the soft Iambic " might have a good effect in unrhymed lyric measures. Byrom answered with a verse epistle in defence of rhyme, containing a rhymed version of Comberbach's ode. With Byrom's permission and Comberbach's reply to the reply these were published in 1754 or 1755. [7] No doubt is left in the reader's

---

[1] Ed. Edith J. Morley, 1918, pp. 26-7.

[2] *Ibid.*, p. 37.

[3] His library included John Mason's *Two Essays on the Power of Numbers* (1761). Byrom had apparently read them on their first publication (1749). They do not bear much on the question of rhyme.

[4] In 1725 he made a blank-verse paraphrase of 1 *Corinthians* xv, but otherwise he always rhymed.

[5] *An Epistle to a Friend on the Art of English Poetry*, 18.

[6] *An Epistle to a Gentleman of the Temple*, 427-8.

[7] As *A Dispute, consisting of a Preface in favour of Blank Verse, [and] an Ode . . . by Roger Comberbach, . . . an Epistle from Dr Byrom . . . in Defence of Rhyme ; and Mr Comberbach's Reply.*

mind as to Byrom's own sentiments and preferences. He is the
" friend to rhyme "[1] and prizes the numbers of his " plain,
familiar, honest, rhyming Muse . . . far beyond all blanks."[2]
In a most amiable way he awards Comberbach's ode " every grace
but one "[3] :—

> That one, however, is a special Grace,
> Tho' Roman Horace could not give it place.
> His Latin language, fill'd with many more,
> Wanted not Rhyme to grace its ample store.
> But in our own . . .
> It would be too too partial to the tongue
> To say that Rhyme was needless in the song ;
> Which, tho' in pompous buskin verse declin'd,
> Is quite essential to the oral kind [4]

—that is to say, to the lyric which, he is convinced, cannot be
" Britishly exempt . . . from Rhyme."[5] He stoutly rejects the
arguments that " Rhyme is certainly false taste "[6] and that the
" learnèd ancients all " avoided rhyme :—

> What " learnèd ancients " ?   Let me ask, what " all "
> Into this taste were so afraid to fall ?
> For, as to those of *Greek* and *Roman* stem
> Avoiding rhyme,—why, rhyme avoided them !
> Nature of language upon rhyming feet
> Forbad the two antagonists to meet "[7]

Nor is it possible to argue that the repetition of the measure is
peculiar to rhyming measures. It is the task of the rhyming and
of the unrhyming poet to achieve recurrence without monotony.

> By your account of Rhyme one would suppose
> That the same sound all periods must close.
> This may be irksome,—but 'tis not the case ;
> For varied Rhyme affords a varied grace

—more varied than the repeated cadences of " your Iambic
soft."[8] The so-called " *Gothic* fetters " are sought by all the
muses,

> In all the tongues but *Latin* and but *Greek* :
> Where verse excels, because they both are blest
> With fetters more than any of the rest.[9]

So far from rule and restriction being disadvantageous, they are

[1] I.   [2] 4-5.   [3] 29.
[4] 33-37, 39-42.   [5] 61-2.   [6] 70.
[7] 76-82.   [8] 225-8, 230.   [9] 121-4.

on the contrary valuable aids. Rejecting Mason's dislike of the dactylic measure which he (Mason) alleges Dionysius of Hali-carnassus to have shared, Byrom declines to admit that ancient authority can legislate for us. There is no reason for forbidding such experiments as Comberbach's ;

> But, when you claim her lyrics to your laws,
> Then she looks blank, and there she makes a pause ;
> As well she may,—if all her stock you vest
> In blank *Iambic*, and its varied rest !
> One edict further if your preface goes,
> Adieu to poetry, and all is prose ;
> Nor *Goth* nor *Vandal* has the muse undone,
> But you, alas, her rhyme-distasting son.[1]

Thoughts on Rhyme and Blank Verse appear to have been written about the same time. But its cantering anapaests are much more outspoken and were probably never meant for general publication. It begins :—

> What a deal of impertinent stuff, at this time,
> Comes out about verses in blank or in rhyme !
> To determine their merits by critical prose,
> And treat the two parties, as if they were foes !—
> Its allotting so gravely, to settle their rank,
> All the bondage to rhyme, all the freedom to blank,
> Has provok'd a few rhymes to step forth, and repress
> The pedantical whim, grown to such an excess.

Byrom has no wish to debar " the dupes of this fanciful wit " [2] and " partial . . . taste " [3] from expressing their views, but only to save young poets from supposing that rhymes cannot be as free as blanks and free with their own delight superadded. The allegations of " fetters and jingles " [4] can be substantiated only from the work of feeble writers ; and " a blockhead's a blockhead, with rhyme or without." [5] Rhyme :—

> came, as they tell us, from ignorant Moors,
> And by growth of fine taste will be turn'd out o'doors :
> Two insipid conceits, at a venture entwin'd,
> And void of all proof both before and behind :
> Too old its reception, to tell of its age ;
> Its downfall, if taste could but fairly presage,
> When the bees of the country make honey no more,
> Will then certainly come—not a moment before.[6]

---

[1] 193-200. [2] 9. [3] 12.
[4] 18. [5] 56. [6] 57-64.

Blank verse is like an aloe from a hot-house that occasionally shoots a head and makes people stare, but rhyme is in continual flower and fruit. After a fling at the classically prejudiced " finetasters " [1] and a piece of obscure theatrical history which appears to mean that rhyme (? in the Restoration period) abandoned the stage because of the rant and general deterioration of the drama, leaving

> poor blank, in its fetters held fast,
> To bemoan its hard fate in romantic bombast,[2]

Byrom concludes the whole matter with :—

> 'Tis the subject, in fine, in the matter of song,
> That makes a blank verse, or a rhyme to be wrong.[3]

He is thinking, however, not of the appropriateness or inappropriateness of metre to theme, but of the propriety and decency of the matter versified :—

> the possessor of tunable skill
> Unfetter'd, unjingled, may take which he will :
> Any plan to which freedom and judgment impel—
> All the bus'ness he knows, is to execute well.[4]

Robert Lloyd's *On Rhyme : A Familiar Epistle to a Friend* is in the colloquial octosyllabic couplet in which some of the eighteenth-century minors did their best work. Some critics, he says, may blame these easy rhymes, ostensibly because the muse requires rule and law, but really because they themselves have not the gift :—

> Nay, e'en professors of the art,
> To prove their wit betray their heart,
> And speak against themselves to show,
> What they would hate the world should know,
> As when the measur'd couplets curse,
> The manacles of Gothic verse,
> While the trim bard in easy strains,
> Talks much of fetters, clogs, and chains ;
> He only aims that you should think,
> How charmingly he makes them clink . . .
> From Boileau down to his translators,
> Dull paraphrasts, and imitators,
> All rail at metre at the time
> They write and owe their sense to rhyme.[5]

---

[1] 76.   [2] 87-88.   [3] 89-90.   [4] 93-6.   [5] 107-16, 131-4.

But the fact is that if the unready poet has to labour for his rhymes, the ready is the better for some restraint. Those who have gone " Milton-mad " [1]

> Approve no verse, but that which flows
> In epithetic measur'd prose,
> With trim expressions daily drest
> Stol'n, misapply'd, and not confest,
> And call it writing in the style
> Of that great Homer of our isle . . .
> Blank, classic blank, their all in all.[1]

Lloyd readily admits Milton's sublimity without rhyme ; but he asserts also Dryden's with it and Milton's own rhyming harmony. That is to say, good poetry can be written either way, though no doubt the couplet " falls in works of epic length." [2] Of rhyme itself Lloyd demands more

> Than the two catch-words in the rear,
> Which stand like watchmen in the close,
> To keep the verse from being prose . . .
>   No poet flows
> In tuneful verse, who thinks in prose ;
> And all the mighty secret here
> Lies in the niceness of the ear.[3]

This account of Milton's influence on metrical practice and theory may give an impression that the result was greater than indeed was the case. Rhyme was the rule, and blank verse the exception in the eighteenth century as it had been before. Just as Bysshe had expressed the general opinion on rhyme at the beginning of the century, so a greater than Bysshe and one no less authoritative stated it towards the end. This was Dr Johnson.

XVIII

He may be taken as summing up the debate on rhyme *versus* no-rhyme, which I have outlined ; and his views for that reason deserve to be fully stated. He recurs to the subject frequently and always consistently in his *Lives of the Poets* (1779-81), and never with more than qualified or ambiguous praise for blank

---

[1] 175, 177-83.   [2] 206.   [3] 246-8, 267-70.

verse.[1] There is, he says, in Mallet's *Amyntor and Theodora* (1747) " copiousness and elegance of language, vigour of sentiment, and imagery well adapted to take possession of the fancy. But it is blank verse " [2]—with which damning admission he leaves it. Or again he attributes the failure of Dyer's *Fleece* (1757) almost as much to its vehicle as to its contents :—" the disgust which blank verse, encumbering and encumbered, superadds to an unpleasing subject, soon repels the reader, however willing to be pleased." [3] Indeed only three practitioners of blank verse are partially excepted—Milton, and his two most distinguished followers, Thomson and Young. *The Seasons* (1726-30) is allowed to be " one of the works in which blank verse seems properly used. Thomson's wide expansion of general views, and his enumeration of circumstantial varieties, would have been obstructed and embarrassed by the frequent intersection of the sense, which are the necessary effects of rhyme." [4] On the other hand, Thomson's *Liberty* (1734-6) Johnson found unreadable. The *Night Thoughts* (1742-5) of Young, however, is also " one of the few poems in which blank verse could not be changed for rhyme but with disadvantage. The wild diffusion of the sentiments, and the digressive sallies of the imagination, would have been compressed and restrained by confinement to rhyme." [5] As for Milton, " whatever be the advantages of rhyme," Johnson says, " I cannot prevail on myself to wish that [he] had been a rhymer ; for I cannot wish his work to be other than it is,"—which would be handsome, if he had not added " yet, like other heroes, he is to be admired rather than imitated. He that thinks himself capable of astonishing may write blank verse; but those that hope only to please must condescend to rhyme." [6] One almost hears Johnson adding

[1] Cf. *Boswell's Life of Johnson*, ed. G. Birkbeck Hill and L. F. Powell, 1934, i, 427-8 :—" He enlarged very convincingly upon the excellence of rhyme over blank verse in English poetry. I mentioned to him that Dr Adam Smith, in his lectures upon composition . . . had maintained the same opinion strenuously. . . . JOHNSON. " Sir, I was once in company with Smith, and we did not take to each other ; but had I known that he loved rhyme as much as you tell me he does, I should have HUGGED him." "

[2] *Life of Mallet* in *The Works of Samuel Johnson*, ed. 1792, xi, p. 352.

[3] *Life of Dyer* in *The Works of Samuel Johnson*, ed. 1792, xi, 275.

[4] *Life of Thomson* in *The Works of Samuel Johnson*, ed. 1792, xi, 235.

[5] *Life of Young* in *The Works of Samuel Johnson*, ed. 1792, xi, pp. 343-4.

[6] *Life of Milton*, ed. cit., ix, pp. 181-2.

after each of the three verdicts, " Not guilty, but don't do it
again." He recognises certain extenuating circumstances in
each case. But *a priori* blank verse is disallowed ; and though
he has to make exceptions of Thomson, Young, and Milton yet
he never thought " it safe to judge of works of genius merely
by the event." [1] Thomson's blank verse may be right for his
purpose, and Young's right for his, the description of wide
landscapes and the indulgence of the discursive imagination
respectively. But Johnson's criticisms of Thomson's diction as
" too exuberant, and sometimes . . . filling the ear more than
the mind," [2] and of Young's style for similar features point to
the very faults which he condemned blank verse for encourag-
ing :—" The exemption which blank verse affords from the
necessity of closing the sense with the couplet betrays luxuriant
and active minds into such self-indulgence, that they pile image
upon image, ornament upon ornament, and are not easily
persuaded to close the sense at all. Blank verse will therefore,
I fear, be too often found in description exuberant, in argument
loquacious, and in narration tiresome." [3] Milton's justification
is his presentation of majestic, superhuman persons and events
in a style appropriate and not to be confused with prose. To
show how much Johnson regarded Milton as an exception, not
a precedent, it is enough to note his dismissal of Philip's *Cider* :—
" he unhappily pleased himself with blank verse, and supposed
that the numbers of Milton, which impress the mind with
veneration, combined as they are with subjects of inconceivable
grandeur, could be sustained by images which at most can rise
only to elegance. Contending angels may shake the regions of
Heaven in blank verse ; but the flow of equal measures, and the
embellishment of rhyme, must recommend to our attention the
art of engrafting, and decide the merit of the *redstreak* and
pearmain." [4] Similar views are expressed by Johnson in the *Life
of Roscommon* :—" Blank verse, left merely to its numbers, has
little operation either on the ear or mind : it can hardly support
itself without bold figures and striking images. A poem frigidly

---

[1] *The Rambler*, no. 156, in *The Works of Samuel Johnson*, ed. 1792, vi, p. 99.
[2] *Life of Thomson*, ed. cit., xi, p. 236.
[3] *Life of Akenside* in *The Works of Samuel Johnson*, ed. 1792, xi, p. 361.
[4] *Life of J. Philips* in *The Works of Samuel Johnson*, ed. 1792, ix, pp. 301-2.
In the *Life of Somerville*, ed. cit., x, p. 280, Johnson remarks that " One
excellence of the *Splendid Shilling* is, that it is short."

didactic, without rhyme, is so near to prose, that the reader only scorns it for pretending to be verse " ; [1] and again in the *Life of Somerville* :—" If blank verse be not timid or gorgeous, it is crippled prose ; and familiar images in laboured language have nothing to recommend them but absurd novelty, which, wanting the attractions of Nature, cannot please long." [2]

Naturally it was in the *Life of Milton* that Johnson had most to say on the question. He rather unjustly asserts that Milton wanted to persuade himself that blank verse was better because he knew it to be easier. It is true, says Johnson, that rhyme is no necessary adjunct of true poetry " as a mental operation." [3] But, he goes on, neither is metre nor music ; " it is however by the musick of metre that poetry has been discriminated in all languages." [4] Some languages may be such that metre without rhyme is enough of itself to make verse and distinguish it from prose. " But one language cannot communicate its rules to another : where metre is scanty and imperfect, some [other] help is necessary. The musick of the English heroick line strikes the ear so faintly, that it is easily lost, unless all the syllables of every line co-operate together ; this co-operation can be only obtained by the preservation of every verse unmingled with another as a distinct system of sounds ; and this distinctness is obtained and preserved by the artifice of rhyme. The variety of pauses, so much boasted by the lovers of blank verse, changes the measures of an English poet to the periods of a declaimer ; and there are only a few happy readers of Milton, who enable their audience to perceive where the lines end or begin. *Blank verse*, said an ingenious critick, *seems to be verse only to the eye*.

" Poetry may subsist without rhyme, but English poetry will not often please [without it] ; nor can rhyme ever be safely spared but where the subject is able to support itself. Blank verse makes some approach to that which is called the *lapidary style* ; has neither the easiness of prose, nor the melody of numbers, and therefore tires by long continuance. Of the Italian writers without rhyme, whom Milton alledges as precedents, not one is popular ; what reason would urge in its defence has been confuted by the ear." [5]

Thus, to put Johnson's objections briefly, when the subject was of sufficient, intrinsically poetic interest, it would require

---

[1] *Ed. cit.*, ix, p. 220.   [2] *Ed. cit.*, x, p. 280.   [3] *Ed. cit.*, ix, p. 180.
[4] *Ibid.*, ix, p. 180-1.   [5] *Ibid.*, ix, p. 181.

a diction and style quite distinct from prose, though not from sense and " nature " ; therefore on the score of both matter and manner there could be no confusion of the blank verse with prose. But when the subject was of a lower poetic interest and therefore gave occasion for a lower-pitched style, Johnson who disliked inversion of the normal word-order and novelties of diction [1] felt that without rhyme the verse would not have the necessary poetic distinction. The verse would be merely prose arbitrarily cut into lengths ; and it would have little of the beneficial restrictive power rhyme has over exuberance and garrulity.

With Johnson we come to the end of a chapter in metrical history. A new chapter began before he had said his last word, indeed when the pre-romantic movement was gathering momentum with Gray and Collins and the Wartons, and still more with Macpherson, Percy, and Chatterton, for one of the most obvious signs of their innovating was their metrical and rhythmical experimentation. But they went about their experiments with no Miltonic sanction or classical bias ; they did not carry on the centuries-old discussion which I have summarised, but by their examples of metrical freedom and innovation rather than by anything said in justification of these examples they originated an entirely new discussion on a different ground altogether, which was taken up by Blake, Wordsworth, Coleridge, and Southey and may be said to be still continuing at the present day.

[1] Cf. *Life of Cowley* in *The Works of Samuel Johnson*, ed. 1792, ix, pp. 43-44 :—" The artifices of invention, by which the established order of words is changed, or of innovation, by which new words or meanings of words are introduced, [are] practised, not by those who talk to be understood, but by those who write to be admired " ; and *Life of Collins* in *The Works of Samuel Johnson*, ed. 1792, ix, p. 270 :—" his diction was often harsh [*i.e.* not according to usage], unskilfully laboured, and injudiciously selected. He affected the obsolete when it was not worthy of revival ; and he put his words out of the common order, seeming to think, with some later candidates for fame, that not to write prose is certainly to write poetry."

THE RHYMING ANCIENTS

[D]ire per rima in volgare tanto è quanto dire per versi in latino, secondo alcuna proporzione.

Dante, La Vita Nuova, xxv, 4.

What " learned ancients " ? Let me ask, what " all "
Into this taste were so afraid to fall ?
For, as to those of *Greek* and *Roman* stem
Avoiding rhyme,—why, rhyme avoided them !
Nature of language upon rhyming feet
Forbad the two antagonists to meet.

John Byrom, Dr Byrom's Letter to Mr Comberbach, 68-82.

Rhyme, that exquisite echo which in the Muses' hollow hill creates and answers its own voice ; . . . rhyme, which can turn man's utterance to the speech of gods ; rhyme, the one chord we have added to the Greek lyre.

Oscar Wilde, The Critic as Artist in Intentions, 1909, pp. 102-3.

I

ONE of Milton's reasons for rejecting rhyme in *Paradise Lost* was that " the jingling sound of like endings . . . [was] avoyded by the learned Ancients both in Poetry and all good Oratory." [1] But the statement needs more than a little qualification, especially as regards Latin. Rhyme was not unknown either to the Greeks or to the Romans, as indeed was inevitable from the fact that, whether men like it or not, there can be only a limited number of syllables, and fortuitous, not to mention deliberate, rhymes are bound to occur, especially in highly inflected languages.

II

In Greek poetry ὁμοιοτέλευτα are certainly rarer than in Latin, but they are nevertheless common enough. There are enough of them, for example, in Homer, such as :—

ἠΰτε ἔθνεα εἶσι μελισσάων ἀδινάων,
πέτρης ἐκ γλαφυρῆς αἰεὶ νέον ἐρχομενάων,[2]

---

[1] *The Verse* of *Paradise Lost*, 1668.　　　　[2] *Iliad*, ii, 87-8.

and

> Ζεὺς δέ σφι Κρονίδης ἐνδέξια σήματα φαίνων
> ἀστράπτει· Ἕκτωρ δὲ μέγα σθένεϊ βλεμεαίνων
> μαίνεται ἐκπάγλως,[1]

for the anonymous writer of a *De Vita et Poesi Homeri* to adduce corresponding endings of lines as one of the σχήματα of the Homeric style.

On the other hand, it is clear that when Euripides brings in the tipsy Herakles rhyming four gnomic lines together :—

> βροτοῖς ἅπασι κατθανεῖν ὀφείλεται,
> κοὐκ ἔστι θνητῶν ὅστις ἐξεπίσταται
> τὴν αὔριον μέλλουσαν εἰ βιώσεται·
> τὸ τῆς τύχης γὰρ ἀφανὲς οἷ προβήσεται,
> κἄστ’ οὐ διδακτὸν οὐδ’ ἁλίσκεται τέχνῃ,[2]

he intended a comic effect, as if the wine had made the hero's tongue trip into rhyme. From my point of view, however, the important fact is that, whether comic or not, the rhymes were deliberate.

They were as deliberate in these lines from Aristophanes's *Acharnians* :—

> κᾆτ’ ἐπειδὰν ὦ μόνος,
> στένω κέχηνα σκορδινῶμαι πέρδομαι,
> ἀπορῶ γράφω παρατίλλομαι λογίζομαι,
> ἀποβλέπων ἐς τὸν ἀγρὸν εἰρήνης ἐρῶν,
> στυγῶν μὲν ἄστυ τὸν δ’ ἐμὸν δῆμον ποθῶν,
> ὃς οὐδεπώποτ’ εἶπεν, ἄνθρακας πρίω,
> οὐκ ὄξος, οὐκ ἔλαιον, οὐδ’ ᾔδει πρίω,
> ἀλλ’ αὐτὸς ἔφερε πάντα χὠ πρίων ἀπῆν.[3]

But we must go to the Alexandrian poets to find rhyme in more frequent use. They delighted in patterns, correspondences, and symmetry, not to mention such japes as poems which when written had the shape of an axe, a pair of wings, a shepherd's pipe, or an altar. As their poetry was written to be recited rather than sung to a musical accompaniment, they tried to make up for the absence of music by introducing new kinds of verbal melody.

---

[1] *Iliad.*, ix, 236-8.   [2] *Alcestis*, 782-6.
[3] 29-36. Other and perhaps better examples will be found in *The Clouds*, 709-15, *The Wasps*, 133-5 and *Ecclesiazusæ*, 219-28.

In order to set off their unsung cadences they brought in their metrical returns and rhythmical recurrences at briefer intervals. They had a partiality for strophic arrangements and often punctuated their poems with refrains. Now the refrain is cousin to rhyme ; and of the same kin are other favourite devices of the Alexandrians, such as anaphora, alliteration, antithesis, parisosis or parallelism of structure, and paromoiosis or parallelism of sound, all of which can be seen in Bion's *Lament for Adonis*. Of rhymes between successive verses or between two halves of a single verse one might give a considerable number of examples :—

θᾶσαι μάν· θυμαλγὲς ἐμὶν ἄχος. αἴθε γενοίμαν
ἁ βομβεῦσα μέλισσα καὶ ἐς τεὸν ἄντρον ἱκοίμαν
τὸν κισσὸν διαδὺς καὶ τὰν πτέριν, ᾇ τὺ πυκάσδεις.[1]

τετόρταιος ἔχει παῖδος ἔρος μῆνά με δεύτερον,
καλῶ μὲν μετρίως, ἀλλ᾽ ὅποσον τῷ ποδὶ περρέχει
τὰς γᾶς, τοῦτο χάρις, ταῖς δὲ παραύϝαις γλύκυ μειδίᾳ.
καὶ νῦν μὲν τὸ κακὸν ταῖς μὲν ἔχει, ταῖσι δέ μ᾽ οὐκ ἔχει
τάχα δ᾽ οὐδ᾽ ὅσον ὕπνω 'πιτύχην ἔσσετ᾽ ἐρωῖα.[2]

φοιτῇς δ᾽ αὖθ᾽ οὕτως, ὅκκα γλυκὺς ὕπνος ἔχῃ με,
οἴχῃ δ᾽ εὐθὺς ἰοῖσ᾽, ὅκκα γλυκὺς ὕπνος ἀνῇ με,
φεύγεις δ᾽ ὥσπερ ὄις πολιὸν λύκον ἀθρήσασα.[3]

οὐ γάρ μιν πολλοὶ καὶ ἐπημοιβοὶ γανόωσιν
ἀστέρες, οἵ μιν πᾶσαν ἐπιρρήδην στιχόωσιν.[4]

ταὶ Μοῖσαι τὸν Ἔρωτα τὸν ἄγριον οὐ φοβέονται
ἐκ θυμῶ δὲ φιλεῦντι καὶ ἐκ ποδὸς αὐτῶι ἕπονται.[5]

III

But on the whole, Greek poetry was less given to rhyme than was Latin, for two connected reasons. In the first place natural stress accent (not tonic accent) is light or non-existent in Greek and heavy in Latin. In the second place—and this is the main factor in the different weights of accent in the two languages

---

[1] Theocritus, iii, 12-14.
[2] *Ibid.*, xxx, 2-6.
[3] *Ibid.*, xi, 22-4 ; *cf.* also viii, 66-70.
[4] Aratus, *Phænomena*, 190-1 ; *cf.* also 77-86, 264-7, 364-79, 778-81, 916-7, 1062-3, 1114-21.
[5] Bion, v, 1-2 ; *cf.* also Moschus, iii, 98-104 ; Dosiadas, *The Altar*, 1-18 ; Callimachus, *Epigrams*, xx, 3-6.

—the proportions of vowels to consonants are strikingly different in Greek and in Latin. Greek is highly vocalic; indeed the average proportion of vowels to consonants is 54·4 to 45·6. In Latin, on the other hand, the proportion is almost exactly reversed, 45·7 vowels to 54·3 consonants. The proportion of vowels to consonants in English is 42·4 to 57·6. Now when there are more vowels than consonants, the consonants are fairly evenly scattered among the vowels and do not often form obstructive clusters. The voice, therefore, passes evenly along from vowel to vowel and the accents tend to be slight or negligible. Thus Greek scansion came to be based on the comparative duration of syllables, classified into long and short, not on the varying amounts of force with which the syllables were uttered. But in Latin, and, still more, English, which are thickly strewn with consonants, the somewhat infrequent vowels are separated by grouped consonants, and the voice in forcing its way is likely to develop strong accents before the obstructions and an accented-unaccented modulation generally. This being so, such languages naturally tend to an accentual prosody. They need not, of course, combine rhyme with accent, though, for reasons which I shall discuss later, they generally do.

"When the same modification of sound recurs at definite intervals," says Guest, "the coincidence very readily strikes the ear; and when it is found in accented syllables, such syllables fix the attention more strongly than if they merely received the accent. Hence we may perceive the importance of rhyme in accentual verse. It is not, as it is sometimes asserted, a mere ornament: it marks and defines the accent, and thereby strengthens and supports the rhythm."[1] But the low percentage of consonants in Greek also discouraged rhyme. For rhyme is more dependent on the consonants than on the vowels; at least it is the consonants which give frictional character to the rhyming syllables, whereas the vowels may be slightly, or even considerably, different.

Though the natural tendency of Latin was towards an accentual prosody, the tendency was deflected at the dictates of a Hellenising fashion and by the hypnotic influence of the great Greek models. Thus an alien way of versifying according to quantity was accepted. Nevertheless Latin poetry began with

[1] *A History of English Rhythms*, ed. W. W. Skeat, 1882, i, p. 113.

K

accent ; and it reverted to accent whenever it escaped from the rules of quantity, in *populares versus* appearing at all periods of Latin literature, and in the poetry of the early Church when the quantitative system was in decay. Latin poetry, too, seemed to have a hankering after occasional rhymes, for they crop up in every Latin poet from first to last almost as if they could not be kept out.

IV

In the earliest period, before Greece had led captivity captive and taught her arts to victorious Rome, the rude verses of the Latins, as of all the Italic peoples, were accentual. The commonest scheme, and the only one with a distinguishing name, is the *versus Saturnius*. This was a six-beat line with a middle caesura and an indeterminate number of unaccented syllables, as in :—

> Malum dabunt Metelli / Naevio poetae,[1]

chosen as the most perfect Saturnian line by Macaulay who gave as an exact metrical equivalent :—

> The queen was in her parlour eating bread and honey.[2]

This primeval metre was akin to early Teutonic verse, and indeed, like it, was probably derived from an Indo-European prototype.[3] There are enough Saturnians and similar early accentual verses in existence to show that end-rhymes, middle or leonine rhymes, and scattered jingles of one sort or another were regarded as a legitimate ornament. It has even been maintained, though not I think by any recent scholar, that rhyme was systematic.[4] In addition to rhymes, we also come on alliteration, which may be called fore-rhyme, and refrains, which may be regarded as a groping towards rhyme. Thus the Song of the Arval Brethren, which is so archaic that it was unintelligible

---

[1] Aemilius Baehrens, *Fragmenta Poetarum Romanorum*, 1886, p. 53.

[2] *Lays of Ancient Rome*, 1848, p. 19.

[3] The Anglo-Saxon variant had only two beats in each half-line with alliteration to bind the halves together. But the alliterative line of the *Nibelungenlied* had six accents. It is possible that the six-beat line of the *Poema del Cid*, the earliest Spanish line, and even the French Alexandrine, first used in the *Roman d'Alexandre*, are of the same kin.

[4] G. Lange, *Jahrbuch der Philologie*, 1830, p. 256.

even in the time of Varro, has some attempts at sound-identities, not to mention the ritual repetitions :—

> Enos, Lases, iuvate. (thrice)
> Neve lue rue, Marmar, sins incurrere in pleores. (thrice)
> Satur fu, fere Mars. Limen sali. Sta. Berber. (thrice)
> Semunis alternei advocapit conctos. (thrice)
> Enos, Marmor, iuvato. (thrice)
> Triumpe. (five times) [1]

Probably no less ancient and certainly more striking from my point of view are three charms, two recorded by Cato, as cures for dislocations :—

> motas uaeta daries dardares astataries dissunapiter ;

and

> huat hanat huat ; ista pista sista ;
> domiabo damna ustra ; [2]

and the third by Varro as a cure for aching feet :—

> terra pestem teneto, / salus hic maneto.[3]

The same kind of jingling can be heard in other popular verses, such as this scrap of weather-lore :—

> hiberno puluere, / uerno luto,
> grandia farra, / camille, metes ; [4]

or this lullaby :—

> lalla lalla lalla ! / i, aut dormi aut lacta.[5]

Much more interesting, however, than these relics are the more strictly poetical remains, as for example the following lines from Naevius's *Bellum Poenicum* :—

> bicorpores Gigantes / magnique Atlantes ; [6]

> liquidum mare eunt fugantes / atque sectantes ; [7]

---

[1] *Corpus Inscriptionum Latinarum*, 1863, i, p. 9.

[2] *De Agri Cultura*, clx.

[3] *De Re Rustica*, I, ii, 27.

[4] J. Wight Duff, *A Literary History of Rome from the Origins to the Close of the Golden Age*, 1914, p. 79.

[5] Aemilius Baehrens, *op. cit.*, p. 34.

[6] *Ibid.*, p. 46.

[7] *Ibid*, p. 48.

V

According to Horace, the introduction of Greek literary standards drove out the Saturnian verse :—

> Graecia capta ferum victorem cepit, et artes
> intulit agresti Latio.   Sic horridus ille
> defluxit numerus Saturnius et grave virus
> munditiae pepulere.[1]

The new metres were alien, not only in the simple sense of coming from another land, but in the sense of being contrary to the genius of Latin.   " Great results," says Archbishop Trench, " came of the change, and of the new direction in which the national taste was turned.   Everything, in short, came of it but the one thing, for the absence of which all else is but an insufficient compensation ; namely, a thoroughly popular literature, which should truly smack of the soil from which it sprung, which should be the utterance of a nation's own life ; and not merely accents, which, however sweet or musical, were yet caught from the lips of another, and only artificially fitted to its own." [2]

The first of the new metres to arrive was the hexameter, probably introduced by Ennius,[3] who despised the rugged Saturnians of his predecessors :—

> quos olim Fauni vatesque canebant
> cum neque Musarum scopulos [quisquam superarat],
> nec dicti studiosus erat quisquam erat ante hunc.[4]

Ennius also used the pentameter in elegiac couplets.   As for the various metres in the dramas of Plautus, Ennius, and their followers, though they were of Greek origin, they cannot be scanned according to strict quantitative rules.   It was Catullus and Horace who first composed iambic metres with the correctness demanded in hexameters and pentameters.   It was they also who brought in the chief lyric metres, Catullus the more simple, and Horace the more elaborate.[5]   Moreover, though the hexameter and the pentameter were naturalised, " the lyric metres

---

[1] *Epistles*, II, i, 156-9.

[2] *Sacred Latin Poetry*, 1874, p. 20.

[3] *Cf*. Cicero, *De Legibus*, II, xxvii, 68, and Isidore of Seville, *Origines*, I, xxxix, 6.

[4] Quoted by Cicero, *Brutus*, xviii, 71.

[5] *Cf*. Horace, *Epistles*, I, xix, 21-34.

remained exotics to the end, [and] were never truly acclimated,—
nothing worth reading or being preserved having been produced
in them, except by those who first transplanted them from Greek
to Italian ground." [1] Quintilian, in fact, ignoring Catullus, goes
the length of saying that " lyricorum . . . Horatius fere solus
legi dignus." [2]

The substitution in cultured circles of quantitative, for
accentual, verse coincided with the beginning of the separation
of literary Latin from the Latin of everyday speech. In this
departure, too, Ennius was the leader. To some extent the one
involved the other, because, quite apart from the endeavour
of the Latin poets to emulate the style of their Greek models,
the new versification necessarily excluded straight away a great
many words for metrical reasons. As time went on, the vocabulary
of poetry—and, as an inevitable consequence, the vocabulary of
prose though to a lesser degree—became more and more fastidious
and exclusive for reasons no longer merely metrical. The
excluded words did not by any means all drop out of use, though
they may have been rejected in literary use ; for many words
which the dictionaries degrade as " pre-Ciceronian " were also
" post-classical," having survived below the literary level.

VI

Though Ennius was the reformer of Latin numbers on
quantitative principles, he did not forgo the native tradition of
occasional rhymes, jingles, assonances, and alliterations. The
following examples are from his *Annales* :—

> ac Volturnalem, Palatualem, Furinalem,
> Floralem, Falacrem et Pomonalem, hic facit idem ; [3]
>
> o Tite tute Tati tibe tanta tiranne tulisti ; [4]
>
> at tuba terribili sonitu taratantara dixit ; [5]
>
> flentes plorantes lacrimantes optestantes ; [5]
>
> maerentes flentes lacrimantes ac miserantes ; [5]
>
> bellipotentes sunt magis quam sapientipotentes.[6]

---

[1] R. C. Trench, *op. cit.*, p. 16.

[2] *Institutio Oratoria*, X, i, 96. Out of the goodness of his heart he adds :—
" Si quem adiicere velis, is erit Caesius Bassus, quem nuper vidimus ; sed
eum longe praecedunt ingenia viventium."

[3] Aemilius Baehrens, *op. cit.*, p. 72.

[4] *Ibid.*, p. 69.   [5] *Ibid.*, p. 74   [6] *Ibid.*, p. 78.

I quote the next passage, which occurs in the *Saturae*, not for any rhyming but for the rather childish playing with the same root through four lines :—

> nam qui lepide postulat alterum frustrari,
> quem frustratur, frustra eum dicit frustrasse ;
> nam qui se frustrari quem frustra sentit,
> frustratur, si frustrast ; ille non est frustra.[1]

Such a trick is obviously of the same class as rhyme.   But the most remarkable pure rhymes by Ennius are found in the fragments of his tragedies :—

> haec omnia vidi inflammari,
> Priamo vi vitam evitari,
> Iovis aram sanguine turpari ; [2]

> coelum nitescere, arbores frondescere,
> vites laetificae pampinis pubescere,
> rami bacarum ubertate incurvescere ; [3]

> rex ipse Priamus somnio mentis metu
> perculsus, curis sumptus suspirantibus
> exsacrificabat hostiis balantibus.[4]

> vidi videre quod sum passa aegerrume
> Hectorem curro quadriiugo raptarier
> Hectoris natum de muro iactarier.[5]

The comic writers, too, as was natural, sported with rhymes and jingles and made them contribute to their wit and word-play:—

> Chrysalus med hodie laceravit
> Chrysalus me miserum spoliavit ; [6]

> Prolatis rebus parasiti venatici
> sumus, quando res redierunt, molossici,
> odiosicique et multum incommodestici ; [7]

---

[1] Aemilius Baehrens, *op. cit.*, pp. 119-20.

[2] From *Andromacha Aechmalotis*.   The passage has been preserved by Cicero, who quotes it twice in his *Tusculanae Disputationes*, I, xxxv, 85, and III, xix, 45.   He also quotes two of the lines in the *De Oratore*, III, lviii, 217, and one in *Pro Sestio*, lvii, 121.

[3] Probably from *Eumenides*.   Cicero quotes the passage in *Tusculanae Disputationes*, I, xxviii, 69, and a phrase from it in *De Oratore*, III, xxxviii, 154.

[4] Probably from *Alexander* (*i.e.* Paris) ; quoted by Cicero in *De Divinatione*, I, xxi, 42.

[5] From *Andromacha Aechmalotis*.   Cicero quotes the first two lines in *Tusculanae Disputationes*, I, xliv, 105, and Varro the third in *De Lingua Latina*, x, 70.

[6] Plautus, *Bacchides*, V, i, (1097-8).   [7] Plautus, *Captivi*, I, i, (85-7).

Si nunc me suspendam, meam operam luserim
et praeter operam restim sumpti fecerim
et meis inimicis voluptatem creaverim ; [1]

nisi ego teque tuamque filiam aeque hodie obtruncavero,
poste autem cum primo luci cras nisi ambo occidero,
et equidem hercle nisi pedatu tertio omnis efflixero ; [2]

Mihi ad enarrandum hoc argumentum est comitas,
si ad auscultandum vostra erit benignitas. [3]

The same comic or grotesque use of rhymes can be illustrated
from the early satirists :—

depoclassere aliqua sperans inde ac deargentassere,
decalauticare, eburno speculo despeculassere ; [4]

non esse arquatos ? surgamus, eamus, agamus ! [5]

Ante auris nodo ex crobyli subparvuli
intorti emittebantur sex cincinnuli ;
oculis suppaetulis nigelli pupuli,
quantam hilaritatem significantes animuli ! [6]

The coming of the Golden Age did not cause the banishment
of rhyme ; and the Silver Age was no less tolerant. Indeed,
verses with middle or final rhymes occur in every classical Latin
poet from Lucretius to Ausonius and Claudian. According to
Archbishop Trench, such jingles were " no doubt only with
difficulty avoided by those writers, whose stricter sense of beauty
taught them not to catch at ornaments which were not properly
theirs ; and easily attained by those who with a more questionable
taste were well pleased to sew it as a purple patch on a garment of
altogether a different texture. Thus we cannot doubt that these
coincidences of sound were sedulously avoided by so great a
master of the proprieties as Virgil in whose works therefore
rhyming verses rarely appear : while it is difficult not to suspect
that they were sometimes sought, or, if not sought, yet welcomed

---

[1] Plautus, *Casina*, II, vii, (424-6).
[2] Plautus, *Cistellaria*, II, i (524-6).
[3] Plautus, *Miles Gloriosus*, II, i (79-80).
[4] Lucilius in Aemilius Baehrens, *op. cit.*, p. 205.
[5] Lucilius, *ibid.*, p. 240.
[6] Varro, *Papia Papae*, in John Wordsworth, *Fragments and Specimens of Early Latin*, 1874, p. 362.

when they offered themselves, by Ovid, in whom they occur far more frequently, and whose less severe taste may have been willing to appropriate this as well as the more legitimate adornments which belonged to the verse he was using." [1] This passage, however, is not in my opinion quite an accurate reading of the facts. While it would be absurd to maintain that all the instances of rhyming in the classical Latin poets were deliberate, yet many of them in Virgil no less than in other poets undoubtedly were, as for example :—

Furi et Aureli, comites Catulli,
sive in extremos penetrabit Indos,
litus ut longe resonante Eoa
    tunditur unda ; [2]

limus ut hic durescit, et haec ut cera liquescit
uno eodemque igni, sic nostro Daphnis amore ; [3]

    summo cum monte videmus
ipsum inter pecudes vasta se mole moventem
pastorem Polyphemum, et littora nota petentem ; [4]

    effusa si quando grandine nimbi
praecipitant, omnis campis diffugit arator,
omnis et agricola ; et tuta latet arce viator ; [5]

non satis est pulchra esse poemata ; dulcia sunto,
et quoncunque volent animum auditoris agunto ; [6]

tot tibi tamque dabit formosas Roma puellas,
    haec habet, ut dicas, quicquid in orbe fuit.
Gargara quot segetes, quot habet Methymma racemos ;
    aequore quot pisces, fronde teguntur aues ;
quot coelum stellas, tot habet tua Roma puellas :
    mater et Aeneae constat in urbe sui ; [7]

      nec invenimus
dignum tam tenera virum puella.
hanc ne lux rapiat suprema totam,
picta Publius exprimit tabella :
in qua tam similem videbis Issam,
ut sit tam similis sibi nec ipsa.

---

[1] *Op. cit.*, pp. 27-8.

[2] Catullus, xi, 1-4.

[3] Virgil, *Eclogues*, viii, 80-1.

[4] Virgil, *Aeneid*, iii, 656-7.

[5] *Ibid.*, x, 804-5. For other Virgilian rhymes, see *Aeneid*, i, 625-6; ii, 124-5, 456-7 ; iii, 549 ; iv, 256-7 ; viii, 620-1, 646-7 ; ix, 182-3 ; *Eclogues*, iv, 50-1 ; and *Georgics*, ii, 500-1.

[6] Horace, *De Arte Poetica*, 99-100.

[7] Ovid, *De Arte Amatoria*, i, 55-60.

Issam denique pone cum tabella :
aut utramque putabis esse veram,
aut utramque putabis esse pictam.[1]

Of the Augustan poets alone, Ovid, as might have been expected, is the most partial to rhyme. Thus in the *Tristia* no less than 380 out of the 1766 pentameters have leonine rhymes of sorts.

After the Golden and the Silver Ages rhymes were not less but more numerous. Thus Hadrian's so-called dying address to his soul is full of sound correspondences :—

Animula, vagula, blandula,
hospes comesque corporis,
quae nunc abibis in loca,
pallidula, rigida, nudula,
nec ut soles dabis iocos ? [2]

And his friend Florus took a similar pleasure in rhyme :—

nulla fit exinde finis uel quies cupidinis :
crescit arbor, gliscit ardor : animus implet litteras.[3]

As time goes on, rhymes—not least leonine rhymes which in some ways are more significant because almost certainly deliberate —become more and more common. They abound in Ausonius who loved all kinds of verbal jugglery :—

huic ego, quod nobis superest ignobilis oti,
deputo, sive legat, quae dabo, sive tegat ; [4]

possem absolute dicere,
sed dulcius circumloquar
diuque fando perfruar ; [5]

fleta prius lacrimis, nunc memorabo modis ; [6]

quae Numa cognatis sollemnia dedicat umbris,
ut gradus aut mortis postulat aut generis.[7]

---

[1] Martial, I, cix, 15-23.

[2] Milton might have animadverted that Hadrian's indulgence in rhyme was but a poor argument for it since he had so little judgment as to prefer Cato the Elder, Ennius, and Caelius Antipater to Cicero, Virgil, and Sallust, not to mention his preference in Greek for Antimachus to Homer and Plato. (*Cf.* B. W. Henderson, *The Life and Principiate of the Emperor Hadrian*, 1923, p. 242.)

[3] *De Qualitate Vitae*, v, 3-4.   [4] *Epigrammata*, I, i, 15-16.

[5] *Epistolae*, xii, 7-9 (of the part in verse).

[6] *Parentalia*, verse preface, 2.   [7] *Ibid.*, pp. 7-8.

And Claudian, last of the classical Latin poets and so far as metrical quantity was concerned much more correct than any predecessor since Statius, begins his *Fescennine Verses* on the marriage of the Emperor Honorius with a string of rhymes :—

> Princeps corusco sidere pulchrior,
> Parthis sagittas tendere doctior,
> eques Gelonis imperiosior,
> quae digna mentis laus erit arduae ?
> quae digna formae laus erit igneae ?

VII

So much for " the jingling sound of like endings " in classical poetry. But what about them in " good oratory " ? The answer is that many orators and prose-writers in Greek or in Latin were quite willing to use them to gratify the ear or to enliven the style.

Curiously enough, one of those who indulged in rhyme and the other devices of a like nature, even to excess, was Isocrates, " that Old man eloquent " of Milton's tenth sonnet,[1] as for example in :—

> τοῦ μὲν ἐπίπονον καὶ φιλοκίνδυνον τὸν βίον κατέστησεν,
> τῆς δὲ περίβλεπτον καὶ περιμάχητον τὴν φύσιν ἐποίησεν.[2]

He had acquired his partiality for such rhetorical graces from the Sicilian school of oratory and in particular from his master, Gorgias ; and he in his turn handed it on to his pupil, Theopompus.

Thucydides is an example of a prose-writer as distinct from an orator who was likewise given to what Dionysius of Halicarnassus calls the " showy " (θεατρικῶν)[3] or " affected " (μειρακιώδεις)[4] figures, including rhyme :—

> ἐν αἷς ἐπλεόνασε Γοργίας ὁ Λεοντῖνος καὶ οἱ περὶ Πῶλόν καὶ Λικύμνιον καὶ πολλοὶ ἄλλοι τῶν κατ᾽ αὐτὸν ἀκμασάντων.[5]

Dionysius's depreciation of these euphuistic figures was far from absolute rejection. Indeed in his *De Compositione Verborum*

---

[1] 8.

[2] *Helen*, xvii. In his *Panathenaicus*, ii-iii, written when he was ninety-four, he says that he had given up such ornaments because they were unsuited to one of his years.

[3] *Epistola ad Ammaeum*, II, ii, 792.

[4] *Ibid.*, II, xvii, 808.   [5] *Ibid.*, II, ii, 792.

he not infrequently uses them to sweeten his style, as for example
in this piece of studied prose :—

ἀλλὰ ποίημα μὲν καὶ γέννημα παιδείας καὶ ψυχῆς τῆς ἐμῆς, κτῆμα
δὲ σοὶ τὸ αὐτὸ καὶ χρῆμα πρὸς ἁπάσας τὰς ἐν τῷ βίῳ χρείας ὁπόσαι
γίνονται διὰ λόγων ὠφέλιμον.[1]

Like the other classical rhetoricians he accepted rhyme, called
by the Greeks ὁμοιοτέλευτον and by the Romans *similiter
desinens*,[2] as one of the recognised figures. It might not be
suitable in emotional passages because it would look artificial,
says Demetrius ; but, he adds, it may be used with propriety to
heighten expression.[3] Dionysius regarded παρομοίωσις of which
ὁμοιοτέλευτον was a species, as indicative of youthful exuberance
and as bringing the style of panegyric to its highest
perfection.[4]

Of all the classical orators and rhetoricians Cicero was
among the most lenient to exuberance of style :—" volo enim se
efferat in adulescente fecunditas ; nam facilius sicut in vitibus
revocantur ea, quae se nimium profuderunt, quam, si nihil
valet materies, nova sarmenta cultura excitantur ; item volo esse
in adulescente, unde aliquid amputem ; non enim potest in eo
sucus esse diuturnus, quod nimis celeriter est maturitatem
exsecutum." [5] From his quotation no less than four times of a
particularly florid passage of rhyme from Ennius [6] and his high
praise of it as " Praeclarum carmen ! est enim et rebus et verbis
et modis lugubre," [7] it is clear that he was not a " learned
ancient " who had any objection to " like endings . . . in
poetry." Nor had he any dislike of them in oratory or in his
other prose, as for example :—" sine re, sine fide, sine spe, sine

---

[1] i.

[2] *Cf.*, *e.g.* :—Dionysius of Halicarnassus, *De Compositione Verborum*,
xxiii ; Aristotle, *Rhetoric*, III, ix, 9-11 ; Demetrius, *De Eloquentia*, I, xxvi-
xxix ; *Rhetorica ad Alexandrum*, xxvii-xxix ; Cicero, *De Oratore*, III, liv,
206, and *Orator*, xxxix, 135 ; *Rhetorica ad Herennium*, IV, xx ; Quintilian,
Institutis Oratoria, IX, iii, 77. See also Christian Walz, *Rhetores Graeci*,
1832-36, viii, pp. 475, 517, 562, 687, 710 ; ix, p. 16 ; and Carl von Halm,
Rhetores Latini Minores, 1863, pp. 11, 18-19, 30, 67-8, 433, 481, 610.

[3] *De Eloquentia*, xxvii-xxix.

[4] *De Compositione Verborum*, xxiii.

[5] *De Oratore*, II, xxi, 88.

[6] See *supra* for it and for other rhyming passages from Ennius quoted by
Cicero.

[7] *Tusculanae Disputationes*, III, xix, 46.

sede " ; [1] " Abiit, excessit, evasit, erupit " ; [2] " Intelliges nihil illius liniamentis nisi eorum pigmentorum . . . florem et colorem defuisse " ; [3] " nomen ut nostrum illustretur et celebretur tuis " ; [4] " At haec etiam servis semper libera fuerunt, timerent, gauderent, dolerent suo potius, quam alterius arbitrio." [5] When in the *Orator* he discusses the means of giving pleasure to the ear he cites a particularly jingling passage from his own speech *Pro Milone* :—" Est igitur haec, iudices, non scripta, sed nata lex, quam non didicimus, accepimus, legimus, verum ex natura ipsa adripuimus, hausimus, expressimus, ad quam non docti, sed facti, non instituti, sed imbuti sumus." [6] And he complacently remarks of it :—" Haec enim talia sunt, ut, quia referuntur eo quo debent referri, intellegamus non quaesitum esse numerum, sed secutum." [7] If, he admits, certain *lumina verborum* are to be used only sparingly and unobtrusively in forensic contests, yet there are many other kinds of prose, epideictic oratory and its derivatives, in which these deliberate figures have a proper place and give pleasure :—" Ab hac [sc. nutrice] et verborum copia alitur et eorum constructio et numerus liberiore quadam fruitur licentia ; datur etiam venia concinnitati sententiarum et arguti certique et circumscripti verborum ambitus conceduntur, de industriaque non ex insidiis, sed aperte ac palam elaboratur, ut verba verbis quasi demensa et paria respondeant, ut crebro conferantur pugnantia comparenturque contraria, et ut pariter extrema terminentur eundemque referent in cadendo sonum." [8]

VIII

Since quantitative verse was an alien imposition on Latin which had naturally strong accents, it was likely, or even bound to lose its hold when the circumstances which had favoured its tyranny changed. Quantitative verse with its carefully selected vocabulary and its arbitrary classification of longs and shorts was appreciated only by the lettered few whose culture was Hellenised and civic, and who used for most literary purposes— the exceptions were in the spheres of comedy, satire, and the familiar letter—a dialect different from the speech of the un-

---

[1] *Pro Caelio*, xxxii.   [2] *In Catilinam*, ii,   [3] *Brutus*, lxxxvii, 298.
[4] *Epistulae ad Familiares*, V, xii, 1.
[5] *Ibid.*, XI, xxviii, 3.   [6] *Pro Milone*, iv, 10.   [7] *Orator*, xlix, 165.
[8] *Orator*, xii, 37-8 ; cf. *ibid.*, xxxix, 135, and *De Oratore*, III, liv, 206.

lettered many and the peasants.   But in the later periods the
literary dialect began to lose ground and the dialects of non-
literary occasions, the *sermo cotidianus*, the *sermo plebeius*, and
the *sermo rusticus*, reasserted themselves.   They entered into
bolder competition with the dialect of culture, partly as a result
of the disintegration of stylistic standards in the latter, but still
more because many persons in high places spoke metropolitan
Latin imperfectly.   Thus Hadrian, though born in Rome,
made the Senate laugh when he first spoke in it by the rusticity
of his pronunciation,[1] and Septimius Severus never lost his
African accent, and had to blush for his own sister's ignorance
of Latin.[2]   The spread of Latin as a *lingua franca* all over
the Empire—a spoken Latin which abounded in provincial
variations and in which the natural tendencies of the language
had free play far from the restraints of metropolitan *littérateurs*
—the flooding of the vocabulary with new words from many
sources, the decay of Greek studies and fashions, the study,
citation, and imitation by revivalists from the time of Hadrian
of pre-Ciceronian writers, and the general exhaustion of literature
were other factors in the undermining of metrical conventions.

As early as the second century A.D., long and short vowels
were tending to be pronounced more and more alike, and poets
were beginning to relax the quantitative rules.   The difficulties of
deciding whether a syllable was long or short increased in the
third century, as can be seen in the work of Nemesianus (*floruit*
280), and by the end of the fourth century Ausonius (*c.* 310-95),
Avianus (*floruit* 390) and Rutilius Namatianus (*floruit* 410)
show that the distinction between long and short had probably
been largely lost as regards unstressed syllables, though it may
have survived for the stressed during the next century.

That is to say, the accent inherent in the nature of the language
more and more prevailed.   It had never in verse lost its appeal
to the masses.   A popular accentual verse, derived from the
ancient Saturnian, had run alongside the quantitative all through
the Golden and the Silver Ages, even as in England the old
alliterative verse of the Anglo-Saxons survived in popular use
from the Conquest till its reappearance in literature in the second
half of the fourteenth century.   Of such *populares versus* naturally
only a few have been recorded as having been sung by soldiers

[1] Aelius Spartianus, *Hadrianus*, iii.
[2] Aelius Spartianus, *Severus*, xix and xv.

at triumphs, shouted by cat-calling citizens, or scribbled on statues and walls by the disaffected. I shall quote one or two of them which happen to contain rhymes or jingles :—

> Urbani, seruate uxores : moechum calvom adducimus.
> Aurum in Gallia effutuisti, hic sumpsisti mutuum ; [1]

> Gallos Caesar in triumphum ducit, idem in curiam ;
> Galli bracas deposuerunt, latum clavum sumpserunt ; [2]

> Pater argentarius, ego Corinthiarius. [3]

These specimens belong to the camp, the forum, and the tavern. But it was probably in the rural districts of Italy that accentual verses, *versus rhythmici* as they were called to distinguish them from *versus metrici*, flourished. After referring to the expulsion of Saturnian verse from polite literature by the conquering metres of Greece, Horace adds :—

> sed in longum tamen aevum
> manserunt hodieque manent vestigia ruris. [4]

And there are many other allusions to these rustic melodies. [5]

IX

Contemporaneously with the waning of classical Latin literature especially with the decline of the Empire after Marcus Aurelius's death in 180 A.D., a new Christian Latin literature was gaining strength. It began with apologetics in prose and spread to poetry only in the second half of the third century.

Both in prose and in verse the Christian writers had something new and vital clamouring for expression. They had to find an utterance at once fitting, and intelligible for vaster and less easily defined concepts than had concerned their pagan predecessors, the tremendous truths of Omnipotence, Omniscience, and Omnipresence, of Trinity in Unity, of Incarnation and

---

[1] Sung, according to Suetonius, *Julius Caesar*, li, by the troops at Caesar's Gallic triumph.

[2] Sung by the populace ; *cf*. Suetonius, *ibid*, lxxx.

[3] Scribbled on Octavian's statue ; *cf*. Suetonius, *Augustus*, lxx.

[4] *Epistles*, II, i, 159-60.

[5] See L. A. Muratori, *Antiquitates Italicae medii aevi*, 1773-78, dissertatio 40, *De Rythmica Veterum Poesi et de Origine Italicae Poeseos*, viii, 214-306.

Resurrection, of the Eternal Logos, and of Infinite Love. But they were hampered by the inadequacy of the current Latin.

By this time, as Archbishop Trench says, Latin " had reached its climacteric, and was indeed verging, though as yet this fact was scarcely perceptible, toward decay, with the stiffness of commencing age already upon it . . . something to which a new life might perhaps be imparted, but the first life of which was well-nigh overlived. . . . And we do observe the language under the new influence, as at the breath of a second spring, putting itself forth anew, budding and blossoming afresh, the meaning of words enlarging and dilating, old words coming to be used in new and higher significations, obsolete words reviving, new words being coined—with much in all this to offend the classical taste, which yet, being inevitable, ought not to offend, and with gains which far more than compensated the losses." [1] The chief monument of Vulgar Latin is the Vulgate Bible of St Jerome (*c.* 340-420). He took as his basis the language of the masses in his day, which, if it admitted many neologisms, also retained words not at all new though studiously avoided by classical writers. Master of expression as he was, he practically created a new language out of it. The stiff, inflexional Latin acquired an unexpected suppleness and scope, while it kept much of its original dignity and strength. On this foundation the liturgy of the Church was built and therefore the Latin of the medieval world. [2]

Finding the metres of pagan poetry ready to their hands, the Christian poets naturally adopted them. These metres, however, had two defects. In the first place they were too rigid. They were struck out for the carriage of certain restricted emotions and certain circumscribed concepts : they pertained peculiarly to the classical view of life and the classical response to life. But " [t]he boundless could not be content to find its organ in that, of which the very perfection lay in its limitations and its bounds . . . a versification . . . attached . . . by no living bonds to the thoughts, in which sense and sound had no real correspondence with one another." [3] Since the rhythm of vital

---

[1] *Op. cit.,* pp. 5-6.

[2] *Cf.* H. H. Milman, *History of Latin Christianity, including that of the Popes to Nicholas V,* 1854-5, i, 74 ; and Frederick Brittain, *The Medieval Latin and Romance Lyric to A.D 1300,* 1937, p. 6.

[3] R. C. Trench, *op. cit.,* p. 8.

poetry is an intimate and inalienable possession, Christian poetry was forced to find a versification with an intellectual value, " which should associate it with the onward movement of the thoughts and feelings, whereof it professed to be . . . the expression." [1]

The other defect of the quantitative measures for Christian purposes was more practical, in that they excluded a vast number of words for metrical reasons, many of them words of the utmost importance for Christian thought and feeling. " One has but to turn to the lyrical poems of Horace, to become at once aware of the wealth of words, which, for the writer of the hexameter and pentameter may be said not to exist. What a world, for example, of noble epithets—tumultuosus, luctuosus, iniuriosus, formidolosus, fraudulentus, contumax, pervicax, insolens, intaminatus, fastidiosus, periculosus—with many more among the most poetical words in the language, are under the ban of a perpetual exclusion.[2] The very word *ecclesia* could never appear in the pentameter, and in the hexameter only in one of its cases.[3] The Latin poets of the classical period had themselves been only too conscious of the metrical restrictions on their choice of words, and had been forced to adopt ingenious circumventions without, however, being able thereby to solve all their problems. Thus Ovid has to admit the impossibility of bringing the name of his friend Tuticanus into his elegiac verse except by unworthy subterfuges :—

> Quo minus in nostris ponaris, amice, libellis,
>   nominis efficitur condicione tui . . .
> lex pedis officio fortunaque nominis obstat,
>   quaque meos adeas est via nulla modos.
> nam pudet in geminos ita nomen scindere versus,
>   desinat ut prior hoc incipiatque minor.
> et pudeat, si te, qua syllaba parte moratur,
>   artius adpellem Tuticănumque vocem.
> nec potes in versum Tŭticani more uenire,
>   fiat ut e longa syllaba prima brevis,
> aut producatur, quae nunc correptius exit,
>   et sic porrecta longa secunda mora [4]

---

[1] R. C. Trench,, *op. cit.*, p. 8.

[2] *Ibid.*, p. 10, note 1.

[3] Hence St Paulinus of Nola (353-431) has to scan it *ĕclēsĭă* in his *Carmina*, xv, 117, whereas Venantius Fortunatus (530-609) scans it *ecclēsĭa* in his *Miscellanea*, III, vi, 24.

[4] *Epistolae ex Ponto*, IV, xii, 1-2, 5-14.

,imilarly Horace could only allude to a little town on the
oad to Brundisium without naming it :—

> quod versu dicere non est,
> signis perfacile est ; [1]

oth Horace [2] and Lucilius [3] had to have recourse to a circum-
ocution because the nominative of Valerius cannot be accom-
nodated in a hexameter ; and Lucilius had to take the same
vay to indicate a certain festival :—

> Servorum est festus dies hic
> quem plane hexametro versu non dicere possis.[4]

Martial's " Musae severiores " would not allow him to fall back
on a Greek licence in order to fit Earinus into a hendecasyllabic
ine.[5]

It was natural, therefore, in view of the less strict observance
oy classical poets themselves of the quantitative rules and in
view also of the cramping effect of these same rules on the
expression of the Christian *ethos* that even from the outset the
Christian poets, with Lactantius (*c.* 260-*c.* 340) as a notable
exception if the poems generally attributed to him are really
his, made greater or less departures from the time-honoured
moulds. The signs of their emancipation were two :—" the
first being the [further and more thorough] disintegration of
the old prosodical system of Latin verse, under the gradual
substitution of accent for quantity ; and second, the employment
of rhyme, within, or at the close of the verse, as a means of
marking rhythm, and a device for the producing of melody." [6]

Though these two processes were interdependent and con-
current, for the sake of clarity I shall take them separately,
beginning with the substitution of accent for quantity.

X

The first Christian poet in Latin belonged to Africa—" ex
Africa semper aliquid novi " [7]—; this was Commodianus who
wrote as an elderly man probably in the second half of the third

---

[1] *Satires*, I, v, 87-8.   [2] *Ibid.*, I, vi, 12.
[3] E. H. Warmington, *Remains of Old Latin*, 1938, iii, p. 404-5.
[4] *Ibid.*, iii, 78-9.   [5] IX, xii, 13-17.
[6] R. C. Trench, *op. cit.*, p. 2.
[7] *Cf.* Pliny, *Historia Naturalis*, viii, 42.

L

century.[1]   His poems show the almost complete collapse o
quantity and the restoration of accent in full vigour.   Th
Instructiones, consisting of seventy-nine poems, are in verse whic
maintains the apparent framework of the hexameter but fills i
out on the accentual principle :—

> Praefatio nostra viam erranti demonstrat
> respectumque bonum, cum venerit saeculi meta,
> aeternum fieri, quod discredunt inscia corda :
> ego similiter erravi tempore multo. [2]

The same kind of *versus politici*, as they have been called, ar
found in the pseudodactyls [3] of Commodian's *Carmen Apolo
geticum* in which only 26 out of the 1060 lines are quantitativel
correct.   He is generally right in his stressed syllables, anc
negligent in his unstressed.   Almost certainly these poems wer
not isolated phenomena.

In the fourth century the Church itself recognised the valu
of verse in its services.   Gradually it built up a written liturg
to take the place of extemporary worship, and to that liturg
were admitted hymns which like the *Gloria in excelsis* and th
Te Deum were at first in rhythmical prose or free verse, bu
which before the end of the fourth century were assuming fixec
verse and stanzaic forms to be sung to a recurring melody by a
congregation.   Such were the hymns of St Hilary of Poitier
(*c.* 300-367)

Certainly the next hymnodist, St Ambrose (*c.* 340-398), wa
strictly correct in his quantities.   But he chose the iambi
dimeter which, as Archbishop Trench points out,[4] is the least
markedly metrical and the most nearly rhythmical of all th
ancient metres appropriate to his purpose.   Thus his auster
hymns, like the *Veni, Redemptor gentium*, have a strong rhythm
which takes its force from the accents, so that the " rhythmic
syllabic character of the poetry of Ambrose marks in reality
the beginnings of Romance versification, not because it was no
known before him, but because of his constant adherence to th

[1] Perhaps, however, in the fourth century ; *cf.* Frederick Brittain, *op. cit.*,
pp. 2-3.

[2] I, i, 1-4.

[3] The lines are meant to end with a dactyl followed by a spondee, but as a
rule he achieves only accentual dactyls and spondees.

[4] *Op. cit.*, p. 14.

system on account of its popularity and effectiveness with the mass of the faithful." [1]

Such verse as St Ambrose's catechumen, St Augustine (353-430), wrote was not in the form of hymns, but of didactic poetry in pretty much the same class as that of his fellow-countryman, Commodian. It departed metrically even further than did Commodian's from classical rules. It is not only regulated entirely by accent, but it is generally isosyllabic with a norm of sixteen syllables and a middle caesura. St Augustine was what in modern parlance might be called a realist in language, deliberately rejecting a Ciceronianism of style and diction in favour of the more effective appeal of contemporary idiom.[2] It is therefore not surprising that he was a realist in versification as well. He distinctly says that he chose for his *Psalmus contra partem Donati* a rhythm which would not hamper or restrict him in his choice of words.

His slightly older contemporary, Prudentius (348-*c*. 410), was scarcely less emancipated from classical rules and puts whatever words he needs into his verse in defiance of quantity. The " Horace and Virgil of the Christians," as Bentley called him, was by no means so classical as that title implies. " He still affects to write, and in the main does write, prosodically ; yet with largest licences. No one will suppose him . . . ignorant . . . of the quantitative value which the old classical poets of Rome, with whose writings he was evidently familiar, had attributed to words ; yet we continually find him attributing another value, postponing quantity to accent, or rather allowing accent to determine quantity. . . . The whole scheme of Latin prosody must have greatly loosened its hold, before he could have used the freedoms which he does use, in the shifting and altering of syllables." [3]

The change from quantitative to accentual verse was helped by the liturgical developments of the fourth, fifth, and later centuries. More and more hymns were required for the canonical hours daily—the Rule of St Benedict (*c*. 480-*c*. 544) directed that

---

[1] H. F. Muller and Pauline Taylor, *A Chrestomathy of Vulgar Latin*, 1932, p. 115.

[2] Not from any superstitious fear such as confirmed his contemporary, St Jerome, in his use of Vulgar Latin. St Jerome had been alarmed by a vision of damnation for being too Ciceronian.

[3] R. C. Trench, *op. cit.*, p. 9, note 1.

every hour should have its hymn—and for the many new festivals, for saints' days, and for other occasions. As the hymns from the time of St Hilary of Poitiers were generally in stanzas to be sung to recurring melodies, it· was natural to prefer metres which, unlike most classical ones, had a fixed number of syllables and did not need to be continually accommodated to the melodies.[1]

The process I have been tracing was completed at least as early as the hymns attributed to the Venerable Bede (672-735). If after the time of Bede correct enough hexameters, pentameters, sapphics, and other quantitative verses were occasionally written during the dark and the middle ages, accentual verse was by far the commoner and more popular.

XI

The history of the adoption of rhyme is almost exactly parallel to, and contemporaneous with, the history of the substitution of accent for quantity. Though new to Latin verse, at least in the degree in which it came to figure in the Latin poetry of Christianity, yet rhyme, as I have tried to show, was by no means unknown at any period of Latin literature. It seemed to agree well with Saturnian verse. Even after the introduction of quantitative verse in Ennius it looked at first as if it might be going to flourish. Though it did not do so and was indeed checked, it remained common enough and became more frequent in the later classical period.

In the Christian poetry of the third and fourth centuries it was subconsciously adopted by the poets to compensate for their quantitative deficiencies. This was the stage it had reached in Commodian who introduced rudimentary rhymes in -e and -ae, sporadically but frequently and deliberately. One section of his *Instructiones* ends every line with -o. St Ambrose, St Augustine, and Prudentius rhyme in the same occasional way.

In these writers and in their successors we can see the slow and uncertain evolution of a systematic use of rhyme. " At first the rhymes were often vowel or assonant ones, the consonants being required to agree ; or the rhyme was adhered to, when this was convenient, but disregarded as often as the needful word was not readily at hand ; or the stress of the rhyme was suffered to fall on an unaccented syllable, thus scarcely striking the ear,

[1] *Cf.* Frederick Brittain, *op. cit.*, pp. 7-8.

or it was limited to the similar termination of a single letter ;
while sometimes, on the strength of this like ending, as sufficiently
sustaining the melody, the whole other construction of the verse,
and the arrangement of syllables, was neglected." [1]   But at last
in the twelfth and thirteenth centuries, when it had triumphed in
Provençal poetry and was bringing the prosodic systems of the
other vernaculars to their medieval perfection, it took full
possession also of Latin verse, as in Adam of St Victor's sonorous
De Sanctis Evangelistis :—

> Jucundare, plebs fidelis,
> cuius Pater est in caelis,
> recolens Ezechielis
>   Prophetae praeconia :
> est Iohannes testis ipsi,
> dicens in Apocalypsi,
> vere vidi, vere scripsi
>   vera testimonia.[2]

[1] R. C. Trench, *op. cit.*, pp. 37-9.   [2] 1-8.

THE DIFFICULTY OF RHYMING

Rime the rack of finest wits,
That expresseth but by fits
    True Conceipt,
Spoyling Senses of their Treasure,
Cosening Judgement with a measure,
    But false weight.
        Ben Jonson, *A Fit of Rime against Rime*, 1-6.

Wer Grosses will muss sich zusammenraffen ;
  In der Beschränkung zeigt sich erst der Meister,
  Und das Gesetz nur kann uns Freiheit geben.
        Goethe, *Natur und Kunst* 12-14.

Ou plutôt, fée au léger
    Voltiger
Habile, agile courrière
  Qui mènes le char des vers
  Dans les airs
Par deux sillons de lumière !
        C. A. Sainte-Beuve, *À la Rime*, 43-48.

Ave, o bella imperatrice,
    O felice
Del latin metro reina !
Un ribelle ti saluta
    Combattuta,
E a te libero s'inchina.
        Giosue Carducci, *Alla Rima*, 55-60.

I

IN asserting that rhyme is an arbitrary requirement much to the poets' " vexation, hindrance, and constraint to express many things otherwise, and for the most part worse than else they would have exprest them," [1] Milton puts forward the commonest and most plausible argument in the case against rhyme. He was thereby perhaps rationalising a dislike which drew its main strength from his respect for classical modes and his scorn for

---

[1] *The Verse* of *Paradise Lost*, 1668.

the monkish and medieval. But this objection to rhyme on the score of difficulty is the only one which has any apparent weight at the present day, when æsthetic problems can no longer be solved as in Milton's time by appeals to authority and to classical prejudice. For it is the ground of the modern plea, not only for blank verse and other rhymeless metres (which, by the way, are no easier than rhyme if they are to be any good at all), but for the varieties of free verse which discard rhyme, metre, and stanza in order to isolate a supposed poetic essential and to capture some elusive poetic reality in a lightning flash.

(Incidentally, it is a curious commentary on Milton's objection to the restricting and distorting effect of rhyme that his predecessor Campion was disgusted rather by its facility. According to him, it was a " vulgar and easie kind of Poesie " which arose in " lack-learning times, and in barbarized Italy." [1] On the one hand, its " facilitie and popularitie " created " as many Poets, as a hot sommer flies " ; [2] and on the other, " many excellent wits " have been " deter'd . . . from the exercise of English poesy," by a custom so " vulgar and vnarteficiall," [3] so " lame and vnbeseeming " [4] compared with the difficult beauty of classical versifying.)

II

In actual practice Milton has no rival in his respect for, and command of, the architectonic of poetry. Nevertheless his objection to rhyme as a clog on expression implies, as do later demands for the emancipation of poetry from some or all metrical requirements, a debatable theory of the nature of poetry, namely that it is a matter of substance rather than of form. The implication is that a poem is distinct from the words and the organised design in which it subsists, since it may be better or worse according as the poet is free from, or constrained by, " the troublesom . . . bondage of Rimeing." [5] Having devoted himself for years to the composition of an epic " doctrinal and

---

[1] *Observations in the Art of English Poesy* in *Elizabethan Critical Essays*, ed. G. Gregory Smith, 1904, ii, p. 329.

[2] *Ibid.*, ii, p. 330.

[3] *Ibid.*, ii, p. 327.

[4] *Ibid.*, ii, p. 330. Campion (*ibid.*, ii, p. 331), however, also refers to rhyme as a Procrustean bed which " inforceth a man oftentimes to abiure his matter and extend a short conceit beyond all bounds of arte."

[5] *Op. cit.*

exemplary to a nation," [1] a great didactic poem of the utmost religious significance as a justification of the ways of God to man, Milton conceived of poetry as pre-existing material which might be damaged in its transmission from the poet to his public.

The sole duty of the poet who accepts this conception of poetry will be not beauty, but the most straightforward communication. In order to achieve his end with the least possible loss, however, he will have to abjure more than rhyme. He must give up metre as well because it is just as much of an encumbrance. He must guard against ambiguity and obscurity, understatement and overstatement by the abundant use of qualifying and saving clauses, modifiers, parentheses, connectives and transitions, definitions and technical terms, cross-references and footnotes. In short, he must drop the graces of rhetoric and the seductive charms of formal arrangement and anything that savours of art or the emotions or the transfiguring power of the imagination. He must write not poetry but gaunt, colour-less, Euclidean prose to make his readers, if he can, pursue one straight and narrow way to the truth, the whole truth, and nothing but the truth.

All this must he do. But the result will be only a compromise. Let the poet, if he can still be so named, not for one moment suppose that he will be able to express all his message in the baldest prose. The most conscientious and competent writer of prose knows only too well how, despite all his scruples and all his skill, it is but a poor vehicle for the carriage of ideas : there is always a precious residuum which prose cannot convey, not only discrete ideas which elude expression, but subsidiary and qualifying ideas to all degrees of subtlety, the delicate nuances and bloom of thought. For the prose-writer recording his ideas is like a man counting the stars who can tell those of the first, second, third, and perhaps lesser magnitudes, but has to give up exact enumeration when he comes to the star-clusters and the Milky Way.

> If all the pens that ever poets held,
> Had fed the feeling of their maisters thoughts,
> And every sweetness that inspir'd their harts,
> Their minds, and muses on admyred theames :
> If all the heavenly Quintessence they still
> From their immortall flowers of Poesy,

---

[1] *The Reason of Church Government* in *The Student's Milton*, ed. F. A. Patterson, 1930, p. 525.

Wherein as in a myrrour we perceive
The highest reaches of a humaine wit :
If these had made one Poems period
And all combin'd in Beauties worthinesse,
Yet should there hover in their restlesse heads,
One thought, one grace, one woonder at the least,
Which into words no vertue can digest.[1]

III

When Milton inspected the channel of ideas in the poet's mind, he penetrated no farther back than the parting of the ways into rhymed or unrhymed verse. But he was then, as it were, only at the beginning of an infinite regress. Before that last bifurcation of the channel there was an earlier one into metre or prose ; and before that again who knows how many others at each of which an idea would have to pause and choose which way it would go ? At some medial stage of the journey in " the dark backward and abysm "[2] of the poet's mind it existed only in some nondescript, fluid, and pre-verbal shape,

If shape it might be call'd that shape had none
Distinguishable in member, joynt, or limb,
Or substance might be call'd that shadow seem'd,
For each seem'd either.[3]

At what stage between an idea's first conception in the mind and its birth in expression is it at its prime, entire yet undistorted ? In some ways the answer is Never. For to force an idea from the less to the more defined is always to change it, and while it may gain steadily in definition it will lose steadily in freedom. As Carlyle says, " The faithfulest, most glowing word of a man is but an imperfect image of the thought . . . that dwells in him."[4]

But whereas the fullest possible communication is normally the primary purpose of prose as distinguished in spirit from poesy rather than merely in form from verse, communication is not the primary purpose of poetry, even the poetry of statement.

[1] Marlowe, 1 *Tamburlaine*, V, ii, 98-110.
[2] Shakespeare, *The Tempest*, I, ii, 50.
[3] Milton, *Paradise Lost*, ii, 667-70.
[4] *Latter-day Pamphlets* in *The People's Edition of Thomas Carlyle's Works*, 1888, xx, p. 172.

Or rather what poetry tries to communicate is itself, not something else for which it is only the vehicle.

> Forget not, brother singer ! that though Prose
>   Can never be too truthful or too wise,
> Song is not Truth, not Wisdom, but the rose
>   Upon Truth's lips, the light in Wisdom's eyes.[1]

As Archbishop Whately puts it, " Poetry is not distinguished from Prose by superior Beauty of thought or of expression, but is a distinct kind of composition ; and they produce, when each is excellent in its kind, distinct kinds of pleasure." [2] They happen to use the same medium of language but in quite different ways and for quite different purposes ; as the stonemason uses stone and the house-painter paint in ways and for purposes entirely different from those of Meštrović and Cézanne respectively.

Language is of such a nature that a statement can, strictly speaking, be made only in one way : any change in the words or their order, even in the punctuation or the emphasis, results in another statement more or less different. The task both of the poet and of the prose-writer is to choose the optimum out of an infinite number of arrangements. But each must also ask himself, The best for what ? The prose-writer's answer will be, For the clearest and most adequate expression of an idea requiring only definition by words, which are purely instrumental. The poet's answer, however, will be, For the achievement of the most artistic synthesis of thought, emotion, and perception, which can be completed only in the words and the design expressing it and of which the words and the design form an integral part. (Such at least is the ideal distinction, on which for the sake of clarity I would insist. At the same time I recognise that there can be no rigid line of demarcation. It may be possible for poetry to be pure and without any infusion of the prosaic ; but it is not possible for prose, even the simplest, to be without some admixture of the poetic by way of emotion or imagination or artistic management.) Thus whereas prose is a means to an end (*ratio prima*), poetry is an end in itself (*ratio ultima*), the creation in words of a design—an æsthetically satisfying coherence of parts. Or, in other words, prose is the useful, and poetry the fine, art of words.

---

[1] Sir William Watson, *To* ——, 1-4.
[2] *Elements of Rhetoric*, 1850, p. 216.

IV

Now in none of the fine arts does the artist conceive of a work of art in a spiritual abstract utterly apart from the contamination of the physical medium. The artist's experience is conceived in terms of his medium ; he is peculiarly sensitive to its characteristic qualities ; and his desire to create is a desire directed to, and conditioned by, the possibilities and the resistances of the medium. The originating idea longs for union with the physical and is nothing till that union is consummated. For art is the quality of spirit sensuously apprehended and made sensuously apprehensible. It is something beyond sense, yet experienced through sense and laying a double spell on spirit and sense alike.

Thus what any artist has to " say " can be " said " in terms of his art and its medium, but not otherwise. A musician, a sculptor, or a painter does not " say " anything except his music, his sculpture, or his painting, and there can be no other way of " saying " it, for what the artist " says " and his way of " saying " it are one and the same. Similarly poetry is also something as said, not a thing apart from the saying.

In poetic creation an idea does not spring from nowhere into the poet's mind to be dressed up in words by him trying and rejecting them like a man trying on boots or hats. The creative process is more like the way in which spiders spin their webs :— just as from the spider's spinnerets exude several glutinous streams of silk which coalesce to form the gossamer thread, so in the poet's mind the several streams of thought, emotion, perception, and expression coalesce in one complex but indissoluble thread which we call a poem. The union of the diverse constituents is as complete and mysterious as the interaction of soul and body.

As in Spenser's Garden of Adonis—

> there is the first seminary
> Of all things that are borne to live and dye,
> According to their kynds [1]—

there exists in the poet's mind a state of creative flux in which the fluid sap rises up into poems, each poem springing from a unique seed which grows by its own laws into its own otherwise

---

[1] *The Faerie Queene*, III, vi, 30.

incommunicable self. The true poem has its form, not as a thing arbitrary, but as a thing vital and essential, " the manifestation and utterance of its innermost life . . . the making visible, so far as that is possible, of its most essential spirit." [1] The form of a poem is its incarnation.

But artistic incarnation of any kind is always the result of struggle against the obstruction offered by the medium on the one hand and against the formal limitations on the other. An artist's creativeness thus functions only within constraint and through opposition ; and a work of art is the result of a drawn battle between the energy of the artist and the stubbornness of his medium and his form.

V

And the poet is not content with the line of least resistance. In the words of Hobbes, he seeks " glory from a needlesse difficulty." [2] For in the height of his creative energy he must command difficulties he has himself invented and make them, if possible, contribute to his triumph. The poet is ποιητής, a maker or shaper, a creator on a minor scale who abhors the inchoate and from the welter devises, not a mere lump like a piece of dough or butter, but the most beautiful and significant shape in which spirit and form grow one with delight. He has an imperative desire to get the whole right with an entire absence of frustration. So far, however, from his being a lawless ranger and the better the freer he is from restrictions, he has adopted instinctively law and order, long before he deliberately (and much less successfully) experimented in prosodic and formal anarchy. He has voluntarily fettered himself not only with rhyme and its kin, assonance, alliteration, refrains, and the like, but with metre and all its exigencies. He has invented complicated rhyme schemes, the sonnet, the ballade, the canzone, and other schemes like the Sapphic and the strophic odes which are not less complicated for being unrhymed.

> If by dull rhymes our English must be chain'd,
> And, like Andromeda, the Sonnet sweet
> Fetter'd, in spite of pained loveliness ;

[1] R. C. Trench, *Sacred Latin Poetry, chiefly Lyrical*, 1874, p. 1.
[2] *The Answer of Mr Hobbes to Sr Will. D'Avenant's Preface before Gondibert* in *Critical Essays of the Seventeenth Century*, ed. J. E. Spingarn, 1908-9, ii, p. 57.

Let us find out, if we must be constrain'd,
   Sandals more interwoven and complete
      To fit the naked foot of poesy ;
   Let us inspect the lyre, and weigh the stress
Of every chord, and see what may be gain'd
   By ear industrious, and attention meet ;
      Misers of sound and syllable, no less
         Than Midas of his coinage, let us be
         Jealous of dead leaves in the bay wreath crown ;
      So, if we may not let the Muse be free,
         She will be bound with garlands of her own.[1]

VI

It is a mistake, too, to regard the resistances offered either by
the poet's medium or by his chosen form only as obstacles and
not also as supports. They are indeed like the water through
which a swimmer has to force his way but which at the same
time buoys him up and without which he could not swim at all.[2]

Though poets often complain of the obstinacy of words in
particular, their complaints are like the murmuring of fascinated
lovers : language may indeed be a difficult mistress,

> Hard, but oh the glory of the winning were she won.[3]

Words are for them not mere symbols which stand for things but

---

[1] Keats, a sonnet on the sonnet. I have tried to indicate by indenting the
complexity of the rhyme-scheme which, according to an alphabetical notation,
is as follows :—a b c a b d c a b c d e d e. *Cf.* Wordsworth's similar sonnet
on the sonnet in *Miscellaneous Sonnets*, Part I, i. :—

Nuns fret not at their convent's narrow room ;
   And hermits are contented with their cells ;
   And students with their pensive citadels ;
Maids at the wheel, the weaver at his loom,
Sit blithe and happy ; bees that soar for bloom,
   High as the highest Peak of Furness-fells,
   Will murmur by the hour in foxglove bells :
In truth the prison, unto which we doom
      Ourselves, no prison is : and hence for me,
         In sundry moods, 'twas pastime to be bound
         Within the Sonnet's scanty plot of ground ;
      Pleased if some Souls (for such there needs must be)
      Who have felt the weight of too much liberty,
         Should find brief solace there, as I have found.

[2] Cf. *Immanuel Kant's Critique of Pure Reason*, ed. Norman Kemp Smith,
1929, p. 47.

[3] Meredith, *Love in a Valley*, 16.

are themselves nothing. As the wind makes no music till it sings through the trees, so the wind of the poet's inspiration is dumb till it is entangled in the thickets of words. " [I]n poetry of the first order," says F. W. H. Myers, " almost every word (to use a mathematical metaphor) is raised to a higher power. It continues to be an articulate sound and a logical step in the argument ; but it becomes also a musical sound and a centre of emotional force. It becomes a musical sound ;—that is to say, its consonants and vowels are arranged to bear a relation to the consonants and vowels near it,—a relation of which accent, quantity, rhyme, assonance, and alliteration are specialised forms, but which may be of a character more subtle than any of these. And it becomes a centre of emotional force ; that is to say, the complex associations which it evokes modify the associations evoked by other words in the same passage in a way quite distinct from grammatical or logical connection." [1] The poet, therefore, must try to use all the possibilities, declaratory, musical, and emotive, of his medium and organise it to the highest degree for his purpose :—" not speaking (table talke fashion or like men in a dreame) words as they chanceably fall from the mouth, but peyzing each sillable of each worde by iust proportion according to the dignitie of the subiect." [2]

Moreover the poet, wrestling with his words like Jacob with the angel, often wins a blessing beyond his expectation. For by some mere arrangements of sound he will secure an effect which neither he nor any one else could have predicted. Like a magician accidentally stumbling on a magic formula, he some-times releases some mysterious power in his medium which no known laws can explain but which conduces miraculously to his intention. A similar surprising spontaneity is found from time to time in the media of the other arts as well. There is in them all now resistance, now support, and yet again an unexpected generosity. They are sometimes tyrants whom nothing can bend, sometimes slaves who can be made more or less willingly to obey, and sometimes the friendliest of spirits or bottle imps who guide the artist's hand in a way better than his best. The artist is, therefore, an adventurer going out to seek what he can find, not a pedlar who knows exactly all that his bundle contains

---

[1] *Virgil* in *Essays Classical and Modern*, 1921, p. 115.
[2] Sidney, *An Apology for Poetry* in *Elizabethan Critical Essays*, edited by G. Gregory Smith, 1904, i., p. 160.

before he unties it. His medium is not an easy vehicle to carry
what he wants and whither. It will carry, but in its own way
and in a direction which is something of a compromise ; and
what is carried will be shaken to fit into its receptacles.

VII

In the very nature of language, which has to ring the changes
on a limited number of sounds, there inheres the certainty of
occasional jingles. In several, perhaps all, languages they are
also instinctively struck out in jingling compounds and proverbial
phrases, of which English is full :—hugger-mugger, high and
dry, health and wealth, near and dear, namby-pamby. Rhyme
in verse is the deliberate use of this latent characteristic and the
regularising of this innate tendency.

It is to be classed with other means employed by poets for
the exalting of their language. The poet who like Spenser writes
in what Ben Jonson called " no Language "[1]—and most poets
write in a diction differentiated from the speech of the day by
its mere accommodation to metre, by selection and omission, by
archaisms, innovations, and the like—lays restrictions on his
language, just as much as does the poet who demands of his
language that it shall rhyme. A conditioned language has no
doubt greater negative restrictions ; but it has also greater
positive virtues for poetic purposes.

The management of a conditioned language might be likened
to the dragging of a magnet through sand sown with iron grains.
Even so the poet drags his attractive concept through the riches
of his vocabulary. From right and left the relevant words and
phrases fly, and the irrelevant are passed over as mere grit
pro hac vice. Of the vast heap of words only a handful is valid :
many indeed are called but few are chosen. The poet who adds
rhyme to his other requirements in expression is merely making
more rare and precious what he selects ; he is doing something
analogous to Dante's advice to his brother poets—to put their
words through a sieve until only the combed out and shaggy
urban words were left for use in the illustrious vulgar tongue.[2]
But whatever conditions the poet imposes on his diction, it is

---

[1] *Timber, or Discoveries* in *Critical Essays of the Seventeenth Century*,
ed. J. E. Spingarn, 1908-9, i, p. 34.

[2] *De Vulgari Eloquentia*, II, vii.

nearer the truth to say that from the outset he works in the conditioned style than that he is always translating from the unconditioned to the conditioned. Thus the need of rhyming, like any other of his requirements, is so actively present in his mind that when he is working spontaneously he does not begin to look for a rhyme after he has written the previous line : the rhyme-scheme inheres in his idea of the poem-to-be and regulates the movement of his mind *ab initio*.

In any case language which has to rhyme is far more pliable to the poet than we might think, even though at times he groans at its stubbornness. When a poet rhymes well, he has mastered his medium thoroughly. The result is as if he had *invented* a language which has rhyme as one of its natural characteristics and which by an unforeseen luck turns out to be intelligible to his readers. He makes the language which is the daily drudge of ordinary life and prose also the servant of the highest art, like Prospero controlling the willing-unwilling spirits by his "rough magic." [1] He makes the language anew : in his hands it is born again with rhymes as graces of the new birth. Dante often declared, according to his son and first commentator, that never did a rhyme force him to say anything otherwise than he wanted to, and that frequently by means of his rhymes he had made words to express what they were not wont to express for other poets. For language finds a new harmony when a master of it makes its instruments call each to each.

VIII

It is a fact that poets have not only written great poetry without rhyme—a feat remarkable enough—but they have also written great poetry with it. What then ? Are we to say in the face of a great poem like *Lycidas* that because of the necessity of building "the lofty rhyme" [2] it is less great than it might have been ? Surely not ; for quite apart from the loss of the graces of rhyme—and most enemies of rhyme would concede it some absolute beauty if it did not in their opinion cost too much —we have no means whatever of estimating the compensating gain.

Moreover, though there may be lapses in even the greatest

---

[1] Shakespeare, *The Tempest*, V, i, 50.
[2] Milton, *Lycidas*, 11.

poets when the exigencies of rhyme have proved too much for them or they have been careless, rhyme is no more a detachable element in a poem than any of the others in it are. And none of these elements can be retained by the poet except at a price, and that sometimes exorbitant. When rhyme is handled as it ought to be, as it can be, and as it generally is by the poets who have any right to the name, the reader has no feeling whatever that the poets have been forced by a pre-existing and therefore rigid language, made still more rigid by the necessity of rhyming, " to express many things otherwise, and for the most part worse than else they would have exprest them." [1] I do not deny the difficulty of composition in rhyme : I only assert the triumph when the difficulty is surmounted, the real beauty of the accomplishment, and its seeming inevitability. *Omnia praeclara difficilia.*

[1] Milton, *The Verse* of *Paradise Lost,* 1668.

M

RHYME AND NO RHYME

Tho' I should wander *Terra* o'er,
    In all her climes,
Grant me but this, I ask no more,
    Ay rowth o' rhymes.
          Robert Burns, *Epistle to James Smith*, 123-6.

I

By its very nature rhyme is primarily an appeal to the ear, and it is probably, in some degree at least, pleasing in all languages. But its delectability and therefore its artistic value vary from language to language. It is likely to be more agreeable and valuable in languages in which it is not too common and easy on the one hand and in which accent rather than quantity is the basis of versification on the other. Such, I think, are the most fundamental conditions for its natural adoption.

But every language is a law to itself. It can neither receive the practice of another nor communicate its own ; it has not only a genius of its own and a peculiar speech-habit, but also a tradition and a history which are just as powerful. And " no method of gratifying the ear by *measured sound*, which experience has found pleasing, is to be neglected by the poet ; and although, from the different structure and genius of languages, these methods will be different, the studious application of such methods, as each particular language allows, becomes a necessary part of his office. He will only cultivate those methods most, which tend to produce, in a given language, the most harmonious structure or measure, of which it is capable." [1]

But though every language, if given free play, will be true to its own nature and faithful to its past, a literature may be deflected from its course by the experiments and examples of a few influential poets. These poets may be more influential than great or wise, and their examples may seriously mislead. For poetry is not always or often irresistible and unconscious

---

[1] Richard Hurd, *On the Idea of Universal Poetry* in Q. *Horatii Flacci Epistolae ad Pisones, et Augustum*, 1776, ii, pp. 156-7.

inspiration : it is generally more or less deliberate and artificial. But the experimentalist often thinks of strong reasons for doing the wrong thing, and the innovator often convinces himself that whatever is new is therefore good. The fact is, however, that the more theoretical and new-fangled a poet is, the more chancy the result.

II

Thus the classical versifiers in the sixteenth and seventeenth centuries did not sufficiently recognise the genius of English and its difference from Greek. Ascham, for example, supposed that " by right *Imitation* of the perfit Grecians " [1] English could be brought, as Latin had been, to " trew versifiying." [2] Sidney considered English to be more suited than any other vernacular for both quantity and accent.[3] Webbe patriotically believed that if only English had enjoyed " the true kind of versifying in immitation of Greekes and Latines " [4] it would long since have equalled the best in any other tongue. Why, indeed, should it not even in that late day proceed to the glory which was its due ? For just as the Latins had done, Englishmen could fit their language to receive the new covenant, and one great example in quantitative verse would be enough to establish its use. With more caution Puttenham, who in his heart of hearts preferred accent and rhyme, came to a similar conclusion.[5] So also did Campion with a subversive enthusiasm for quantity which rivalled Webbe's.[6]

On the other side in the debate Daniel drew his weightiest argument for the continuance of rhyme in English from " Custome that is before all Law, Nature that is aboue all Arte. Euery language hath her proper number or measure fitted to vse and

---

[1] *The Schoolmaster* in *Elizabethan Critical Essays*, ed. G. Gregory Smith, 1904, i, 29.

[2] *Ibid.*, i, 30.

[3] *An Apology for Poetry* in *Elizabethan Critical Essays*, ed. G. Gregory Smith, 1904, i, 204-5.

[4] *A Discourse of English Poetry* in *Elizabethan Critical Essays*, ed. G. Gregory Smith, 1904, i, 278.

[5] *The Art of English Poesy* in *Elizabethan Critical Essays*, ed. G. Gregory Smith, 1904, ii, 117-24.

[6] *Observations in the Art of English Poesy* in *Elizabethan Critical Essays*, ed. G. Gregory Smith, 1904, ii, 327 *et seq.* Campion (*ibid.*, p. 333) and Ascham (*op. cit.*, p. 30) rejected the English hexameter.

delight, which Custome, intertaininge by the allowance of the Eare, doth indenize and make naturall." [1] Very much the same opinion is expressed by Bacon in the magisterial Latin of the *De Augmentis Scientiarum* :—" Illud reprehendendum, quod quidam antiquitatis nimium studiosi linguas modernas ad mensuras antiquas (heroïcas, elegiacas, sapphicas, etc.) traducere conati sunt : quas ipsarum linguarum fabrica respuit, nec minus aures exhorrent. In huiusmodi rebus sensus iudicium artis praeceptis praeponendum. . . . Neque vero ars est, sed artis abusus, cum illa naturam non perficiat sed pervertat." [2]

III

In Greek and Latin, which are highly inflected languages loaded with identical terminations indicating case, gender, number, tense, and mood, rhyming is easy. But even so, though the Greeks generally avoided it, the Latins had a hankering after it and did not altogether reject it, the reason being as I have suggested elsewhere, that whereas Greek accent is light, Latin accent is heavy and there is a natural affinity between accent and rhyme. If Latin had been left to follow its own bent, the heavy accent would have produced spontaneous rhyming despite its ease, as indeed is proved by the poetry of the early period before the introduction of Greek measures and by the poetry of the late period after these measures had lost their authority. As it happened, Latin forwent accent and incipient rhyme and adopted an artificial prosody, not however (*pace* Milton) in order to be freer but to bind itself hand and foot or foot and foot by metres so complex, especially in the lyrical measures, that the values of many or most of the syllables was predetermined and verse composition was of the lapidary kind.

Now in all the languages in which it occurs, rhyme is a well-nigh spontaneous result of the natural desire for periodic recurrences, proportion, and limitation. All metre, accentual or quantitative, comes from the realisation that if passion is to have its maximum momentum and not run to waste it requires

[1] *A Defence of Rhyme* in *Elizabethan Critical Essays*, ed. G. Gregory Smith, 1904, ii, 359. This is also very much Puttenham's opinion (*op. cit.*, ii, pp. 117-18, 123-4), though he was prepared to discuss the possibility of English quantity.

[2] *The Works of Francis Bacon*, ed. James Spedding, R. L. Ellis, and D. D. Heath, 1870-2, i, pp. 656-7.

restraints; and these restraints which poetry accepts for its own ultimate good must be somehow made distinctly noticeable to the ear.

The quantitative poetry of the ancients was just as much obliged to do so as is the rhyming poetry of the moderns, though in another way. The Greek or Roman listener knew when the turns of the lines came because of the identically weighted syllables. The hexameter interchanged spondees and dactyls within the line, but normally closed on a dactyl followed by a spondee. Likewise the pentameter, the choliambic, and the Sapphic, Alcaic, and Asclepiadean, to name a few other examples, had each an invariable ending, whatever metrical options they allowed within the body of the line. Had dactyls and spondees been used promiscuously anywhere in, let us say, the hexameter, no satisfying token would have indicated the close of the line to the ear; and if the hearer had once missed the close, he would have had some difficulty in detecting it again. But the arrangement of fixed dactyl and spondee for the close answered the same purpose as rhyme. The turn of the verses was thus marked by quantitative identities—similitude in time with dissimilitude in sound, or a kind of muffled or quantitative rhyme.

IV

In the modern languages the consonance of final syllables is less frequent than in Greek or Latin, and the quantities of syllables either are not so distinctly marked as of themselves to afford a satisfactory metrical basis or are overpowered by the strength of the accents. Accordingly the modern prosodic systems have come to be based on accent or what one might call isometric syllabification; and the lines are made up of metrically identical units consisting of groups of syllables or of separate syllables, and do not end on a sequence which clearly indicates the close. The turns of the lines, therefore, are inaudible when there are no rhymes to mark them off and to regulate the rhythm.

V

Thus the recitation of blank verse, unless a perceptible pause is made at the ends of the lines (a pause which is often at odds with the running-on of the thought), tends to become indiscriminate, and as a result the melodic line is blurred. Those who read blank verse only silently to themselves and do not listen to it being read aloud may not realise this. But it is a fact that, as Dr Johnson says, " The musick of the English heroick line strikes the ear so faintly that it is easily lost, unless all the syllables of every line co-operate together ; this co-operation can be only obtained by the preservation of every verse un-mingled with another as a distinct system of sounds ; and this distinctness is obtained and preserved by the artifice of rhyme. The variety of pauses, so much boasted by the lovers of blank verse, changes the measures of an English poet to the periods of a declaimer ; and there are only a few happy readers of Milton who enable their audience to perceive where the lines end or begin. *Blank verse*, said an ingenious critick, *seems to be verse only to the eye*." [1] At least one might say that it too easily sounds like an endlessly recurring and unbroken rhythm instead of a series of verse-units, each with its separate interest and yet each approximating to a recognisable norm.

As for the unrhymed measures in English other than the decasyllabic, the only ones which succeed in being true verse as distinct from a more or less agreeable and uninterrupted rhythm are those which imitate such classical verses as warn the listener when they turn back on themselves. The better examples of hexameters (Clough's *Amours de Voyage* and *The Bothie of Tober-na-Vuolich* or Kingsley's *Andromeda*), of Sapphics (Swinburne's " All the night sleep came not upon my eyelids "), of Alcaics (Tennyson's " O mighty-mouth'd inventor of harmonies "), of hendecasyllabics (Tennyson's " O you chorus of indolent reviewers "), and of galliambics (Tennyson's *Boadicea*) are at any rate unmistakable verse, whatever one may think of the wisdom of trying to naturalise alien measures. But even in the poems mentioned one cannot help noticing how often the verse is " end-stopped," how often a rhetorical pause in the sense coincides with and confirms the end of the line.

From English unrhymed measures which do not indicate the ends of the lines by particular metrical sequences, one gets a feeling of verse in the strict sense only when the ends are marked by distinct pauses. The listener to such "verse" sooner or later, and rather sooner than later, gets lost, however good his ear may be.

---

[1] *Lives of the English Poets : Milton* in *The Works of Samuel Johnson*, 1792, ix, p. 181.

VI

But in fact metrical sensibility is a rare gift among listeners. By far fewer of them than one might realise are the internal rhythm of lines and the value of syllables, natural, rhetorical, and rhythmical, appreciated ; and much of the modulation between the beginning and the end of a line necessarily escapes their ears. But for such people, that is, for the great majority of listeners rhyme is unmistakable and reassuring. Though they may reel to and fro like a drunken man along the *coulisses* of verse, they are always brought up sharp by the pillars of rhyme at the ends, and thus a periodic steadiness is given to their otherwise stumbling and erratic progress.

Not only does rhyme steady the average listener and clarify his metrical sense, but on one occasion at least it saved our poetry. In the century and a half between the death of Chaucer and the publication of *Tottel's Miscellany* (1557) there had been a time of prosodic welter when the verse-makers were mumbling something between decayed Middle English and immature Modern English. In that transitional period it was rhyme which kept the tradition of poetry from utter extinction, and it was from the support of rhyme that the new poetry recovered its step. Indeed it would almost look as if Skelton made his lines shorter and shorter in order to have more rhymes to lean on and shorter distances between them to traverse on his own hobbling feet. But it was touch and go. The decadence of rhyme, says Saintsbury, " in the Time of Staggers, is almost as remarkable as the decadence of rhythm, and shows the intimate connection between the two in poetry." [1] The situation was saved, however, because the vitality of rhyme carried it through. " From being at worst a series of irregular detonations, at best a sort of typewriter bell announcing that a certain number of words or syllables have gone before, Rhyme recovers, and more than [recovers, its proper place as Moderatress of Harmony within line and line-group, and as bestower of wonderful additional graces from without, that fill the air around and about the syllabic structure." [2]

[1] *A History of English Prosody from the Twelfth Century to the Present Day*, 1906, i, p. 416.

[2] *Ibid.*, i, p. 416.

VII

Of all the modern languages French is the one most dependent on rhyme for its versification. Though French verse is not accentual, French being like Greek practically devoid of stress-accent, neither is it quantitative. The basis of French verse is what I have called isometric syllabification, the syllables being grouped in agreeable rhythmical phrases. But what distinguishes French verse more than anything else from French prose is rhyme. Hence Théodore de Banville defines French verse as " seulement l'assemblage d'un certain nombre régulier de syllabes, coupé, dans certaines espèces de vers, par un repos qui se nomme *césure*, et toujours terminé par un son qui ne peut exister à la fin d'un vers sans se trouver reproduit à la fin d'un autre ou de plusieurs autres vers, et dont le retour se nomme LA RIME." [1] Elsewhere in the same book he is even more emphatic as to the primary importance of rhyme in French poetry :—" la RIME . . . est l'unique harmonie des vers et elle est tout le vers . . . la RIME est seule et elle suffit. C'est pourquoi *l'imagination de la Rime* est, entre toutes, la qualité qui constitue le poëte." [2] The nature of the language is such that rhyme as judged by the liberal English standards would be rather too easy. But the rules of rhyme are much stricter in French than in English ; and besides the actual prohibitions there are desirable refinements and subtleties which have the effect of still further restricting the French poet's choice. These absolute or virtual regulations raise and keep up the price of rhyme.

On the other hand the facility of rhyming in Italian was probably as much the cause of Trissino and his contemporaries resorting to rhymeless verse as was their reverence for ancient practice. But even though rhyming was easy, easier indeed than in any other modern language, it still remained sufficiently difficult to be worth the trouble. For the examples of unrhymed verse outside the drama are exceptional, even when we include Leopardi and Carducci ; and certainly, as Dr Johnson says, " Of the Italian writers without rhyme, whom Milton alledges as precedents, not one is popular ; what reason could urge in its defence has been confuted by the ear." [3] Probably

---

[1] *Petit traité de poésie française*, 1909, p. 10.   [2] *Ibid.*, p. 47.
[3] *Lives of the English Poets : Milton* in *The Works of Samuel Johnson*, 1792, ix, p. 181.

rhyme retained its esteem for two reasons, one of which at least
counterbalances its facility.   In the first place Italian has a
marked stress-accent which attracts rhyme to it by a kind of
gravitational pull.   And in the second place Italian rhymes are
nearly always double or triple, and the stanzas and forms favoured
generally require more identical endings than would be convenient
in English.

Spanish has a stress-accent of about the same weight as
Italian has ; and in their general characteristics the two languages
are not unlike, especially as regards ease in rhyming.   But
unrhymed metres have appealed even less to Spanish than to
Italian poets.   No doubt something like the reasons I have given
for the persistence of rhyme in Italian will account for its hold in
Spanish also.   Perhaps another factor has some obscure bearing
on the place of rhyme in Spanish poetry.   That is the poet's
partiality for assonance and its survival in full strength alongside
of rhyme down to the present day.   It may be that assonance
provides the poets not so much with a just-tolerable substitute
as with a really agreeable variant on rhyme.   Certainly in a
language with such open vowels as Spanish has, assonance can
probably resist the competition of perfect rhyme more successfully
than it could in English with its somewhat flattened and smothered
vowels.

In German the emphatic stress-accent led as naturally to
rhyme in the modern periods as it once did to alliteration.   Rhyme,
too, is easy because German is nearly as highly inflected as Latin
and Greek.   The superfluity of inflectional rhymes, however,
may have been partly responsible for the numerous and not
unsuccessful rhymeless experiments of the German poets.   But
possibly the strength of the old alliterative tradition also helped
to keep alive an interest in unrhymed verse.   Possibly, too, the
fact that some of the most influential German poets were also
the most experimental, especially in the light of classical models,
is to be noted as likely to spread and establish a taste for poetry
without rhyme.

VIII

In English rhyme is comparatively rare ; and therefore it is
a valuable property of our language, not a bad habit or a nuisance.
It is a pleasant thing, to be sought and treasured as a stylistic
charm or a poetic grace.   Partly because of the hybrid origin

of English and partly because of their multiform shapes, our
words, especially the Anglo-Saxon ones which form the core
and to a large extent the substance of our poetic diction, have a
much greater variety of terminations than have the vocabularies
of less mixed and more uniform languages.   Indeed it is because
there are more ways in which words can end in English that
our rhymes are the rarer.   Unlike the rhymes in highly inflected
languages with their constantly recurring grammatical terminations or in languages like Italian and Spanish in which the same
parts of speech have often the same suffixes, English rhymes are
rarely due to mere inflexions and are generally between words
belonging to different categories, as can be seen from any passage
chosen at random :—

> 'Mid the mountains Euganean
> I stood listening to the pæan
> With which the legion'd rook did hail
> The sun's uprise majestical :
> Gathering round with wings all hoar,
> Through the dewy mists they soar
> Like gray shapes, till the eastern heaven
> Bursts, and then,—as clouds of even,
> Fleck'd with fire and azure, lie
> In the unfathomable sky,—
> So their plumes of purple grain,
> Starr'd with drops of golden rain,
> Gleam above the sunlight woods,
> As in silent multitudes
> On the morning's fitful gale
> Through the broken mist they sail.[1]

Moreover in English, which has a high proportion of mono-
syllables, frequently one or both members of a rhyme are
monosyllabic, and as a result strong and positive.   Even when
the rhyming words are dissyllabic or polysyllabic, the rhymes
themselves are generally masculine, falling on the last syllables
of the lines and not weakened as in feminine or triple rhymes by
trailing unaccented syllables.

Nevertheless, just because English rhymes are predominantly
masculine, double or triple rhymes, when they do occur, are
likely to be used more deliberately than in French which has
complicated rules for the interchange of masculine and feminine
rhymes, or in Italian which is practically restricted to double and

---

[1] Shelley, *Lines Written among the Euganean Hills, North Italy*, 70-85.

triple ones only.   Thus the single double rhyme at the crisis
of *The Rape of the Lock*—there is only one other in the whole
poem [1]—communicates a comic sob to the verse and a mock-epical
finality to the severance of the lock from its owner's head :—

> The peer now spreads the glittering forfex wide,
> To inclose the lock ; now joins it, to divide.
> Even then, before the fatal engine closed,
> A wretched sylph too fondly interposed ;
> Fate urged the shears, and cut the sylph in twain,
> (But airy substance soon unites again)
> The meeting points the sacred hair dissever
> From the fair head, for ever, and for ever.[2]

Or again at the crisis of another story, *Isabella*, Keats uses
double rhymes to suggest the tenuous communion between the
living and the dead, the spiritual remoteness of Lorenzo, and his
dragging weakness of utterance :—

> I am a shadow now, alas ! alas !
>   Upon the skirts of human-nature dwelling
> Alone : I chant alone the holy mass,
>   While little sounds of life are round me knelling,
> And glossy bees at noon do fieldward pass,
>   And many a chapel bell the hour is telling,
> Paining me through : those sounds grow strange to me,
> And thou art distant in Humanity.[3]

Often, however, the effect intended by the use of double rhymes
is stylistic and superficial, rather than a confirmation of the
thought expressed : they are meant to give a witty liveliness
of manner, a general comicality of style, from their apparent
dexterity and speed, as in *Don Juan* :—

> My poem's epic, and is meant to be
>   Divided in twelve books : each book containing,
> With Love, and War, a heavy gale at sea,
>   A list of ships, and captains, and kings reigning,
> New characters ; the episodes are three :
>   A panoramic view of Hell's in training,
> After the style of Virgil and of Homer,
> So that my name of Epic's no misnomer.[4]

Probably triple rhymes are even more restricted to purely comic
effects ; they have a slickness about them out of keeping with

---

[1] v, 115-16.   [2] iii, 147-54.   [3] xxxix.   [4] I, cc.

anything but light verse and they naturally tend to go with reckless anapæstic measures as in the Colonel's song in *Patience* :—

> The dash of a D'Orsay, divested of quackery—
> Narrative powers of Dickens and Thackeray—
> Victor Emmanuel—peak haunting Peveril—
> Thomas Aquinas, and Doctor Sacheverell—
> Tupper and Tennyson—Daniel Defoe—
> Anthony Trollope and Mr Guizot ! [1]

The comparative rarity of English rhymes has resulted in our poets using rather simple rhyme-schemes, with more variety of terminations and less cloying effects. Our rhymes are most commonly only in pairs (as in the octosyllabic and heroic couplets, the elegaic quatrain, the *In Memoriam* stanza, the Shakespearian sonnet, and the common, short, and long measures, as well as in a great many stanzas which have no specific names) ; much less often in threes (as in the *ottava rima* and rhyme royal) ; and rarely in groups of four or more (as in the Burns metre and the Spenserian stanza, both of which like the *ottava rima* and rhyme royal also contain twin rhymes).

IX

But much as I like and believe in the virtues of English rhyme in the abstract, I am not prepared to maintain that all English poetry must be rhymed, or ought to be, and that such extant poetry as there is without rhyme would be improved by being tagged with it. For example, I would go well beyond Dr Johnson's extorted admiration for Milton's blank verse :— " whatever be the advantage of rhyme, I cannot prevail on myself to wish that Milton had been a rhymer ; for I cannot wish his work to be other than it is ; yet, like other heroes, he is to be admired rather than imitated. He that thinks himself capable of astonishing may write blank verse ; but those that hope only to please must condescend to rhyme." [2] I would not warn poets off blank verse, as Johnson was inclined to do, or exclude from full critical approval all already written except what can be found in Milton and in the dramatists. Indeed there seem to me to be, in addition to much good non-Miltonic and non-dramatic

---

[1] Sir W. S. Gilbert, *Original Plays*, Third Series, 1924, p. 96.
[2] *Lives of the English Poets : Milton*, ed. cit., ix, pp. 181-2.

blank verse, examples of other unrhymed measures (in Collins, Blake, Tennyson and Kingsley), and even specimens of " free verse," which actually give pleasure and are not merely *tours de force*.

X

For on the whole, there appear to be purposes and occasions for which rhyme is more or less unsuitable, just as there are others for which it is more or less proper. But which are which ? For what sort of communication or expression is it essential or valuable or possible, and what sort does it either falsify or impair ? It is by no means easy to reach any kind of general agreement ; and such apportionments as I have seen of poetry, according to its " kinds " or to its degrees of greatness, intensity, subtlety, and the like into the rhymable and the unrhymable are all too simple to be satisfactory.

For the sake of convenience I would suggest the following classification :—first by a disjunction into the objective poetry of events in time and the subjective poetry of feelings and opinions ; and secondly by a subdivision of the objective according to the manner of handling into the narrative and the dramatic, and by a subdivision of the subjective according as the poet is stirred emotionally or involved intellectually into the expressive and the conceptual. In other words I would classify poetry into four main categories :—narrative poetry ; dramatic poetry ; lyrical poetry ; and the poetry of ideas. (I quite realise that these are not water-tight compartments. For an epic, like *Paradise Lost*, may contain a metaphysic ; a drama may be superficially objective and fundamentally subjective, like some of Ibsen's ; a lyric may be " dramatic " like Browning's and expressive of a character other than the poet's ; almost any form of poetry may be a receptacle for satire ; and some parts of a poem which is predominantly of one kind may belong to quite a different one.)

XI

To begin with narrative poetry and in particular with the epic. How diverse opinions are on the propriety of rhyme in the epic can be seen by putting alongside the last quotation from Dr Johnson another from Bishop Hurd :—" if we set aside some learned persons, who have suffered themselves to be too easily prejudiced by their admiration of the Greek and Latin languages, and still more, perhaps, by the prevailing notion of the monkish or Gothic original of rhymed verse, all other readers, if left to themselves, would, I daresay, be more delighted with this poet [Milton], if, besides his varied pause and measured quantity, he had enriched his numbers with *rhyme*." [1]   The direct negative to Hurd's general view that " our epic . . . compositions are found most pleasing when clothed in rhyme " [2] is put emphatically by Joseph Warton :—" An epic poem in rhyme appears to be such a sort of thing, as the *Æneid* would have been if it had been written, like Ovid's *Fasti*, in hexameter and pentameter verses ; and the reading of it would have been as tedious as the travelling through that one long straight avenue of firs that leads from Moscow to Petersburg " ; [3] or by Edward Young who lamented that in translating Homer Pope succumbed to " the temptation of that Gothic dæmon, which modern poesy, tasting, became mortal. . . . [R]hyme . . . in epic poetry is a sore disease." [4]

I am not sure, however, that these opinions for and against the rhymed epic give us much help. Either they are of the *a priori* order or they vainly speculate on what effects *Paradise Lost*, Pope's Homer, and the *Aeneid* would have had if they had been written in quite different metres. They are much too conjectural for a subject so empirical as literary criticism.

We are on safer ground when we take our stand by extant heroic poems. When we do so, we have to admit, even if we pass over epics in Italian, Spanish, French, and Portuguese and limit ourselves to English, that *The Faerie Queene* alone would make a kind of case for the rhyming epic. But few as the English epics are, it is not alone. Giles Fletcher's *Christ's Victory and Triumph*, Phineas Fletcher's *Apollyonists*, Shelley's *Revolt of Islam*, Morris's *Lovers of Gudrun, The Life and Death of Jason*, and *Sigurd the Volsung*, and Swinburne's *Tristram of Lyonesse* are, if not all unquestionable epics, sufficiently epical and sufficiently great to compare with anything unrhymed in the heroic vein except Milton's own.

And indeed, when we recognise the inviolable greatness of Milton's majestic blank verse, we have also to admit that it has

---

[1] *Op. cit.*, ii, p. 158.   [2] *Ibid.*, ii, p. 158.
[3] *An Essay on the Genius and Writings of Pope*, 1752-82, ii, pp. 211-12.
[4] *Conjectures on Original Composition*, ed. Edith J. Morley, 1918, pp. 26-7, 37.

a good deal more in it than its blankness. The verse of *Paradise Lost* is most closely wrought with innumerable subtleties of verbal music such as must have cost Milton more trouble by far than mere rhyme would have required. It is not simply straightforward blank verse, but blank verse enriched by every compensating artifice of the master-metrist. The reduction of the metrical interest in *Paradise Regained* is perhaps one of the reasons why most readers find it less satisfactory.

So far as the other narrative varieties are concerned, the English poets from Chaucer and the anonymous balladists and romance-writers to Marlowe, and Shakespeare, and Drayton, from Dryden to Crabbe, and from Burns to Mr Masefield have preferred rhyme in no uncertain way. Their choice is an implicit critical verdict ; and the taste of the generality of readers has confirmed it.

The fact is that only certain kinds of story are suitable for telling in verse. Such narratives as we feel to be rightly in verse, from *Paradise Lost* to *Tam o' Shanter*, have one common characteristic distinguishing them from others which, we feel, are or ought to be rightly in prose. That common characteristic can best be described as a fitness for being stylised. In order to justify a metrical vehicle, the story, be it epical, idyllic, satiric, decorative, comic, or what you will, must be told less for the intrinsic interest of the events and their credibility than for their wider significance and for the unity and depth of impression which they can make. The apprehension of the matter should be ideal rather than real, typical and significant and tending to universals, not factual and photographic and limited to particulars. It should be a story which puts a certain distance between itself and life, by simplification, abstraction, artistic distortion, exaggeration, and emphasis, or by imaginative rearrangements and composition. It must be easily reducible to a patterned unity, however much the outline may be overlaid by description or commentary as in *The Eve of St Agnes* or *The Nonne Prestes Tale*. Similarly, in diction it will not aim at a reproduction of the language actually used by men (unless some degree of beauty can thereby be achieved), because " A poem is that species of composition, which is opposed to works of science, by proposing for its *immediate* object pleasure, not truth ; and from all other species (having *this* object in common with it) it is discriminated by proposing to itself such delight from the *whole*, as is compatible with a distinct gratification from each component *part*." [1]

Certain stories with the qualities I have described are singularly impressive in blank verse. If we pass over Milton's two epics, the best examples are naturally Wordsworth's, especially *Michael* and *The Ruined Cottage*.[2] But there are not many others, and even Wordsworth's blank-verse tales are special cases. Each of them is, like *Michael*,

A story unenriched with strange events.[3]

The austerity of style common to them all is gaunt and even monotonous, but peculiarly fitting ; for we feel that any sort of incidental beauty, such as rhyme or metaphor or antithesis, would impair the effect. But without the profound Wordsworthian emotion, the style would at once become flat and garrulous. Wordsworth himself used rhyme for narrative purposes far oftener ; perhaps because he instinctively felt, despite his theories of poetic diction, that in blank-verse narrative the pleasure which the reader gets from the parts is too little a reward ; and because blank verse with its laxer organisation and its easy reception of words in their prose order too readily provokes the question, Why is all this not in prose ?

That is a question which the narrative poet must try to preclude. But it may be difficult to avoid, because a narrative by its very nature requires so many merely structural links and transitions and so much of the explanatory and the circumstantial. No doubt the poet economises in this unpoetic cement. But some he must have. And by rhyme, far more than by verse alone, he can either disguise this irreducible residuum or give an extrinsic interest to it. Moreover, a rhyme-scheme will make a more harmonious whole of all the parts, principal and subordinate, important and transitional, and thus go far to justify telling the story in verse at all.

XII

The drama is now nearly always in prose. On the rare occasions when it is not, it is almost certain to be in blank verse in the wake of the overwhelming example of Shakespeare. As a result there has been little or no divergence of opinion among

---

[1] Coleridge, *Biographia Literaria*, ed. J. Shawcross, 1907, ii, p. 10.
[2] Incorporated in *The Excursion*, i.   [3] 19.

the critics as to the propriety of excluding rhyme from the drama, since Shakespeare's greatness was generally recognised as an article of poetic faith, that is, since the beginning of the eighteenth century or somewhat earlier. Thus Bishop Hurd, who strongly prefers rhyme for all non-dramatic purposes, admits in a non-committal way that " our tragedies are usually composed in blank verse." [1] Young, who on the other hand regards rhyme as at the best a necessary evil, pronounces it " absolute death " to tragic poetry above all.[2] Since the eighteenth century it has scarcely occurred to anybody even to mention the possibility of rhyme in the drama.

But that there is much to be said for it in theory at least can be seen from those essays of Dryden written when he was in love with his mistress Rhyme.[3] And perhaps still better arguments— for Dryden in these essays was a special pleader and not very consistent at that, to say nothing of his later rejection of dramatic rhyme in the prologue to *Aureng-zebe* (1676)—can be found in actual plays which rhyme in whole or in part and are not unsuccessful, as for example *Everyman* and *The Faithful Shepherdess*. That rhyme is much commoner in the French, Italian, and Spanish theatres can no doubt be partly explained by the natures of these languages and by the temperaments of these nations. But the fact that dramas so great as those of Corneille, Racine, and Molière, Ariosto and Tasso, Calderón and Lope de Vega admit rhyme is also an argument of general theoretic scope that rhyme is not wholly incompatible with at least some dramatic varieties. But that Mr Shaw, or Mr Maugham, or Mr O'Casey ought to have written their plays in rhyme scarcely follows. They, like most modern dramatists, and indeed like many in an increasing number from Gascoigne and Lyly in the sixteenth century, have made a colourable imitation of extemporary and colloquial speech an essential element in their idea of a play; whereas in most earlier drama, especially of the more serious kind though also of the comic, the criticism of life was at several removes, and the vehicle of that criticism could therefore be without incongruity verse or even rhyme. When realism is not a primary

[1] *Op. cit.*, ii, p. 158.   [2] *Op. cit.*, p. 37.
[3] Epistle Dedicatory of *The Rival Ladies*, 1664 ; *An Essay of Dramatic Poesy*, 1668 ; *A Defence of an Essay of Dramatic Poesy*, the preface to *The Indian Emperor*, 1668 ; *Of Heroic Plays*, the preface to *The Conquest of Granada*, 1672. All of these essays are included in *Essays of John Dryden*, ed. W. P. Ker, 1900, 2 vols.

aim of the dramatist, the proper vehicle for his play has to be determined by other considerations than the likeness of the dialogue to actual speech.

It was to some such conclusion that Dryden was moving in the essays I have mentioned, although he never actually got there. In his day the drama was certainly regarded as an " imitation " in the Aristotelian sense and the dramatist was supposed to hold a kind of mirror up to nature. But *vraisemblance* was only occasionally attempted, and that only in comedy. It was, moreover, very far from being an untouched photograph of men as they lived. The idea of a realism so unemphatic as Mr van Druten's or so much an echo of colloquial speech as Mr Noel Coward's had never occurred to anybody even for comedy. In serious plays the taste was still pretty much what elsewhere I have described it as being in the Elizabethan theatre, a taste " for the romantic, the extreme, the paradoxical, the sensational,

> the dangerous edge of things,
> The honest thief, the tender murderer,
> The superstitious atheist, demireps
> That love and save their souls." [1]

At any rate the majority of the plays were sufficiently remote from life for verse to be the commonest vehicle without appearing incongruous. It is true that more prose was used than had been by the Elizabethan playwrights ; but drama was still reckoned naturally a department of poetry and therefore more appropriately in verse. Nevertheless the general tendency was towards a lower pitched drama. Before the end of the seventeenth century a working compromise had been reached by which the classification into comedies and serious plays coincided with the classification into prose and verse. Congreve, for example, used prose for all his comedies of manners and blank verse for his *Mourning Bride*. Eighteenth-century drama almost to the end was ruled by the same compromise ; and traces of it persist into the nineteenth.

XIII

But earlier in the Restoration period, during the years when Dryden was most prolific as a dramatist, verse, either rhymed or

---

[1] *Thomas Heywood, Playwright and Miscellanist*, 1931, p. 233. The verse quotation is from Browning, *Bishop Blougram's Apology*, 395-8.

blank, was in frequent use for comedies, tragicomedies, heroic plays, and tragedies. The blank verse was an inheritance from the Elizabethans and the heroic couplets an attempt to emulate the French Alexandrines.

As the name indicates, the heroic plays were meant to be dramatic parallels to the contemporary heroic poems and heroic romances. They were supposed to transfer the epic ideals to the stage. That the ideals, as understood by the Restoration, were decidedly shabby goes without saying. But the important fact for my purpose is that the plays are rather narrative than dramatic ; and rhetorical argumentation and declamation, extravagant conceits and similes, and excessive epigram and antithesis, all smacking of the Metaphysical manner, were employed to give a dramatic effect by other than dramatic means. No doubt the heroic drama would never have reached its gross perfection if the playwrights had not kept glancing at the nobler perfection of the French stage. But it owed far more to the melodramatic varieties of later Elizabethan drama, especially in Beaumont and Fletcher, Massinger, Ford, and Davenant, with their complicated and often pseudo-historical plots, startling incidents, surprising dénouements, exaggerated passions about love and honour, and hectic style.

Even the heroic couplet, which in the fully developed heroic drama tried to catch the effect of the French Alexandrines, was a common feature in Elizabethan drama from the first. The Elizabethans often emphasised a remark or rounded off a speech or a scene with rhyme, long before Corneille's *Le Cid* (1636) inaugurated the French classical theatre. Davenant himself, to whom Dryden gave the credit of inventing the heroic play, was partial to resounding, antithetical couplets from the time of his first play, *The Tragedy of Albovine* (1629). It was not, however, till *The Siege of Rhodes* (1656), after a sojourn in France, that he made the heroic couplet the staple of a play and thus completed the evolution of a *genre*.

No other metrical mould could have been more fitting, and without it the heroic would never have become the characteristically Restoration variety of serious play, sweeping all before it.

For a time Dryden, born rhymer and verse-rhetorician that he was, was dazzled by the heroic play, especially by its all-conquering couplets. It seemed to him that his age had produced a kind of play peculiarly its own and challenging equality with the classical, the Elizabethan, and the French. His views were at first countered by his brother-in-law, Sir Robert Howard, with whom he was not on the best of terms. In Dryden's later remarks on dramatic rhyme he seems to be defending the drama of the Restoration against the literary conservatives of his day. The issue, therefore, is crossed by a desire to score debating points and by some special pleading.

By common consent the question was restricted to the suitability of rhyme for serious plays. Dryden proposed to reduce it even further, to its propriety for the speeches of great and noble characters on fit subjects, especially scenes " of argumentation and discourse, on the results of which the doing or not doing some considerable action should depend." [1] On the other hand, he allowed that blank verse was also permissible in serious plays, though as a *sermo pedestris* it was more fit for comedies, in which rhyme in his opinion was improper. [2]

Dryden's arguments for rhyme in drama are of varying worth. The plea that its adoption was in accord with the practice of the most polished nations on the Continent, and even of English dramatists before Shakespeare " invented " blank verse " to shun the pain of continual rhyming," [3] may be dismissed. And so may his contention that rhyme is more memorable; [4] for, while it is true, rhyme is not for that reason the more suitable for drama, except from the actor's point of view. The argument that rhyme circumscribes a too luxuriant fancy [5] comes appropriately from the copious Dryden upon whom " thoughts, such as they are, come crowding in so fast . . ., that my only difficulty is to choose or to reject, to run them into verse, or to give them the other harmony of prose." [6] But it is not very pertinent to the matter in hand. Howard rightly remarked that " the dispute is not which way a Man may write best in, but which is most proper for the Subject he writes upon ; . . . he that wants Judgment in the liberty of his Phancy may as well shew the

---

[1] Epistle Dedicatory of *The Rival Ladies*, ed. cit., i, p. 9.

[2] *An Essay of Dramatic Poesy*, ed. cit., i, p. 97.

[3] Epistle Dedicatory of *The Rival Ladies*, ed. cit., i, p. 6.

[4] Epistle Dedicatory of *The Rival Ladies*, ed. cit., i, p. 7.

[5] Epistle Dedicatory of *The Rival Ladies*, ed. cit., i, p. 8 ; cf. *An Essay of Dramatic Poesy*, ed. cit., i, pp. 93, 106-7.

[6] Preface to *Fables, Ancient and Modern* in *Essays of John Dryden*, ed. W. P. Ker, 1900, ii, p. 249.

defect of it in its Confinement." [1]   Moreover, so far from rhyme having actually confined Dryden's fancy, there are no more turgid passages anywhere in his work than one finds only too easily in his heroic plays.

The most important of all Dryden's pleas for dramatic rhyme was the need for heightening the dialogue in a serious play.   Like the epic, he says, a serious play " is indeed the representation of Nature, but . . . Nature wrought up to an higher pitch. The plot, the characters, the wit, the passions, the descriptions, are all exalted above the level of common converse, as high as the imagination of the poet can carry them, with proportion to veri-simility." [2]   That last phrase, however, begs the question.   The need for idealisation in dialogue can be readily conceded.   But how far should it go ?   Ought it to be the same in kind and in degree as in the epic ?   And is rhyme the means by which to get it ? Dryden appears to think so, because he holds " that if rhyme be proper for one it must be for the other," [3] not recognising that the fact of stage presentation ought to have some considerable effect on the " proportion to verisimility." [4]

In order to meet Howard's shrewd objections,[5] Dryden speciously argued that blank verse itself was an initial departure from nature which justified the further departure of rhyme, and (in order to have it both ways) that rhyme in skilful hands was just as natural as prose or blank verse and more effective than either—as natural as Aristotle could desire dramatic verse to be,[6] and more effective by reason of its higher organisation and by reason of its modifications in the order of words in " the negligence of prose " [7] often making for grandeur, sonority, and variety.   He ingeniously circumvents the stricture that rhyme, especially in repartee, is too like something premeditated, by replying that the same objection might be taken to blank verse and that in any case while rhyme is truly " not the effect of sudden thought . . . this hinders not that sudden thought

---

[1] Preface to *Four New Plays* in *Critical Essays of the Seventeenth Century*, ed. J. E. Spingarn, 1908-9, ii, p. 102 ; cf. *An Essay of Dramatic Poesy*, ed. cit., i, p. 93.

[2] *An Essay of Dramatic Poesy*, ed. cit., i, pp. 100-1.

[3] *Ibid.*, i, p. 102.

[4] *Ibid.*, i, p. 101.

[5] Preface to *Four New Plays*, ed. cit., ii, pp. 97-104.

[6] Cf. *Aristotle on the Art of Poetry*, ed. Ingram Bywater, 1909, pp. 13-15.

[7] *An Essay of Dramatic Poesy*, ed. cit., i, p. 98.

may be represented "[1] in it and mightily enhanced thereby, especially in repartee. As for Howard's cavil that rhyme draws too much attention to such necessary trivialities in a play as calling a servant or ordering a door to be shut, Dryden suggests that they would be as mean in blank verse and that the artful dramatist can either disguise them in pompous words or contrive to get them in the middle of a line or avoid them altogether.

Dryden, however, did not convince even himself on the naturalness of rhyme in dramatic dialogue. In his *Defence of An Essay of Dramatic Poesy*, cheerfully admitting that it is impossible to prove or disprove it, he falls back on his main line of defence, the need for idealisation :—" I am satisfied if [rhyme] cause delight ; [and thereto] a bare imitation will not serve." [2] Or as he put the argument finally in his essay *Of Heroic Plays*, once verse of any kind is admitted in a serious play, " You have lost that which you call natural, and have not acquired the last perfection of Art," [3] which is of course rhyme.

Even this apparently impregnable position was abandoned when, in the prologue to *Aureng-zebe*, he took farewell of his " long-loved mistress Rhyme," at least in her dramatic avatar. The Shakespearian passions which he was thereafter to imitate were too fierce to be bound. Thus Dryden had nearly discovered that rhyme has only a relative, not an absolute, value for one kind of serious play, namely the heroic, and that what had fascinated him so long was its rhetorical effectiveness.

XIV

But what of the other kinds, lyrical poetry and the poetry of ideas ? I shall take these two divisions of subjective poetry together.

Joseph Warton supposes that " rhyme may be properest for shorter pieces : for didactic, lyric, elegiac, and satiric poems ; for pieces where closeness of expression and smartness of style are expected ; but for subjects of a higher order, or for poems of a greater length, blank verse may be preferable." [4] With this Edward Young more or less concurs, though with less respect

---

[1] *An Essay of Dramatic Poesy*, ed. cit., i, p. 102.
[2] *Ed. cit.*, i, p. 113.
[3] *Ed. cit.*, i, p. 148.
[4] *Op. cit.*, ii, p. 211.

for rhyme :—" I wish the nature of our language could bear its intire expulsion, but our lesser poetry stands in need of a toleration for it ; it raises that, but sinks the great, as spangles adorn children, but expose men." [1]

There is, I fancy, some confusion of thought in these two passages. To begin with, they hint at several cross-classifications of poetry, according to matter, length, style, spirit, and so on. Then again lyrical poetry, to which comprehensive category the elegiac belongs, certainly consists of " shorter pieces," many of which are rightly to be reckoned among the " lesser " poems ; but some of our lyrics, short as they are, are among the greatest poems in the language and treat the loftiest subjects with intense enthusiasm and deep emotion. Indeed all the most intense and moving poems are, by the very fact of the emotion which begets them and which they express, lyrical either in form or in spirit or in both ; and the more intense they are, the shorter they are likely to be, or at least the less likely they are to be long. Nor is it only the less passionate and enthusiastic lyrics which are properly in rhyme. For in fact the overwhelming majority of lyrics are, lyrics of every degree of intensity and feeling from the deliberate *vers de société* and the sedate odes and the tepid songs which the eighteenth century produced in the way of lyrics to the " happy fireworks " of Crashaw and the tempestuous inspiration of Shelley. The unrhymed lyrics in English are conspicuous only because they are exceptional, not because they are otherwise remarkable. Perhaps most people feel a certain insipidity about rhymeless lyrics, as of champagne that has gone flat. It may be that some of the weightier kinds of lyric can be given enough interest of statement to do without rhyme, even if such poems as " It was a lover and his lass " or " O my luve's like a red, red rose " are inconceivable without their rhyming grace-notes. But, on the other hand, the weightier the lyric and the more it has to say, the less lyrical will it be and the less able will it be to fly on lyrical wings, like the ostrich and the dodo. In the true lyric the feeling is not always intense, but it must always be of a sufficient intensity to carry its load off on wings, to have enough lift and to spare ; and in the true lyric language is most plastic and ready to receive form and pattern, stanza and rhyme. It is a kind in which the manner is peculiarly important, always at least as important as the matter and generally more so.

[1] *Op. cit.*, p. 37.

XV

To return to the above quotation from Warton, " closeness of expression and smartness of style " are hardly characteristic of the true lyric, though he seems to think they are. Be that as it may, they are characteristic of satire in all its verse species, and perhaps also of didactic and metaphysical poetry. Now the poets, whose choice of any particular style or metre is *caeteris paribus* a stronger argument for it than any amount of theorising, have agreed in practice that satire should rhyme. For much of the sting and rancour and much of the wit and intellectual superiority of the great satirists reside in the trenchant rhymes of their rhetorical verse, the heroic couplets of Dryden and Pope or the *ottava rima* of Byron.

Perhaps we may conclude that satire for one reason and the different kinds of lyric for another are what Hurd calls " sorts, which are more solicitous to please the ear, and where such solicitude, if taken notice of by the reader or hearer, is not resented " ; and in such circumstances " it may be proper, or rather it becomes a law . . . to adopt *rhyme*." [1] All that I would add in qualification is that the law in question is, as it were, common, not statute, law. It derives its authority from the effective practice of the poets and the established traditions of literature, from which there is no appeal.

Are we to include didactic and metaphysical poetry also among the kinds " more solicitous to please the ear " and therefore better when in rhyme ? Certainly some of our best didactic poetry is rhymed, such as Dryden's *Religio Laici* and *The Hind and the Panther*, Prior's *Alma* and *Solomon*, and Pope's *Essay on Criticism* and *An Essay on Man* ; and Goldsmith was indignant that the " pedantry " of blank verse had " found its way into our didactic poetry, and is likely to bring that species of composition into disrepute, for which the English are deservedly famous." [2] But the didactic verse which I have mentioned and which was what Goldsmith no doubt had in mind, as distinguished from such blank-verse poems as Dyer's *Fleece*, and Armstrong's *Art of Preserving Health*, was next-door to satire. It strove after rhetoric, wit, point, and quotability. It was more concerned

---

[1] *Op. cit.*, ii, p. 158.

[2] *An Enquiry into the Present State of Polite Learning* in *The Works of Oliver Goldsmith*, ed. J. W. M. Gibbs, 1885, iii, p. 513.

with effect than with instruction, with the surface play than with real persuasion, argument, and doctrine.   Whether some of the discommendable didactic poems of the eighteenth century were worth writing at all is a question to be asked, but not now.   They might at least have been a little more lively and readable in rhyme, and probably also considerably shorter.   But on the other hand, as their *raison d'être* was what they had to say rather than the way in which they said it, rhyme would have been of less immediate value to them as well as a handicap.

In some kinds of metaphysical poetry also, the manner is less important than the matter, and rhyme may sometimes detract from, or compete with, the interest of the thing said.   This indeed is one of the reasons why Milton rejected rhyme in both of his epics : they were metaphysico-didactic poems, " doctrinal and exemplary to a nation," [1] before they were epics, and therefore their doctrine had to be conveyed through as transparent a medium as was in Milton's opinion still compatible with its utterance in a poetic form.   Perhaps something like the same reason made most of the later writers of metaphysical poetry in the strict sense and on the grand scale prefer blank verse or various kinds of verse that is rhythmical without being strictly metrical.   Except Pope's *Essay on Man*, which in any case is nearer to satire and didactic verse, Shelley's *Triumph of Life*, which is scarcely metaphysical in the full sense, and Tennyson's *In Memoriam*, which is not one long poem but a sequence of short ones, I can recall no important metaphysical poetry in rhyme between Young's *Night Thoughts* on the one hand and Bridges's *Testament of Beauty* on the other.

One might hazard the suggestion that the more unconventional and intuitive the metaphysic as in Blake's prophetic books, the more discursive and reflective as in Wordsworth's *Prelude* and *The Excursion* and Coleridge's *Religious Musings*, the more tentative as in Keats's *Fall of Hyperion*, or the more expository as in Bridges's *Testament of Beauty*, then the more elbow-room a poet likes and the less he wants to be confined to strict forms and a line-by-line interest ; whereas when a poet has to put into verse an already systematised metaphysic like Dante's, a conventional and rhetorical one like Pope's, a lyrically intense one like Shelley's and Tennyson's, he wants to give a more

---

[1] *The Reason of Church Government* in *The Student's Milton*, ed. F. A. Patterson, 1930, p. 525.

definite shape or a more decided stylistic momentum by the use of stanza and rhyme.

The sixteenth- and seventeenth-century poets who philosophised in verse, like Spenser in the Mutabilitie cantos, Sir John Davies in *Nosce Teipsum*, and Henry More in *Psychozoia*, chose rhyme for reasons similar to Dante's and Pope's and confirmed by the taste of their period for complicated patterns in everything from poetry to flower-beds, from architecture to embroidery. The fundamental ideas on which their poems were built were in general familiar enough, however much they were overlaid and diversified by Elizabethan ornament, conceit, and allegory. In the ultimate analysis their poems are ingenious elaborations of commonplaces, or pieces of decorative and even sportive enrichment in which the theme is the occasion for the display. However serious or even sombre their subjects might be, their conception of poetry derives from the old Provençal one which regarded it as *el gai saber* or *la science joyeuse*. As Dante puts it, " omnis qui versificatur suos versus exornare debet in quantum potest " ; [1] and poetry is " fictio rethorica musicaque posita " [2] and has its true sense hidden beneath a rich vesture of rhetorical colouring.[3] Such was the poetic which still lingered. Quite naturally, therefore, rhyme was one of the most prized features of their technique.

So also is it in the poetry, lyrical or non-lyrical, of the unfortunately named Metaphysicals, anti-Petrarchan though their origins may be. The poems of the Metaphysicals have this in common with that of all the followers of the Provençal and troubadour traditions that they are constructions. In every one of them the poet sets himself a two-fold problem of ingenious idea and development and ingenious form and expression. And the characteristic flaws in language and unevennesses in metre of Metaphysical poetry are due to the high-handed methods by which the all-but-baffled poets solved their problems. But, difficult or easy, the problems had to be solved somehow or other without the dropping of any of the factors. If one cannot appreciate the conjuring tricks by which a Metaphysical poet secures a precarious balance, then one is missing his real

[1] *De Vulgari Eloquentia*, II, i, 2.
[2] *Ibid.*, II, iv, 2.
[3] *Cf.* C. S. Lewis, *Donne and Love Poetry in the Seventeenth Century* in *Seventeenth-Century Studies* presented to Sir Herbert Grierson, 1938, p. 65.

achievement. Many modern readers are drawn to Metaphysical poetry by one or other of its separate elements, the ratiocination, the psychological subtlety, the passion, the out-of-the-way learning, and the rest. But it is the totality which counts, the extraordinary reconciliation of opposites, and the interrelation of the theme, its verbal management and illustration, and the metrical form. A severer taste may condemn Metaphysical poetry altogether. But a typical specimen ought not to be taken piecemeal, but as a kind of made-dish or a literary cocktail.

XVI

Having discussed the suitability of rhyme in the four kinds into which I divided poetry, I would now reconsider rhyme in relation to poetry reclassified in other ways, according to length, style, and quality.

Perhaps the most obvious classification of this sort is into good poetry and bad. Now one of Milton's objections to rhyme was that it was " the Invention of a barbarous Age, to set off wretched matter and lame Meeter." [1] It is quite true that it " very often makes an indifferent phrase pass unregarded " [2] and even makes tolerable many whole poems, as for example this sentimental jog-trot of Studdert Kennedy :—

> There was rapture of spring in the morning
>   When we told our love in the wood,
> For you were the spring in my heart, dear lad,
>   And I vowed that my life was good.
>
> But there's winter now in the evening,
>   And lowering clouds overhead,
> There's wailing of wind in the chimney nook,
>   And I vow that my life lies dead. [3]

If for " wood " the reader substitutes " dell " and for " overhead " " in the sky," he will agree with Mr Bonamy Dobrée " that the rhymed version of this poem did at least satisfy the absurd appetencies that it arouses ; whereas in the unrhymed version the poem is completely dead." [4]

[1] *The Verse* of *Paradise Lost*, 1668.

[2] Addison, *The Spectator*, No. 285, in *The Works of Joseph Addison*, ed. Richard Hurd, 1856, iii, p. 194.

[3] *Easter* in *The Unutterable Beauty*, 1927, p. 54.

[4] *An Experiment with Rhyme* in *Life and Letters*, April 1934, p. 69.

But the matter is not quite so simple. Rhyme can expose
as well as disguise, as it does in *The Sailor's Mother* of
Wordsworth :—

> And, thus continuing, she said
> " I had a Son, who many a day
> Sailed on the seas, but he is dead ;
> In Denmark he was cast away :
> And I have travelled weary miles to see
> If aught which he had owned might still remain for me.
>
> " The bird and cage they both were his :
> 'Twas my Son's bird ; and neat and trim
> He kept it ; many voyages
> The singing-bird had gone with him ;
> When last he sailed, he left the bird behind ;
> From bodings, as might be, that hung upon his mind." [1]

I am afraid that here the " wretched matter and lame Meeter "
are, if set off, set off only to their disadvantage. And I confess
with Coleridge that such Wordsworthian poems as " the *Anecdote
for Fathers*, *Simon Lee*, *Alice Fell*, *The Beggars* and *The Sailor's
Mother*, notwithstanding the beauties which are to be found in
each of them where the poet interposes the music of his own
thoughts, would have been more delightful to me in prose, told
and managed, as by Mr Wordsworth they would have been,
in a moral essay, or pedestrian tour." [2]

Rhyme alone no more makes a thing poetry than does
alliteration, antithesis, or any other verbal device. And Milton
might just as reasonably have denounced them for being likewise
tawdry ornaments to catch the uncritical attention. None of
these things is limited to poetry, but all are available for whoever
works in words, from the poet and the orator to the journalist
and the caption-writer. Only when they are effectively used are
they ornaments ; for " nec bovem epiphyatum, nec balteatum
suem dicemus ornatum, ymo potius deturpatum ridemus illum ;
est enim exornatio alicuius convenientis additio." [3]

The point is not whether rhyme improves the bad, which in
any case it only sometimes does, but whether it improves the
good. The finest champagne is not the worse for the sparkle,
even though soda-water is intolerable without it. That rhyme

---

[1] 19-30.
[2] *Biographia Literaria*, ed. cit., ii, p. 53.
[3] Dante, *op. cit.*, II, i, 9.

in the right context does improve the good I have no doubt. The general reasons for that improvement would come more appropriately in another context. But here I might point out that there is in English a great body of poetry which all admit to be good, not bad disguised as good, but good absolutely, that would be nothing without rhyme. Such are many of the most charming lyrics of Herrick, many of the songs of Burns and Shakespeare, and countless other pieces. Turn one of them into unrhymed verse and the result is a *caput mortuum*.

XVII

The next classification of poetry I offer is into long poems and short. Just as one might object to the previous classification into good and bad on the ground that bad poetry is a contradiction in terms, so might one argue that there are no long poems but only short ones which may in some cases be held together by verse below the level of true poetry so as to form a sequence or longer composition.[1] However, as the poets themselves write their sequences in the same metre throughout as a rule, we need not at present consider the variations in quality.

Joseph Warton readily [2] and Edward Young reluctantly [3] admitted that rhyme might be allowed in short poems. Even Milton implies that he had less objection to it in such contexts. But why ? If rhyme is allowed to give any pleasure at all, it is a recurring pleasure which is just the kind of fillip one would expect a long poem to require. There are as many long and great poems in rhyme as in blank verse. While I am not prepared to say that the rhyme is enough to sustain the reader to the end of *The Faerie Queene*, I do believe that the want of it in *Aurora Leigh* makes his way all the wearier. It is perhaps rather the poet than the reader who grows tired of rhyming in a long poem. It might, however, be to the poet's ultimate advantage if he were to submit to the restraints of rhyme and curbed his prolixity

---

[1] Edgar Allan Poe's opinion (in *The Poetic Principle* in *Poems by Edgar Allan Poe*, edited by R. H. Stoddard, 1893, pp. 299-30) is something like this ; except that in his view the excellence and the length are not absolute but variable according to the reader who can sustain his pleasurable excitement only for about half an hour, but who may find enjoyable to-morrow those parts he yawned over yesterday and *vice versa*.

[2] *Op. cit.*, ii, p. 211.

[3] *Op. cit.*, p. 37.

thereby. Long poems like long novels tend to be less exacting in what they admit. Another little bit won't do them any harm, as it were ; whereas the more concentrated or simply the shorter a poem is, the higher the selectivity.

Of course long poems like *Don Juan* and *Night Thoughts* may have very little in common. Length apart from any other characteristic is in fact not a satisfactory differentia.

XVIII

I would turn now to a purely qualitative classification of poetry, according partly to the spirit and partly to the style. As usual I should like to cite a few typical opinions as texts for a commentary.

It has been said by Addison that " Rhyme, without any other assistance, throws the language off from prose . . . ; but where the verse is not built upon rhymes, there pomp and sound and energy of expression are indispensably necessary to support the style and keep it from falling into the flatness of prose." [1] That is to say, Addison would justify blank verse only if the supporting style were sufficiently elevated. Goldsmith similarly believes that " Nothing but the greatest sublimity of subject can render [blank verse] pleasing," though it had come to be used inappropriately " upon the most trivial occasions." [2] Just to complicate matters, let me refer again to Warton and Young. The former would restrict rhyme to less ambitious poems and to those in which " closeness of expression and smartness of style are expected," preferring blank verse for " subjects of a higher order " [3] in which emotion and enthusiasm are to be expressed. The latter believes that rhyme may raise the lesser varieties " but sinks the great, as spangles adorn children, but expose men." [4] Lastly, Mr Bonamy Dobrée speaks of a poetry which plunges us into profundity and of another which bears us up on wings :— " It is possible that the second form may demand rhyme, the first be hampered by it. Take away rhyme from ' Full fathom five,' or add it to the invocation to light in *Paradise Lost*, and both would seem rather foolish." [5]

The first point which I would make in my commentary is

[1] *Op. cit.*, iii, p. 194.
[2] *An Enquiry into the Present State of Polite Learning*, ed. cit., iii, p. 513.
[3] *Op. cit.*, ii, p. 211.   [4] *Op. cit.*, p. 37.   [5] *Op. cit.*, p. 66.

that sublimity of subject and pomp of style do not go together beyond a certain altitude. Just as the Alpine peaks shoot far above the pines which clothe their middle slopes, so the true sublime is always austere. The sublimest passages in any literature are those in which the thought makes the simplest words incandescent by its imaginative awe. Such is the quality of the thought and the words in these lines of Vaughan :—

> I saw Eternity the other night
> Like a great *Ring* of pure and endless light,
>   All calm, as it was bright,
> And round beneath it, Time in hours, days, years
>   Driv'n by the spheres
> Like a vast shadow mov'd, In which the world
>   And all her train were hurl'd ; [1]

or these of Wordsworth :—

> The Rainbow comes and goes,
> And lovely is the Rose,
> The Moon doth with delight
> Look round her when the heavens are bare,
> Waters on a starry night
> Are beautiful and fair. [2]

or these of Blake :—

> Tiger ! Tiger ! burning bright
> In the forests of the night,
> What immortal hand or eye
> Could frame thy fearful symmetry ? . . .
>
> When the stars threw down their spears,
> And water'd heaven with their tears,
> Did He smile his work to see ?
> Did He who made the Lamb make thee ? [3]

Naturally I have chosen rhyming examples of the sublime. But if I had cited others in blank verse from Shakespeare, Milton, Wordsworth, or Arnold, they would also have been as severe and simple in diction. The fact is that one can be simple without poverty either in blank verse or in rhyme, if one knows how. And one can be sublime in either, with the same proviso. Thus Wordsworth's *Michael* has the simplicity and dignity of a

---

[1] *The World*, 1-7.
[2] *Intimations of Immortality*, 10-15.
[3] *The Tiger*, 1-4, 17-20.

narrative in *Genesis*. Tennyson's *Ulysses* is simpler than most, and as dignified as any, of his rhyming poems. On the other hand, Wordsworth's *Solitary Reaper*, or the last chorus in Shelley's *Hellas*, or Housman's *Oracles* prove the power of associated simplicity, dignity, and rhyme.

XIX

It is true, I think, that blank verse is the vehicle of most of the specially pedestrian poems in English. But their flatness is due not merely to a lack of " pomp of sound and energy of expression." [1] Rather they suffer from a vital defect which impoverishes every fibre of their organisms—their rhythm, their structure and coherence, their imaginative vigour, their sensuous appeal, and their intellectual significance, as well as their diction and style. Besides, there are plenty of blank-verse poems or passages in which " pomp of sound and energy of expression " try to do duty for the weightier poetic components and fail the more completely the less their diction and style is supported by theme, passion, and imagination.

So far from blank verse always demanding height of style and being unsuitable for trivial occasions, some of the most satisfying poems in it are quite simple and unassuming in style and as unpretentious in subject. Such are Wordsworth's *Michael* and his *Ruined Cottage* in one direction, and Coleridge's *This Lime-tree Bower my Prison* and *Frost at Midnight* in another.

Indeed, in the right hands blank verse has a considerable range of notes, as can be seen from its flexibility in Browning alone. For " he can use it not only for high poetry but also, very effectively, for the purposes for which Shakespeare used prose. At the one end of the scale he is a master of the slow-moving, artfully composed, highly ornamented style [as in *Rudel to the Lady of Tripoli*.] . . . At the other end of the scale he uses blank verse with unequalled skill and power for humorous conversational purposes [as in *Bishop Blougram's Apology*.] . . . But the best of Browning's blank verse lies in a middle region between *Rudel* and *Blougram*. Its qualities are ease, grace, strength, and chief of all, rapidity." [2]

[1] Addison, *op. cit.*, iii, p. 194.
[2] D. C. Somervell, *The Reputation of Robert Browning* in *Essays and Studies by Members of the English Association*, 1929, xv, p. 133.

I realise, however, that Browning's practice in blank verse, like that of Shakespeare and the dramatists, is an attempt to reach a compromise between metre and psychological truth, between poetry and extemporary utterance. All the different manners which he adopts fall into the generous class of drama, and into the middle reaches of that class. That is, not into the dramatic varieties which reflect life at several removes and can do so in rhyme if they please; nor yet into those realistic kinds of drama which try to catch the very tone and accent of life, necessarily in prose; but into those which keep in touch with life, but poetise it in a metre flexible enough to suggest some of the cadences and irregularities of unpremeditated speech and not so obvious as rhyme would make it. All the poems in which Browning uses blank verse are supposed to be the utterances of men talking, arguing, reflecting, speculating, accusing, justifying; and the differences in the manners, between *Rudel to the Lady of Tripoli* at the one extreme and *Mr Sludge the Medium* at the other, are due entirely to the differences in the characters of the supposed speakers. The several manners, therefore, in Browning's blank verse are only a variety within a larger uniformity. The purpose is essentially the same throughout. (I might add in a parenthesis that Browning could give a plausible colloquialism in rhyme also. Good examples are:—*My Last Duchess* with its rhymes subdued by the frequent enjambement and so somehow in accord with a speech which means so much more than it says; *Pictor Ignotus* with its rhymes similarly restrained and also widely separated so as to suggest a meditative abstraction; and *The Laboratory* with its emphatic, insistent rhymes expressing breathless eagerness. But on the whole, and even in the poems I have just mentioned, whenever Browning uses rhyme, the result is a degree or more above the colloquial and psychological realism of his blank verse. The rhymed " dramatic " lyrics, romances, and other monologues are dramatic in a less direct way.)

To appreciate more accurately the possibilities of blank verse for many purposes one would need to recall its use beyond the sphere of drama and the dramatic monologue. Wordsworth found it the appropriate vehicle in *The Prelude* for anything he had to narrate or describe or explain or exult over. He could make it rise and fall, quicken or brood. But of course Wordsworth, having once chosen his instrument, had to stick to it throughout

O

his long and varied poem, even though it might have been not particularly suitable on some occasions. On the other hand, there is sufficient Wordsworthian blank verse outside *The Prelude* and, one should add, *The Excursion*, to show how various he could make it when he could have chosen other measures if he had so desired. There are, for example, *Tintern Abbey* which is a kind of reflective ode, narratives like *Michael* and *The Brothers*, familiar poems like the *Address to my Infant Daughter*, *Dora*, and several verse letters, and miscellaneous pieces, descriptive, elegiac, and epigrammatic, among the *Poems on the Naming of Places*, epitaphs, and inscriptions.

If it be thought that the Wordsworthian blank verse has all a strong family likeness, one might illustrate the pliability of the medium from the rich variety of narratives in it by Milton and Keats, Arnold, and above all Tennyson, from the odes and meditations, idylls and elegies, epistles, lyrics, and the nondescript in Coleridge, Tennyson again, Landor, Stevenson, and Meredith.

INDEX

O 2

PRINTED IN GREAT BRITAIN BY OLIVER AND BOYD LTD., EDINBURGH